Alec Robins w[illegible] first fascinated by the challenge of crosswords d[illegible] [illegible]ing a long spell i[illegible] service in the [illegible] deeper and m[illegible] [illegible]ng and construc[illegible]

Now firmly established as a compos[illegible] [illegible]word puzzles at all levels of difficulty, he has achieved popularity and distinction in several publications in which he regularly appears.

As well as contributing his long-running series to *Competitors Journal* and the monthly puzzle to *Computer Weekly* under his own name, he also includes among his aliases 'Zander' of the *Listener*, 'Custos' of the *Guardian* and, for six months of each year on alternate months, 'Everyman' of the *Observer*. In all his compositions—over 2000 so far—he combines scrupulous fairness with absolute accuracy, both of which qualities he repeatedly stresses in this book as essential requirements of good crosswords.

Six paperback collections of his own crosswords have already been published, and he collaborated with the late D. S. Macnutt ('Ximenes') in the book *Ximenes on the Art of the Crossword* (Methuen, 1966), for which he wrote three chapters.

A native of Manchester and educated at Manchester Grammar School and Manchester University, Alec Robins is a former Head of Classics at grammar schools in the Manchester area. He and his wife live in Prestwich.

The ABC of Crosswords

Alec Robins

CORGI BOOKS
A DIVISION OF TRANSWORLD PUBLISHERS LTD

To my wife Anne

THE ABC OF CROSSWORDS

A CORGI BOOK 0 552 11843 5

Originally published in Great Britain as *Teach Yourself Crosswords* by Hodder & Stoughton Ltd.

PRINTING HISTORY
Hodder & Stoughton edition published 1975
Corgi edition published 1981

This book is set in 10/11 Times Roman.

Corgi Books are published by Transworld Publishers Ltd., Century House, 61–63 Uxbridge Road, Ealing, London, W5 5SA

Made and printed in the United States of America by Offset Paperbacks, Dallas, Pennsylvania.

Contents

Preface

To the newcomer unacquainted with its rules and conventions, even the simplest riddle is apt to present an insoluble problem. Little wonder, then, that a crossword, consisting as it does of a collection of little puzzles of many different types, is incomprehensible to those who have never been initiated into its secrets and special language.

There are, it is true, some crosswords which on inspection prove to be simply a list of factual or general knowledge questions printed in an unusual format. These seem to be straightforward enough and, even if the questions are sometimes difficult, anyone can tackle them without the need for a lengthy preliminary explanation. But what of those curious concoctions known as 'cryptic' crosswords, which elicit from one's fellow commuters a vacant stare into the distance, followed by a chuckle, perhaps, or a smug beam of self-satisfaction—how on earth does one unlock the door to this house of mystery? The purpose of this book is to provide the key.

As with all forms of entertainment, crosswords display a wide variety of standards and levels designed to suit all tastes. Despite their many differences, however, all of them ought ideally to have certain characteristics in common, paramount among which are accuracy and fairness. One of the main aims of this book is to emphasise these vital qualities, by venturing to draw up a suitable code of laws governing crosswords which, it is hoped, readers may come to accept as reasonable and just.

Beginners have been kept constantly in mind from the outset. For them the crossword puzzle is gradually revealed in its various guises, from the simplest types to those of greater complexity. As each of the many techniques of clue-writing is described in turn and its rules laid down, numerous examples of clues are supplied, every one explained and analysed in detail rather than left to be deduced by the reader. In this way the learner will have ample opportunity to assimilate each new point and to recognise clues of all sorts and conditions.

At the same time the older hand has not been neglected. As he reads, he may perhaps be encouraged to examine crossword clues with a sharper eye, at once more critical and appreciative than before, to find more subtlety in some of them than he may have previously suspected, and to reflect upon whether the views expressed in the course of this book correspond or conflict with his own.

Whenever matters like the principles of clueing or the methods of constructing crosswords are discussed, it is usually the setter who, for the sake of clarity, is being addressed. Yet simultaneously the solver is involved in equal measure; for the more he learns about the ways in which diagrams and clues are produced, the better will he understand the workings of the setter's mind and thus be able to improve his own solving skill. And should this need to be reinforced, a separate chapter comprising hints for solvers is also provided.

But whether my readers are beginners or old hands, setters

or solvers, or maybe a little of each, it is hoped that they may find something in these pages to stimulate thought, and above all that they may derive a genuine enjoyment and satisfaction from the intellectual exercise that crosswords can promote.

The book is arranged in four parts, each having a separate function: Part I presents the historical and factual features of the crossword; Part II is exclusively concerned with cryptic crosswords and the various clueing devices associated with them; in Part III the art and craft of composing crosswords, of both the simple and the more sophisticated kind, are explained and demonstrated; and Part IV consists of actual crossword puzzles of differing styles, types and standards of difficulty, followed by their respective solutions, including a detailed analysis of them wherever this is appropriate.

I should like to record my thanks to the following: the *Sunday Express*, for permission to reproduce the crossword in Chapter 1; Mr John Perkin, Crossword Editor of the *Guardian*, for allowing me free access to that paper's archives and for permission to reproduce its first crossword; Mr L. F. Minter, former Competitions Manager of IPC Magazines Ltd for lending me much useful material about foreign crosswords; Mr Stephen Sondheim, for some facts about the contemporary American crossword scene; the management of the *Observer*, for permission to reprint puzzles by Torquemada and Ximenes and my own 'Everyman' crosswords; the *Listener*, for permission to reuse some of my own crosswords which have appeared in its pages; Frederick Warne & Co., for permission to include a crossword by Afrit from *Armchair Crosswords*; and the late Mr Gerald Abrahams, for much valuable advice.

I am particularly grateful to Mr Robert S. Caffyn for most carefully reading everything at the manuscript stage, and for his many helpful comments.

Alec Robins

Part I

Historical and Factual

1 A history of crosswords

The majority of my present readers, having grown up to recognise crosswords as a regular feature of their newspapers and periodicals, may forgivably have taken it for granted that these puzzles have been flourishing in something like their present form for a couple of centuries at least. It may come as a surprise to many, therefore, to learn that crosswords as we know them in this country are a product of the twentieth century.

Anagrams

The seeds, however, were sown long ago; for despite various features which, as will be seen throughout this book, uniquely distinguish the modern crossword from all earlier types of verbal problem, it may be said to be continuing an ancient and highly respectable tradition. The anagram, for instance, perhaps the most ubiquitous feature of today's cryptic crosswords, can trace its ancestry back to sources almost as old as civilised thought itself. We know that Pythagoras and his disciples of the sixth century BC, and also Plato and his philosophical school of the fourth, constructed anagrams as a regular discipline, and that this practice, first passed on to the highbrows among the classical Romans, had spread throughout Europe by the Middle Ages and was popular in many monastic establishments of the sixteenth and seventeenth centuries.

Mention may perhaps be made here of a Jewish rabbinical sect of the thirteenth century known as the Cabbalists who brought anagram analysis, as it may be called, to a fine art, and may themselves have been drawing upon the precepts of their predecessors from the distant past. They, and other expounders of the Bible who followed them, used to regard it as an exercise of mystic significance to change the normal sequence of the letters of, say, a person's name and read into the new arrangement some indication of that person's character and destiny. Or they might juggle with the numerical equivalents of the Hebrew letters of a disputed phrase in the Bible and, from their computations, produce a novel interpretation of the text.

Although at first an anagram—derived from the Greek *ana*, meaning back, and *gramma*, meaning a letter—was simply a reversal of the order of a word's letters, in practice it was soon extended to include any jumbling of its letters. The technique of adapting the original idea of anagrams to the wording of crossword clues will be explained in detail in Chapter 12.

For all its versatility, however, the anagram is but one of the many devices employed in a crossword's presentation. For the basic ideas which must surely have inspired the crossword itself we must look in particular to two kinds of verbal legerdemain, the acrostic and the word-square, each of which has its own peculiar fascination and has persisted to some extent right up to the present time. A description of the general character and make-up of each will therefore be appropriate at this point.

Acrostics

Like the anagram, the acrostic is of ancient lineage. It works on the principle that the initial letters of successive lines of verse, or of the first lines of each stanza of a poem, or of successive words in a piece of prose, and so on, will themselves spell out a word, name, phrase or sentence. For example, the Latin comedies of Plautus (*c*. 254–184 BC) were prefaced by an Argument, the initial letters of which formed the title of the play.

Hebrew poetry, especially in the form of hymns and psalms, seems to have been obsessed with acrostic techniques. Particularly noticeable is Psalm 119, consisting of twenty-two stanzas corresponding to the number of letters in the Hebrew alphabet. The first line of the first stanza begins with aleph, of the second stanza with beth, and so on until the alphabet is completed. The same initial-letter set-up may also be found in Psalms 25 and 34. Religious verses of this kind, however, although the name of acrostic was applied to them, were usually known as alphabetical or 'abecedarian' hymns.

The monks of the Middle Ages—they had to pass the long hours somehow, and a régime founded on a principle of 'all work and all pray' was scarcely calculated to obviate dullness!—added acrostics to anagrams in their quest for some form of intellectual relaxation. Poets of Germany, France and the Italian Renaissance, including Boccaccio (*c*. 1313–75), indulged in them. But the prize for sheer single-mindedness in this respect must go to Sir John Davies for his twenty-six elegant poems in praise of Queen Elizabeth, written in 1599 and entitled *Hymns to Astraea*. Each one of the poems was of sixteen lines, and in every case the poem's first letters spelled out *Elisabetha Regina*.

Of more relevance to our own subject are those acrostics

which are intended as puzzles, not merely as incidental embellishments to literary compositions. Here is an example of the initial-letter idea in the form of a puzzle:

Acrostic: You'll find me in a book,
Or in your hotel, look!
1 In this she'll keep your wage.
2 You'll see him on the stage.
3 A fruit shaped like a pear.
4 Wide jugs, by no means rare.

It will be seen that the four numbered statements are definitions of the required answers, and that an introductory couplet gives hints about the acrostic. Nor will it have escaped notice that the poetical origins of acrostics have maintained their influence, for it is almost invariable to find doggerel used in puzzles of this kind. The solution is as follows:

1 **P**URSE
2 **A**CTOR
3 **G**UAVA
4 **E**WERS

Note that when the four answers have been written their initial letters, read downwards, form the acrostic **PAGE** which, as the clue indicated, can be found in a book or, with another meaning, as an attendant in a hotel.

A further development of this idea will be apparent if the same four definitions are retained, but the acrostic couplet altered to read as follows:

Uprights: The printed one is what you read,
And here it is The Times you need.

If we examine the previous solution once more, we find:

1 **PURSE**
2 **ACTOR**
3 **GUAVA**
4 **EWERS**

The deviser of this little puzzle has in fact produced one word (**PAGE**) from the initial letters of the four answers and a second word (**ERAS**) from their final letters—PAGE being clued by the first line of the couplet and ERAS by its second line. This is known as a double acrostic, which shows, albeit in a rudimentary form, how certain answers, when written horizontally as a result of solving clues, contribute the letters which vertically form other answers to clues—that is to say, how answers can be obtained by making words cross each other. Further refinements are to be found in acrostics in which not only the initial and final letters of horizontal answers form vertical words but also their central letters, thus making a triple acrostic, a device which prompted the essayist Addison—clearly no potential crossworder—to declare in *The Spectator* that he could not decide whether the inventor of the acrostic or of the anagram was the 'greater blockhead'!

Word-squares

Another form of literal dexterity, also hallowed by time, is the composition of word-squares. The object in these is to construct a square in which the same words run both horizontally and vertically, e.g.:

B E S T
E V E R
S E R E
T R E E

Scholars throughout the centuries have burned an incalculable amount of midnight oil amusing and, at times, torturing themselves by devising such squares, usually aiming at nothing more than the intellectual satisfaction of mastering a tricky problem single-handed, and with no intention of using it as a puzzle for someone else to solve. The Greek philosophers Socrates and Aristotle were both reputed to have enlivened their leisure hours by devising them. It is idle to speculate how many hours or days were consumed by the genius who concocted the following masterpiece, written in Latin on a piece of wall-plaster and unearthed a century ago at Cirencester, Gloucestershire, when the old Roman site there was being excavated:

R O T A S
O P E R A
T E N E T
A R E P O
S A T O R

The sheer brilliance of this word-square will perhaps not be fully appreciated until it is realised that not only can we read the five words horizontally from left to right in descending order of rows, and from right to left in ascending rows, but we can also read them vertically downwards, moving from the left-hand column to the right, and again upwards from the right-hand column to the left. And as a bonus, rare in word-squares, the words actually form a sentence, which may be translated as 'The sower Arepo controls the wheels with an effort'. This futuristic vision of the skilful driver of a motorised seed-spreader leaves one with a sense of wonder at the extraordinary heights of ingenuity to which the human mind is capable of soaring. (The original piece of plaster, incidentally, is still to be seen in Cirencester's Corinium Museum.)

Here again, as in the case of acrostics, we see an arrangement whereby words written horizontally are made to cross and form words vertically, although they turn out in this case to be exactly the same words. It was probably something very similar to the word-square, in fact, perhaps accompanied by very elementary clues, which appeared spasmodically in the late nineteenth century in children's puzzle books and nursery magazines, and then disappeared without trace. But apart from the fact that nowadays the words going across are quite different from those going down, it is a sort of adaptation of several adjacent word-squares which can be detected in crosswords, particularly those found across the Atlantic, in which every letter in the diagram belongs to both a horizontal and a vertical word.

The birth of the modern crossword

For the twentieth-century crossword, as for so many other innovations of modern times, we are indebted to American enterprise, although we may derive a measure of national pride from the birthplace of its inventor. For it was from his native Liverpool that Arthur Wynne, a journalist, emigrated in 1913 to the United States, where he soon persuaded the editor of the *New York World* to publish, in its Sunday supplement called *Fun*, some specimen crosswords that he had devised. That paper continued to run Wynne's crosswords for ten years or so before any other publication took any notice.

Then suddenly, in 1923, a book of fifty simple crosswords was compiled and published by Robert Simon and Lincoln Schuster, two friends who had recently graduated from Harvard. They called themselves the Plaza Publishing Company and sold three-quarters of a million copies of the book within a few weeks. As a result of their obvious popularity, crosswords now began to appear daily in newspapers from coast to coast.

It was not long after this that the crossword made its way to this country, fittingly on the initiative of Arthur Wynne himself. The latter offered a small batch of his puzzles to C. W. Shepherd, a member of a syndicate called Newspaper Features. Mr Shepherd was fascinated by the novelty and persuaded the *Sunday Express* to buy half a dozen. Twenty years afterwards Mr Shepherd himself revealed in a newspaper article that, because the first puzzle chosen, and due for publication next day, happened to contain a word with an American spelling, he took it home in order to make, as he thought, a minor adjustment. In the event he was obliged to make drastic alterations to other words too and, of course, to amend several of the clues accordingly.

As a matter of historical fact, therefore, we can state that the first crossword to be printed in this country, although substantially amended and redrafted by C. W. Shepherd—for whose perspicacity in quickly recognising a potential success we should be grateful—was originated and introduced by the American Arthur Wynne, formerly of Liverpool, who died in January 1945. And the distinction of being first in the field belongs to the *Sunday Express*, who published the Wynne-Shepherd crossword on 2 November 1924. This simple little puzzle, which took Britain by storm on its appearance and which has since developed into the sophisticated cryptic crossword that we know in this country today, is shown below. (The solution appears at the end of this chapter.)

1	2	3	■	4	5	6
7			■	8		
9			10			
■	■	11			■	■
12	13				14	15
16			■	17		
18			■	19		

HORIZONTALS

1 A coin (slang). **4** A tree. **7** Period. **8** Through. **9** Counters of votes. **11** Cosy little room. **12** Drainages. **16** Meaning three (prefix). **17** Snake-like fish. **18** An Oriental coin. **19** Parched.

VERTICALS

1 Wager. **2** Mineral substance. **3** Eminent political figure. **4** Inflicted retribution. **5** A title. **6** Possesses. **10** Grassland. **12** Home of a certain animal. **13** Before (poetic form). **14** Always (poetic form). **15** Cunning.

Once begun, the new pastime gradually spread, as newspapers and periodicals throughout the country in turn made a regular feature of their daily or weekly crossword. The first crossword in the *Sunday Times* appeared in January 1925, and July of the same year saw the start of the long-running series in the *Daily Telegraph*. Torquemada's first crossword for the *Observer* was printed in March 1926, and just one year later the same paper introduced a second and less exacting puzzle, known as 'Everyman's Crossword' (since changed slightly to its present name of the 'Everyman Crossword'). Other papers fell into line until eventually, in February 1930, *The Times* itself bowed to the inevitable and set the seal on the pastime's social respectability by publishing its own crossword puzzle. As a result, men eminent in politics and the professions began to make rival claims, in Letters to the Editor, about the speed with which they normally solved the daily puzzle.

The Guardian

As an indication of the acceptance of the crossword by newspapers of repute, the experience of *The Guardian* may be regarded as fairly typical. After cautiously observing the progress of the new-born infant towards early childhood, the *Manchester Guardian* (as it was then called) launched a weekly crossword on Saturday, 5 January 1929, offering prizes of a guinea each to the senders of the first two correct solutions opened. The first puzzle, with an unsymmetrical arrangement of blocks (which I have included in Part IV as an interesting curiosity), was immediately succeeded by diagrams that were almost or completely symmetrical, although the symmetry was of a type seldom seen today, in which the design of the diagram's right half was a mirror image of that of its left half.

It was also noticeable that, of the first score of puzzles, about half contained a proportion of answers relating to a single subject: for instance, animals in one, birds in another, with fish, trees and plants, characters in Dickens or Shakespeare, and contemporary Test cricketers being represented in their turn. As for the clues, in common with their contemporaries they were predominantly simple definitions, with just here and there a rudimentary attempt at some form of word-play.

By the end of May 1929 the crossword had just begun to appear twice weekly, and from January 1930 onwards it became a daily feature, with the mid-week one made deliberately harder than the rest, and with the addition of a children's crossword every Saturday. The latter lasted for just a year, to be replaced in January 1931 by an extra Saturday crossword for adults, called 'Everest', which now became the one difficult puzzle of the week. When this too disappeared a year later, the paper settled down to the steady routine of a daily crossword aimed consistently at the same kind of solver, as it does today. Exceptionally, a double crossword, with two identical diagrams and a special theme, replaces the normal puzzle on Bank Holiday weekends.

Guardian crosswords have always preserved the traditional anonymity of their setters, as have so many other papers, although for the past few years each puzzle has been headed by the partial identification of a pseudonym. As many as a dozen different setters are responsible for them, some appearing more frequently than others, and they include, besides the usual nucleus of clerics and academics, a carpenter, a retired bank manager and a housewife. The whole operation, as in the case of *The Times* and the *Daily Telegraph*, is coordinated by the overlordship of the Crosswords Editor.

The *Listener*

In April 1930, two months after *The Times*, the *Listener* began printing crosswords as a weekly feature. Whereas *The Guardian* had previously included, in an occasional early puzzle, several answers relating to the same subject, the *Listener* uniquely pioneered the 'single-theme' type of puzzle which has become its characteristic ever since. Among the puzzles of 1930, for instance, one finds the following themes:

music, science, several foreign languages, botany, the motor show and architecture.

Diagram dimensions have ranged from the minute to the very large; and although black and white squares appear from time to time, the use of bars instead of blocks has been typical of *Listener* grids. Many unorthodox shapes of diagram have been devised by setters for special themes, such as a map, an animal, single or multiple circles and hexagons, a firework, a cube and an hour-glass.

The quality common to most *Listener* puzzles is their difficulty, although this is less true today than it was thirty years ago, partly because specialised knowledge was essential then, with clues largely factual, but mainly because today's setters and solvers prefer sophisticated clues which are solvable by ingenuity rather than polymathy.

A practical consideration which affected the standard of difficulty early on was the fact that a book-prize was offered for every correct solution sent in; so that while in one week a dozen prizes might be won, in others no correct solution at all was received. It would be a rare and unintended disaster if that happened nowadays, when the average number of correct solutions each week is a couple of hundred.

Distinguished early *Listener* setters—all now, alas, no more—included Afrit and Ximenes (under his other pseudonym of Tesremos), about both of whom more will be written later in this chapter, and L. E. Eyres, who as Pollux composed thirty-four Latin or Greek crosswords between 1936 and 1948. The number of setters in more recent times has greatly expanded, so that as many as forty or fifty may be regarded as regulars today—too large a number to list here individually.

Alternative-type crosswords

In the late 1920s and early 1930s there appeared a type of prize crossword in which most of the letters of each answer were already supplied and at least two possible alternative letters would fit sensibly into each remaining space. Competitors were required to complete the unfinished words after reading the clues and to send in their solutions with an entrance fee, and large prizes were offered for solutions that corresponded exactly, or most closely, to those of a judging panel. The *Daily Mail* ran a £3000 crossword of this type, while the *Sunday Pictorial* and *News of the World* were each offering £2000.

At first pure guesswork was involved. For example, given the clue 'A quadruped', for which the letters –AT were supplied, one had to choose either CAT or RAT, and only the tossing of a coin could possibly decide between them.

Later, however, when such lotteries were challenged in the courts, and finally declared illegal in 1936, papers like *John Bull* introduced a new kind of clue which could be reasoned out—although not everyone would agree with the mental processes of the judging panel! — and all other crosswords of this kind quickly followed suit.

The recommended method of solving these clues was to make a list of all the possible answers and then find the one word in the clue which the panel of judges would probably concentrate on, since slight but significant differences could be read into such words as 'always', 'usually', 'often', 'sometimes', etc. Here is an example where the letters NE– are already supplied in the diagram:

> **Bride's veil is generally this.** (Possible answers are NEW, NET.)

The panel might argue as follows: a bride's veil is *always* NET and *generally* NEW (unless she wears a borrowed one). Therefore NEW is the more apt answer, on the basis of the word 'generally'.

The popularity of this type of crossword began to wane in the 1960s in favour of trade competitions which were mentally less demanding, and it is now a rarity. Readers who would find it amusing, however, to test their logical reasoning against that of an experienced committee of judges may care to have a shot at a typical example of its kind, which will be found in Part IV, and then compare their findings with the published result, given in the final section of this book.

Crossword championships

Once the crossword habit was firmly established, it was perhaps inevitable that a search for a national solving champion should be periodically mounted. The first such competition, offering a first prize of £5000, lasted for five rounds, each one harder than its predecessor, and was run by the *Daily News* in 1925. An easy first puzzle induced as many as 100 000 hopefuls to compete at an entrance fee equivalent to 5p each round, thus ensuring the venture's viability. Then for the remaining four rounds Gilbert Frankau, a popular novelist of the day, proceeded to reduce the survivors by composing harder and harder puzzles—an exercise, incidentally, which he had never previously attempted.

Three hundred competitors survived the penultimate round by solving a crossword that required some knowledge of German, Spanish, Italian and French words. But no single entrant succeeded in completing the final puzzle, the prize being awarded to a London syndicate who came nearest. That puzzle, measuring 24 × 20 squares and including many reversed or part-answers and an almost incomprehensible system of numbering the clues—clues like 'Curtail and decapitate a diminutive' (Answer, NNETT), 'Ask your tailor about this' (SB), and lots more in similar vein—was outrageously unfair by modern standards. It speaks volumes for the tenacity of solvers—encouraged, it's true, by the alluring prospect of that prize of £5000—that so many persevered and survived almost to the end.

There followed a lull in competitions of that kind for many years, at least on a national scale. Then in 1953 *Competitors Journal* conducted a new series, using cryptic crosswords in every round, and followed it up by a second competition on identical lines in 1954. From 1955–9 other national papers undertook the organisation of a championship, but in 1960–1, and again in 1962–3, it was *Competitors Journal* once more that sponsored two further knock-out tournaments. In more recent years it has been *The Times*, in conjunction with two successive whisky firms that has made the championship an annual event. Correct solutions of some specified crosswords in the paper serve as qualifiers for this, after which the winners of several regional finals held around the country meet in a national final in a London hotel. In both regional and national finals, the winners are those who combine the greatest accuracy in solving with the quickest times.

At all stages of its existence the crossword has been, and continues to be, enlivened by the talent, wit and ingenuity of numerous able (and mostly anonymous) practitioners. From among them, however, there emerge three almost legendary figures who, each in his different way, can be seen in retrospect to have influenced to some extent the thinking and technique of all who have succeeded them. No history of the crossword could be considered complete without some reference to the celebrated trio of Torquemada, Afrit and Ximenes.

Torquemada

Edward Powys Mathers (1892–1939), a gifted scholar from boyhood, with a particular talent for translating Oriental poetry and for original verse composition, was educated at Loretto and Trinity College, Oxford. A voracious reader with a phenomenal memory, he added to his highbrow tastes a love of detective stories, on which he became an expert; and it was as a regular reviewer of such novels that he was first known to readers of the *Observer*.

He noticed the rapid spread of the crossword here at the end of 1924, and although he soon lost interest in clues that were merely dictionary definitions, he toyed with the subject at the back of his mind and in due course produced a dozen crosswords, with the novelty of rhymed clues, which appeared in a paper called the *Saturday Westminster*, under the general title of 'Crosswords for Riper Years', until that paper's demise.

Soon afterwards, in March 1926, he began his long series of 670 puzzles in the *Observer*, adopting the name of Torquemada, a notorious Grand Inquisitor of Spain, as being appropriate for one who intended, but in the most amiable way, to torment his solvers by his devious and often very difficult clues.

Many of his crosswords required specialised literary knowledge for their solution, and often enough an entire puzzle would consist of plain definitions—attractively concealed, however, within ingenious and skilful verse. His diagrams—frequently constructed by his wife from a list of words which he supplied to her—were unsymmetrical in bar arrangement, and commonly contained words to be written in reverse or in two parts appearing in different sections of the diagram. It must be said, too, that a large proportion of his clues would not pass muster today for one reason or another among discriminating solvers.

Viewed solely, therefore, from a modern standpoint, Torquemada's crosswords fall far short of the ideals of fairness and accuracy which will be set forth in the course of this book as desirable goals. In the eyes of his own contemporaries, however, he was a pioneer of genius well in advance of his time, one of the first to use cryptic clues at all extensively, who delighted and puzzled thousands of solvers week after week by his witty and novel approach to what was as yet an imperfectly developed pastime. And when he died, at the early age of forty-seven, after a life of worse than indifferent health, he had kindled the torch which others enthusiastically took over from him.

Afrit

While Torquemada was building his reputation as a puzzler extraordinary among *Observer* readers, another philosopher was founding his own school, gaining new disciples from the lands inhabited by readers of the *Listener*. He was Prebendary Alistair Ferguson Ritchie (1887–1954), Headmaster of Wells Cathedral School from 1924, who appeared as Afrit, the evil demon of Arabian mythology—a pseudonym which, consisting as it did of his own initials and almost half his surname, is indicative of the brilliant exploitation of words and their make-up that was his hallmark.

An outstanding character from his youth, being Head Boy and Games Captain of the Grammar School at King's Lynn, Norfolk, he later graduated from Queens' College, Cambridge. In addition to his fame as a crossword composer, he was also renowned for his other hobby, bee-keeping.

He too, like Torquemada, leaned heavily on literary allusions and references entailing much research; and it was not unusual for no fully correct solution to be received of an Afrit puzzle in the *Listener*. His aim, however, was not merely to test the solver's knowledge or industry but also to entertain. As examples of his inventiveness, the initial letters of the answers in one diagram, when read in sequence, would form an acrostic; in another, the answers might be obtained by subtracting one word from another; or again, the letters of the answers would have to be written in the diagram according to the moves of chess pieces; and so on—fresh ideas poured from his brain as water from a gushing spring.

Afrit later increased his popularity and influence by composing easier puzzles also, some of them in the *Sphere*. A collection of his 'Armchair Crosswords', as he called them, published by Frederick Warne, is unfortunately out of print and virtually unobtainable. In that book's Introduction he laid down rigid standards of fairness and accuracy for setters; and it was his very scrupulousness in applying them to himself that set so many of his successors on the twin paths of idealism and self-discipline.

Ximenes

When Torquemada died in 1939, there followed a period

during which three setters, each working independently, produced puzzles for the *Observer* in rotation. One was F. R. Burrow, a Wimbledon tennis referee, and another B. G. Whitfield, a master at Eton. By 1942 the third setter was calling each of his puzzles 'Torquemada-style Crossword by Ximenes'; and in 1945, now the sole contributor, he launched a completely new series entitled 'Ximenes Crossword'. Thus began the distinguished régime of this master of the genre, who adorned the crossword scene with his ingenuity and skill for more than a quarter of a century.

Derrick Somerset Macnutt (1902–71), educated at Marlborough and Jesus College, Cambridge, was bitten by the crossword bug while still a student in 1924, and within another couple of years he came under the spell of Torquemada. Later, in the 1930s, he contributed crosswords regularly to the *Listener* as Tesremos (reversing his middle name for the purpose), and only ceased to appear in it when his responsibility for the *Observer* crosswords started to consume all his spare time; for, in addition to his role as Ximenes, he was now producing the easier 'Everyman' puzzles as well as being a Housemaster and, later, for many years Senior Classics Master at Christ's Hospital, Horsham.

Following the trend set by Torquemada, he used as his *alter ego* the name of the Cardinal (Ximenes de Cisneros) who succeeded Torquemada in the Spanish Inquisition. (This inquisitorial tradition of the *Observer*, incidentally, has been continued by his present successor, Azed, although this time the Spaniard's real name of Deza has been reversed for alphabetical effect.) For some time he imitated his predecessor closely, having become so familiar with his idol's methods as to consider them the standard. However, when he came into contact with Afrit's puzzles, he realised that he was more in sympathy with the latter's analytical approach, with its intrinsic fairness, than with the less disciplined methods of Torquemada. As a result he developed a new style of his own, producing versions according to the principles laid down by Afrit and gradually discarding any practice, however tempting, that he could not justify by the strict rules of grammar and syntax.

Perfection was always his aim, and seldom did he fail to live up to his own exacting ideal. His diagrams were a model of symmetry, his clues artistic, concise and accurate, with never a word wasted. Nor did he miss an opportunity of injecting humour into his work or of appreciating another setter's wit. He organised and judged regular clue-writing competitions, and circulated among his solvers printed slips giving full details of all highly-commended efforts, often adding pencilled notes of explanation, congratulation or encouragement to individuals. In this way, and by attending periodical dinners organised by one or other of his solvers to mark a milestone, such as the 100th, 500th or 750th crossword, he became personally known to a host of his far-flung admirers. One solver even flew over from New York especially for the dinner held in London in honour of his 1000th crossword!

When Ximenes died he had composed, in addition to numerous other puzzles, an unbroken series of 1200 crosswords in the *Observer*; and the very last of them, fittingly, showed him at the peak of his ingenious form, in a novelty based on the letters MCC (1200 in Roman numerals, and also, of course, the cricket club's initials) in which every single clue in the puzzle had been given a cricketing flavour.

On a personal note, I welcome this opportunity of recording not only my own indebtedness to his precept and example over many years but also my consciousness of the great privilege of having known him as a crossword colleague and friend.

The future

As we have seen, the crossword has undergone a gradual process of evolution until, under the powerful but diverse influence of three talented innovators in particular, it has reached its present highly developed state, at least in this country. But its history is by no means complete; for we anticipate with pleasure the arrival of those future practitioners who will continue the noble tradition of entertaining and puzzling their devoted followers of the next generation and beyond.

Solution of the Arthur Wynne puzzle

1 B	2 O	3 B		4 A	5 S	6 H
7 E	R	A		8 V	I	A
9 T	E	L	10 L	E	R	S
		11 D	E	N		
12 S	13 E	W	A	G	14 E	15 S
16 T	R	I		17 E	E	L
18 Y	E	N		19 D	R	Y

2 Crossword terminology

Although the solution of crosswords does not, by and large, demand any knowledge of technical terminology, the beginner may find it useful at the outset to become acquainted with the following fairly limited number of basic terms, which have a habit of recurring in any discussion of the subject.

The diagram

This is also known as the square, the grid or the grille. It is normally an exact square in shape, most commonly of 15 × 15 small squares in size, with certain squares blacked out to form a symmetrical design. The blacked-out squares are known as 'blocks'. A typical 15 × 15 diagram is shown on the opposite page.

Notice that its symmetry is such that the diagram looks exactly the same when turned upside-down, but not when given a quarter-turn. It is also possible to have the blocks disposed in such a pattern that the design looks exactly the same whichever side of the diagram is uppermost.

It must be conceded that the question of symmetry (or the lack of it) in the arrangement of the blocks or bars of a diagram is irrelevant to the fairness or accuracy of a crossword, to the ease or difficulty of its solution, or to its entertainment value. Nevertheless, ever since the first crossword appeared on the British scene the convention of a symmetrical design has been accepted and perpetuated in most publications as the norm; and I would venture to suggest that, while symmetry alone can never make a poor crossword better, it does invest a good one with the added qualities of neatness and aesthetic attractiveness.

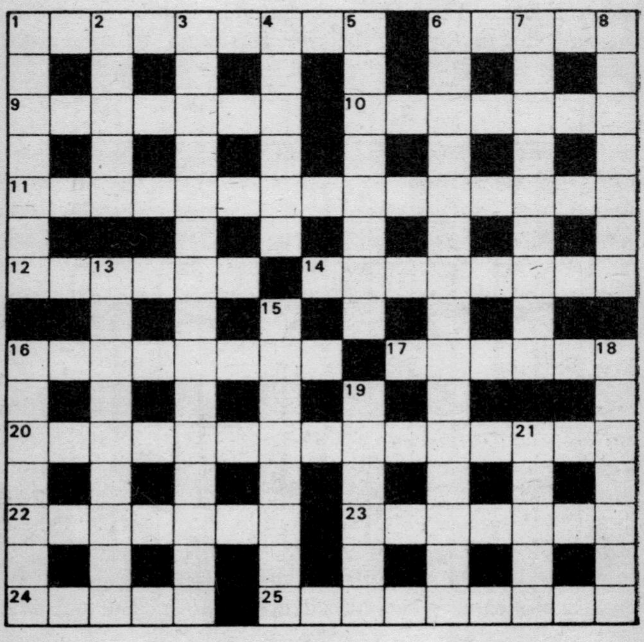

There are bound to be times, for instance in a crossword concerned with a special theme, when it proves in practice to be impossible for the composer to fit in all the necessary items within the framework of a symmetrical diagram of the required size and shape. Far better in that case to sacrifice symmetry than to weaken the theme by the forced omission of the 'awkward' words. Yet it should always be the goal to be aimed at, and it is worth making several experiments, if necessary, before becoming convinced that it can't be achieved after all; and even then it need not be abandoned completely, but rather attempted as nearly as is practicable.

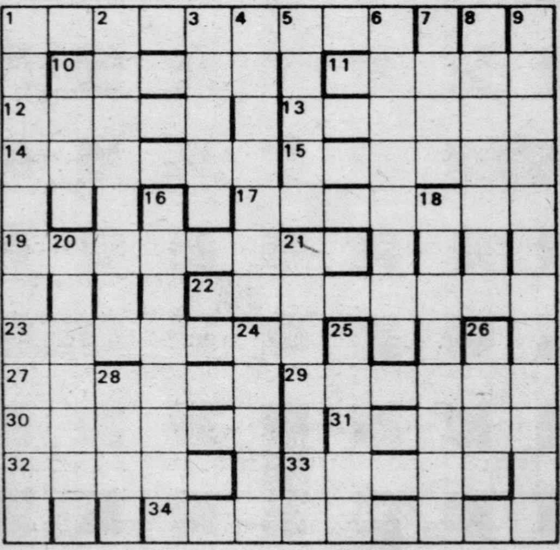

Another type, 12 × 12 squares in size (generally used for the more difficult kind of crossword), has an arrangement of 'bars', or thickened lines, instead of blocks—symmetrical also, ideally, whether in a two-way or four-way design—so that every single square of the diagram is used to accommodate a letter. The bars mark the end of each word in the diagram, thus performing the same function as blocks, as the example opposite will show. In this diagram, the first Across answer has nine letters, after which there is a bar. The second and third Across answers, numbered 10 and 11, are of five letters each, being bounded either by a bar or by the edge of the diagram.

In some newspapers and periodicals, especially those which present a 'quick crossword' in addition to their normal one, the diagram is slightly smaller, with 13×13 squares as against the familiar 15×15; and specialised or novelty crosswords, such as those published weekly in the *Listener*, are, as has been stated in the previous chapter, apt to be of any size and shape.

Clues

The clues are the means by which the setter of a puzzle gives information or hints to the reader, each clue being some kind of problem or teaser to which his reader must find the answer, or which, in other words, he must 'solve'; and it is this answer, in each case, which the reader writes down, or 'enters', in the spaces provided in the diagram. Thus we have clues and answers, the complete set of answers to a crossword being known as the 'solution'. The clues leading to words that must be entered in the diagram horizontally are called 'Across clues' or 'the Acrosses' and those whose answers are inscribed vertically downwards are 'Down clues' or 'the Downs'.

For the convenience of the solver, each clue is concluded by a figure or figures in brackets, from which it is immediately apparent, without having to look at the diagram and count, how many letters there are in the required answer. A clue to FULL, for instance, would finish with '(4)', to FULL HOUSE with '(4,5)', to FULL-DRESS with '(4-5)' and to FULL-DRESS UNIFORM with '(4-5,7)'.

(For several reasons some confusion has arisen over the use of the word 'lights'. They can be apertures for admitting light or divisions of mullioned windows, and in those senses it is understandable that some should think of the small squares of a diagram which contain the answers to the clues, resembling as they do panes of glass, as the 'lights' of a crossword. On the other hand, *Chambers Dictionary* defines 'light' as (*inter alia*) 'a hint, clue or keyword', which would appear to justify it as being synonymous with 'clue'. I suspect, however, that the continued use of the word is a hangover from the crossword's predecessor, the acrostic, in which often the initial and final letters of its words, forming two uprights like goalposts, as well as the horizontal words themselves, constituted the answers and were known as lights; so that reference to the lights of an acrostic could be interpreted with equal reasonableness as meaning either the answers or the hints, or clues, from which to obtain them. In view of this ambiguity, it is surely high time that the word 'lights', which has enjoyed only a limited currency for many years now, was withdrawn from crossword circulation entirely. But if for some reason it should still be considered necessary, then its intended meaning on each occasion ought to be made perfectly clear.)

Checked and unchecked letters

A checked letter is one that is used twice in the same square, occurring simultaneously as part of an Across word and part of a Down word which crosses it. The solver has therefore the opportunity of checking its correctness in the Across word by its equal suitability to the Down word.

An unchecked letter is one that appears in one word only and cannot be checked by an intersecting word because it is restricted by a block or bar. Let us examine the corner of a completed crossword (see opposite page).

The first word going down—DISTRACT—has four checked letters: D, which is used also in the Across word DECIDE; S, which also begins the Across word SLABS; R, the first letter of RISSOLE; and C, which begins CARDINAL. It has its other four letters unchecked: I, T, A and T, each of which

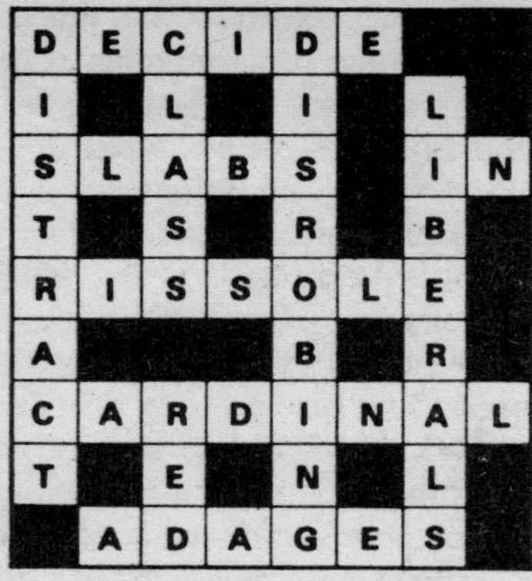

appears in this word only and is prevented from forming part of an Across word by the intervention of a block. Again, the Across word SLABS has S, A and S checked by being used also in DISTRACT, CLASS and DISROBING respectively, and L and B unchecked, being hemmed in by blocks above and below them.

Setter and solver

What shall we call the players in our game of wits known as crosswords? The person who solves them presents no problem: he is the 'solver', pure and simple—his purism (and his demand for it) permanently untainted, one hopes, but his simplicity gradually diminishing as he learns by experience to penetrate every disguise and to sidestep every trap cunningly devised for his undoing.

(My use of the masculine here, in order to avoid the 'he or she' and 'his or her' awkwardness, raises a point deserving a brief digression which may be of interest to psychologists and others: the fact that whereas women solvers are apparently at least as numerous as men, if the names regularly appearing in prize-lists are a reliable guide, there are extremely few female composers of crosswords. This is even more remarkable when one considers the preeminence of women in an allied field of enigmatic artistry, the detective novel. It would appear to be the case that certain types of creativity attract them, while others, for example musical composition, have no established tradition of feminine virtuosity.)

Less satisfactorily designated is the villain of the piece himself, the designer and excogitator of the puzzle. Journalistic tradition and current practice refer to him as the 'compiler': a misnomer, I feel, suggesting as it does the gathering together of the work of others into a single collection, as for example by an anthologist. The appellation, however, has persisted and must therefore be reluctantly acknowledged.

Nevertheless, there are several other and more suitable terms which continue to be used and should be mentioned here. Those who contribute crosswords to the *Listener*, for instance, are almost invariably called 'setters' (as apt a word as any for people who set problems), while in other publications they are known as 'composers' — fittingly, since they compose both the diagram and the clues; and again, if one is discussing the clues alone, 'clue-writers' is both perfectly accurate and self-explanatory.

As a general term for anyone actively interested in crosswords, whether as setter or solver, the name 'crossworder' is clear and unambiguous; but if your preference is for something altogether more grand, you may care to adopt the very impressive title of 'cruciverbalist', formed from the Latin *crux*, *crucis* (a cross), and *verbum* (a word). In this book I shall avoid the word 'compiler' altogether and avail myself at will of any of the other appropriate terms: 'composer', 'setter' and 'clue-writer' for the originator of the puzzle, and the uncontroversial 'solver' for the one who finds the answers and writes them in the diagram.

3 Types of crossword

Crosswords come in such a wide variety of shapes and sizes that it is impossible to describe them all. Moreover, at this very moment some setters may be concocting puzzles of forms or dimensions hitherto untried, whose publication would at once make any such description incomplete. Nevertheless, it is possible to classify with some accuracy the vast bulk of crosswords which appear both in this country and in many others all over the world.

British readers may derive some pleasure, perhaps even pride, from the knowledge that, so far as I have been able to discover, nowhere else has the crossword puzzle developed to such a pitch of sophistication on a national scale as it has in this country. Even those solvers, therefore, who modestly confess that they can manage only easy cryptic crosswords should cast aside any feelings of inadequacy and be comforted by the realisation that the majority of their counterparts in

America and Europe, for instance, have never tackled a cryptic crossword in their lives.

Definition-type

A crossword accompanied by a set of definition clues, to which the answers are purely factual or synonymous, represents all that is required to satisfy the leisure moments or hours of millions of people. In such puzzles, clues like 'European capital (5)' abound, and the solver who quickly inserts the answer PARIS is well content. Or again, to think of SAFETY as the answer to the clue 'Security (6)' requires a certain amount of thought, and to do so with reasonable speed is an exercise in vocabulary not without value or pleasure.

Small wonder, then, that definition-type crosswords enjoy a universal popularity, and few indeed are the national newspapers and periodicals of the world that fail to include such puzzles in their pages. The diagrams may be as small as 10 × 10 squares in a typical French magazine, or of mammoth proportions, occupying a full page in some American Sunday papers for example; they may contain blocks or bars as end-stops to words; and, of course, the standard of difficulty can be made to range from the childishly easy to the very tough general knowledge puzzle for which extensive recourse to learned works of reference is demanded. What they all have in common, though, is the presentation of a list of problems or questions whose answers cross each other, usually within a square or rectangular diagram, so that solving one problem contributes to the solution of others to an ever-increasing extent. Therein lies the fascination, as well as the feeling of achievement as the answers cumulatively build up to a completed diagram.

A typical definition-type crossword in Britain has a diagram of 13 × 13 squares, with a symmetrical arrangement of blocks to separate the answers. An example can be seen in Part IV, complete with a set of clues. As with most such crosswords in this country, every answer has its alternate letters hemmed in by blocks, although in some diagrams short words of three and even four letters are fully cross-checked. Foreign crosswords, on the other hand, including those in America and Canada, regularly have far fewer blocks and consequently very much more cross-checking. (The subject of checked and unchecked letters will be discussed in detail in Chapter 19.)

In some definition-type crosswords, notably in certain magazines in Germany, Finland, Sweden, Denmark and Norway, the clues are actually printed inside the squares which act as blocks, with arrows pointing in the direction of the required answers. It goes almost without saying that in such puzzles the squares are larger than average, and the clues are seldom more than two or three words long. In France, and in Swiss papers printed in French, the numbering of clues is quite different from ours. Here, for example, is a diagram familiar to French solvers:

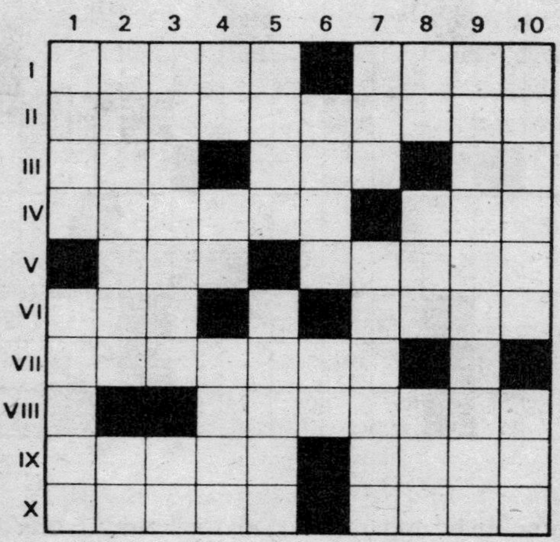

The clues in this *Mots Croisés*, as the French call it, are numbered simply according to the horizontal rows and vertical columns, with Roman numerals for the one set, quite often, and Arabic for the other. All words of two letters and more are clued; and if there are two or more answers in the same row or column, they are clued successively and separated only by a colon or a dash.

Typical of American and many other crosswords is the following diagram:

It will quickly be apparent that all the letters in this diagram are cross-checked by intersecting words, so that solving only half the clues is theoretically enough to fill in the rest automatically. However, to compensate for this, puzzles of this design tend to be much bigger than ours, and diagrams of 25 × 25 squares are not uncommon in a Sunday paper or magazine in the States. This means that, even with a fair number of answers forming themselves, such crosswords have so many clues in them that they are sufficiently time-consuming to keep many Americans pleasantly occupied for most of their day off.

Puzzles with an arrangement of blocks similar to the American ones are the *Crucigrama* of Argentina, the *Kruiswoordpuzzel* of Holland and Belgium, the *Kryssord* of Norway and the *Cruciverba* or *Parole Incrociate* of Italy. Yugoslavia, too, and Lebanese newspapers which are printed in English have large crosswords of this type, while South Africa and Israel often arrange their blocks much more after our own fashion. Of these latter, the South African crossword rejoices in the name of *Blokkiesraaisel* and the Israeli one has its numbers in the diagram printed from right to left, to conform with the way in which words are written in Hebrew. Other countries that have some crosswords with diagrams familiar to us include Denmark, Germany, Jamaica and Spain. Thus we have a mass of evidence testifying to the world-wide popularity of those species of crossword which are served, for all their minor differences in presentation, shape and size, by clues that are virtually the same as questions on general knowledge or on synonyms.

Definition and cryptic

Returning to our own shores once more, we also meet a type of crossword in some publications which is a hybrid, having some of its clues definitive and others cryptic. It is almost as if the setter, having originally intended to produce a straightforward puzzle, has been unable to resist, here and there in the course of his clueing, the injection of a humorous twist suggested by a word's spelling, meaning or associations. This is, of course, what must have happened in the crossword's earliest days when the first few cryptic clues began to trickle into each puzzle, and we still have examples of this mongrel breed today.

Popular cryptic

National and local newspapers in this country, whether Sunday, daily or evening, and a host of weekly and monthly magazines publish a crossword puzzle in every issue. A large percentage of such crosswords are what are known as cryptic—an entirely British invention which is comparatively unfamiliar anywhere else in the world. It is true that some of our own regular cryptic crosswords, by means of an arrangement known as syndication, make their way overseas and are reprinted in some transatlantic or antipodean publications to serve a minority demand; and also some original varieties are devised abroad, for instance in America, for publication in intellectual monthlies and the like for a limited readership. The fact remains that, while elsewhere the cryptic crossword is a national rarity, here it is the staple diet of scores of thousands of regular and enthusiastic solvers.

Standards of such crosswords vary considerably from one paper to another, as do styles of clueing and other features. The entire subject of the cryptic crossword, which is the chief concern of this book, will be treated at length and in depth in the whole of Part II and most of Part III, and will be illustrated by examples of different types and standards in Part IV. Among these the reader will find a number of popular cryptic crosswords, some fairly easy and others of about average difficulty, using the standard 15 × 15 diagram with alternate blocks, similar to the one shown on p. 33.

Ximenes-type

Less popular numerically, but with a most accomplished and devoted following running into several thousands, is the type of cryptic crossword which is avowedly tougher than the average and can rarely be completed without the help of at least a good dictionary. It does not undertake to restrict itself to familiar words, and anything in the nature of an obsolete, dialect or strange-looking word is grist to this kind of mill.

Either through accident or experiment, or by the conscious design of its earliest composers, this harder puzzle has become easily recognisable by its smaller diagram, usually of 12×12 squares but occasionally varying slightly for some special purpose, with bars instead of blocks, as typified on p. 34. The famous Ximenes Crossword of the *Observer* used this format for more than a quarter of a century, and its present successor, the Azed Crossword, is continuing the tradition unchanged. The Mephisto puzzle, too, of the *Sunday Times* invariably appears on similar grids. A point worth mentioning in this connection is that, although the diagram is physically smaller, the fact that every single square in it is occupied by a letter results in a larger total of clues (approximately thirty-six) than the average of thirty in a 15×15 square containing blocks.

Thematic and novelty crosswords

As a change from the normal weekly offering of a fairly stiff but plain puzzle, the *Observer*'s Azed Crossword presents instead a novelty of some kind every couple of months or so, just as Ximenes did regularly in the past. It may be a crossword in which each clue contains a deliberate misprint; one in which the solver has to deduce a hidden theme or work out a code; a blank diagram for which the solver must supply not only the answers to the clues but also the missing bars; or one of many more equally ingenious ideas, culminating in a special puzzle at Christmas, which might be an amalgam of several of the regularly recurring types like those just mentioned.

The *Listener*, referred to in Chapter 1, is the publication which uniquely has a crossword containing some special theme or other novel feature every week of the year, and usually the standard is as challenging as will be found anywhere. This is due partly to the completely different nature of the crosswords from week to week and partly to the fact that, with the regular setters each appearing only a few times in a year, solvers do not have the same opportunity of becoming familiar with their clueing styles as they do with the more frequent or single contributors to other papers.

Novelty crosswords may also be seen in other papers from time to time. Mention has already been made (in Chapter 1) of the special double crossword in *The Guardian*, usually incorporating a literary theme of some kind, skilfully worked into two identical diagrams; and sometimes the same paper has a puzzle that is an alphabetical jigsaw in crossword form. In addition, several monthly magazines, of which more will be said in Chapter 22, specialise in publishing, among other puzzles of various kinds, a number of crosswords in many unusual and intriguing guises.

Part II

The Cryptic Crossword

4 Basic principles

The meaning of 'cryptic'

Among the definitions of the word 'cryptic' in *Chambers Dictionary* we find 'secret, hidden, mysteriously obscure'. There is a real danger that, if all crosswords intended as cryptic adhered strictly to any one or all of these definitions, they would be virtually unsolvable by all but a tiny minority of specially trained experts. Some modification of the word's meaning must therefore be applied to crossword clues if would-be solvers are not to be irrevocably deterred at the outset.

In crossword terms, a cryptic clue is one that seeks to present a riddle, a puzzle or some form of word-game in a manner that is not entirely straightforward—as it would be if merely a familiar synonym or unmistakable definition of the required answer were given. To do so, it relies a great deal on the ambiguous use of words and phraseology. Perhaps the most suitable epithet therefore, strictly within the confines of a crossword context, might be 'misleading', because (as will become evident when all the following chapters dealing with the manifold techniques of deception have been read) the principal aim of the writer of a cryptic clue is to delay its solution temporarily by deliberately disguising the obvious answer by means of some linguistic device or other until, realising that he has been tricked and led up the garden path, the solver returns to the proper route and in due course arrives at the correct destination.

(Let there be no doubt that the intention should be only to postpone the solution, not to prevent it, and that the clue which baffles the solver completely is, in effect, self-defeating and counter-productive, and by no means the triumph for the clue-writer that he sometimes fondly imagines. A battle of wits there may be—and, indeed, should be—between setter and solver, but it is one battle which the setter should plan to lose; for when the struggle is over, the adequacy of the clues is vindicated by the fact of their solution, so that the honours may be said to be equally shared in an atmosphere of mutual respect.

Exceptionally, when crosswords are set with the purpose of progressively eliminating large numbers of entrants, as for example in a knock-out competition where even one incorrect answer disqualifies the participant, the very conditions demand clues that are either vague, unhelpful, extraordinarily tortuous or such that necessitate reference to books which are not easily available. On such occasions the defeat of the solver is the professed aim, but this can be ensured only at the cost of an element of unfairness injected into the clueing. Yet how much more satisfactory it is to both parties when the solver can say, 'You fooled me here and there, but I managed it at last and enjoyed the tussle', to which the setter can reply, 'Well done! And thank you for proving that my clues were solvable.')

Every cryptic clue, then, is a little puzzle on its own which attempts to mislead the solver to some extent; and a cryptic crossword, if it fully aspires to the name, should contain cryptic clues only. Any clue that is a straightforward definition or synonym and nothing else, or a quotation with a missing word to be supplied, cannot qualify as cryptic and, strictly speaking, has no place in a crossword purporting to be such.

Lest there be any misunderstanding here, let it be clearly stated that there is nothing unfair or reprehensible about offering the solver a simple definition or an incomplete quotation; indeed, there are many who thoroughly enjoy having their vocabulary tested, or being reminded in this way of some half-remembered literary experience of the past. It is also readily granted that avowedly literary crosswords, novelty puzzles comprising various different features, general knowledge tests presented in crossword form and the like are perfectly entitled to include any factual question, synonym or quotation within their own terms of reference.

In crosswords that we may call the normal daily or weekly cryptic, however, with which this section is concerned, the quotation and single definition ought never to be found. The reason is that the replacement of one synonym by another and the recollection of some literary passage both call for actual knowledge rather than ingenuity or skill. You either remember the quotation or look it up or guess it, but you certainly don't work it out from the clue's wording, and there is nothing even remotely cryptic about its presentation. Similarly, you may with good reason pride yourself on your versatile vocabulary—and there will be ample scope for such facility during the solving of cryptic clues—but a test of this one facet of language alone is not the object of the exercise.

Helping and misleading

We have now established that a cryptic crossword should consist exclusively of cryptic clues, and that a cryptic clue is one which attempts to delay its solution for a time by misleading the solver in some way. But in what way? It is at this point that we are confronted with an apparent paradox, because what a cryptic clue ought to do, ideally, is both help and mislead simultaneously. It is easy enough to mislead anyone if you supply him with incorrect information, but that is patently unfair. What the ingenious clue-writer must aim at instead is a form of words which is not only misleading but also both accurate and fair, and to that extent genuinely helpful; and it is this combination of accuracy and fairness which lies at the heart of every clue and must take priority over every other consideration. In short, to be able to give perfectly correct information to the solver, but still disguise it sufficiently to mislead him—that is the craft, in two senses of the word, of cluemanship.

Definitions

But let us not become so obsessed with the need to mislead that we neglect the overriding obligation to be helpful in a clear, neat and, if possible, amusing way. The most helpful way to begin is by telling the solver what he is supposed to be looking for, and that means offering him a definition, or at least a very strong hint. If the answer is LADS, we must define it by something like 'Youngsters', which immediately tells the solver that he must find a word that is both a noun and plural; or by 'They are young', say, which amounts to the same thing. If the answer is LARGE, some word or phrase like 'big' or 'of great size' will similarly establish the correct part of speech in the solver's mind, and he will know at once that he is seeking an adjective for his answer. Or again, if the answer is a proper name such as ELIZABETH or MONTREAL, some defining words must be given: e.g. 'girl's name', 'Queen' or 'Bess', and 'city', 'in Canada' or 'place'.

It cannot be too strongly emphasised that a definition is the indispensable minimum requirement of every crossword clue that aims to be fair. If a solver is not told what the problem is, it is quite unfair to expect him to produce the answer with any certainty; and even if he does have a shot at it, he has no sure means of checking that his suggested answer is superior to some possible alternative which also seems to meet the conditions of the clue.

Suppose, for example, that you are confronted with the clue, 'Least damaged (5)'. Imagine, too, that you have S–A–E already entered in your diagram from having solved the intersecting words and that the two missing letters are unchecked, so you can get no further help with this word. You realise quite quickly, having had some experience of such things, that the word 'damaged' suggests that the order of the letters of 'least' has become knocked about in some way, and so you confidently put in the answer STALE. But then it strikes you that if you damage, as it were, the word 'least' it can equally make SLATE, which fits into the space just as well. Which answer did the clue-writer intend? It's impossible to say, because either answer is equally correct on the basis of the scanty information given; and if you find yourself disqualified for having the 'wrong' answer just because the setter was thinking of the other one, you will quite justifiably feel aggrieved. Now if the setter had played fair and written a clue including the vital definition (for instance, '*Roof-cover* that gets least damaged (5)'), the solver, having to choose between the two possible answers STALE and SLATE, would have seen at once that only SLATE satisfied the definition 'roof-cover' and therefore must be the correct answer.

Subsidiary indications

Let us insist, therefore, that a clue must be, or incorporate, a definition at the very least, and that such a definition should accurately show, or hint at, the part of speech used in the answer. But a cryptic clue must do more than merely define: it must give the solver some further help towards working out the answer, but in such a way that the very help contains an element of deception which may require ingenuity, skill or cunning on the solver's part to recognise and overcome. This further help can appear in many guises, which the succeeding chapters dealing with the various techniques of cluemanship will endeavour to explain and exemplify in detail. Whatever device is used, it serves to supplement the basic information supplied by the definition and thus offers the solver a second bite at the cherry. The difference between the definitions and what we may call these subsidiary indications in clues is this: the definition tells you what kind of answer to look for; the subsidiary indication gives you hints or instructions about how to find it. Furthermore, whereas the definition confines itself to the true meaning of the answer, the subsidiary part examines the word's make-up, its component parts, its literary associations, its sound when pronounced, its appearance when written backwards, and so on; and it is this aspect of clueing in particular, with its almost unlimited scope for ingenuity and innovation, that holds so much fascination and enjoyment for the devotees of the cryptic crossword, setters and solvers alike.

Composing a cryptic clue

From the foregoing paragraphs it will be evident that a very high percentage of cryptic clues will consist of two parts: definition and subsidiary indication. (Sometimes other techniques, such as two or three definitions, or a cryptic definition alone, will replace the normal formula, as will be explained later.) Given this premise, the deviser of the clue knows what he must offer and the solver what he must look for. One might say, indeed, that the writing and solving of a cryptic clue is the equivalent of an imaginary dialogue between cluewriter and solver. Let us take a simple example. The cluewriter (C-W) is offering the solver (S) a clue to the placename DONEGAL. The conversation proceeds as follows:

C-W: The answer I want is in Ireland.
S: How many letters?

C-W: Seven.

S: The choice is too wide. Give me some more help, please.

C-W: It's made up of two words, side by side. The first word means 'performed', and the second one means 'girl'.

S: To perform is to act or to do. So performed might be acted, did or done. A girl is a miss, or it may be a girl's name, or perhaps gal. Let's have the whole thing again.

C-W: I'll put all this information together as a complete clue: In Ireland, performed by girl (7).

S: Yes, I see it now. Performed = DONE; and that stands by, or beside, girl, which is GAL. Together they make DONEGAL, which is in Ireland. Very clear, and very helpful, in spite of your attempt to mislead me. Thank you.

Thus we see that in this clue accuracy and fairness have been adhered to: accuracy, because the required answer *is* in Ireland, as has been clearly stated; fairness, because extra help has been offered by the subsidiary information that a word for 'performed' is 'by' a word for 'girl'. What, then, makes this a cryptic clue? The fact that it presents all these correct statements in such a way that on its first impact it is mildly misleading, since it artfully suggests that the solver must try to think of something that a girl performs particularly in Ireland. Or, to put it another way, it is the very abundance of information that disguises the true meaning and leaves the solver temporarily unable to 'see the wood for the trees'.

(It should be added, incidentally, that there is no compulsion upon the clue-writer to present the definition first in the clue's wording if he thinks it will fit in more neatly at the end. The example just considered, for instance, would read quite as naturally, if not a shade more so, if the order of events were reversed, as follows: Performed by girl in Ireland (7).)

Now glance again for a moment, if you will, at the foregoing dialogue. If it had ended after the word 'Seven', this would have represented a straightforward, non-cryptic, definition clue such as one finds in any typical quick crossword, possibly reading as 'A place in Ireland (7)'. As it stands in full, it represents the wording of a cryptic clue, with the deserved addition of the grateful solver's thanks for its helpfulness.

Standards of difficulty

On many occasions one has heard a person with a high degree of competence in solving crosswords make the following complaint, for example with reference to the two different puzzles that appear each Sunday in the *Observer*: 'I can solve the Everyman crossword quite easily, but I can make neither head nor tail of the Azed one.' It must be accepted, of course, that the complainant is speaking the truth as far as he sees it, but really it ought not to be so; for the difference between these two crosswords is mainly one of the standard of difficulty but not of principle, in which they are, generally speaking, identical. In other words, whereas the one confines itself as a rule to vocabulary within the range of everyday usage, and its clues avoid as far as possible the erudite and over-subtle reference, the other does not restrict itself in this way but ranges farther afield into the realms of the dictionary in search of rare, antique or arcane vocabulary, and its clues do not so limit themselves as to exclude greater subtleties or more recondite allusions. And yet in the matter of principle and clueing technique they set out to be equally scrupulous in observing the rules which demand both accuracy and fairness. The following examples will demonstrate a difference, although not an extreme one, in the standard of difficulty and, at the same time, the identity of principle:

(a) Come here, and strike the woman (6)
(b) King's order to page—land the woman one (6)

The answer to both clues is HITHER, which can mean

'Come here' and comprises HIT (strike) and HER (the woman). But whereas in (a) this information is given in simple language and involves easily exchangeable synonyms, rather more thought is needed for (b) before one recalls that it was Wenceslas who was the king who (in the Christmas carol) said 'Hither, page, and stand by me . . .'; nor does HIT HER come so readily to mind from 'land the woman one' as it does from 'strike the woman'. Thus, while both clues are perfectly fair and accurate, and indeed employ the identical principles of cluemanship, the 'average' type used in (a) is of an easier standard than the Ximenes-type given in (b). When you add the fact that a complete crossword of type (b) consists not only of harder clues but also of a high proportion of what one might call 'dictionary words' in the diagram, it is understandable that average solvers may feel initially bewildered and conclude that it is beyond their mental resources. Let me assure them that this is by no means necessarily the case, and that the principles which govern an easy cryptic crossword are equally applicable to harder ones, the main difference being that the latter naturally demand greater perseverance, more time and probably frequent recourse to the dictionary.

Use of dictionaries etc.

Mention of the dictionary in the preceding paragraph has possibly drawn more than a few gasps of incredulity from my readers, as though, at worst, something downright dishonest or, at best, a fairly opprobrious form of cheating were being advocated and encouraged! Allow me to dispose of this misconception without further ado.

If you are taking part in some contest in which the use of dictionaries is not allowed, naturally it is cheating to smuggle one in. It is also realised that solvers don't normally carry dictionaries, atlases and the like about with them on their daily bus and train journeys, so that their favourite crossword tends to confine itself to familiar words and phrases, thus rendering the looking-up of words largely unnecessary. Hence many people regard it as a point of honour to solve crosswords without ever using a dictionary. But that kind of honour is not involved. If you have to put in the name of a place or person of whose spelling you are uncertain—or you can't remember, for instance, whether it's DEPENDANT or DEPENDENT that you want and the vital letter is unchecked—then satisfy yourself on these matters at the earliest opportunity and ensure that your solution is correct. Just as there is no law that compels a mathematician to work out a problem, even for amusement, entirely in his head, so the crossworder may enlist any available help with a clear conscience. What is more, this stubborn and entirely pointless refusal to consult books of reference not only may result in an incorrect solution but also will deprive you of the real pleasure of discovering new words, or unsuspected meanings of common words, which comes from attempting crosswords of a higher standard of difficulty.

It is even more incumbent upon the composer of the diagram to check very carefully both his spelling and his facts. Here again, when everyday words are involved, dictionaries will not normally be required; but should the faintest doubt creep into his mind about a spelling or an allusion, even if he is *almost* positive about either, he should check his references or open his dictionary without delay or compunction; for a good and reliable dictionary is a polymathic mentor, an unbiased arbiter and a friendly companion. Its usefulness may perhaps be underlined by the following anecdotes, which readers may find amusing.

Years ago the *Observer* used to organise a crossword-composing competition every Christmas. The diagram to be used by all entrants had the blocks and numbers already filled in, and contestants were invited to supply their own words to fit the spaces and to compose clues for them. One year, by a strange coincidence, two contestants from different parts of the country both included the misspelt word ASSININE in their diagrams—and, by an even more curious coincidence, at the identical position and clue-number as each other! Now had such a misspelling, due entirely to laziness in failing to look at the dictionary, turned up in a published crossword, complaints about the setter's carelessness would deservedly have come pouring in.

SWITHIN made his saintly appearance in one of my own diagrams. 'No, Sir,' wrote a solver dogmatically; 'the Book of Common Prayer (July Calendar) spells it SWITHUN.' I politely enquired of this correspondent whether I must therefore reject the spelling that everyone else uses, which is given in all the dictionaries in my possession and also, no doubt, in the diary in his own pocket in the space reserved for 15 July.

On the other hand, I was caught out on one occasion (not the only one, I hasten to add) by an alternative answer about whose existence I had forgotten. I had clued the word VICEREGENT by jumbling the letters into an anagram, and, as it happened, it was possible to obtain from solving other clues the letters –I–E–E–E–T. The clue was something like the following:

(c) Crete given, for a change, a deputy (10)

Imagine my surprise when it was soon pointed out to me that both VICEREGENT and VICEGERENT (each in a sense a stand-in or deputy, and each formed by mixing the words CRETE GIVEN) fitted the spaces equally aptly. Of course, both answers were accepted as correct, but it was an unsatisfactory situation; and had I remembered earlier about the alternative word, I would have phrased my clue to fit one answer and to exclude the other. However, all crossword setters must have suffered at some time from the unintended 'red herring'; but so long as care is taken in all foreseeable cases, solvers, who are generally a magnanimous band, will be quick to forgive the occasional lapse which demonstrates our human fallibility.

Afrit's Law

No discussion of cryptic clues should fail to refer to and consider the epigrammatic principle propounded by the celebrated Afrit, whom I mentioned in Chapter 1 as a most powerful influence in the development of this type of crossword. He laid down the following rule for the clue-writer: 'You need not mean what you say, but you must say what you mean.' Brilliantly succinct though this is, it has unfortunately, in common with many epigrams, a cryptic element itself and, as a result, its implications are not always completely appreciated. Let us examine in a little more detail what he intended. Consider the following clue:

(d) Old vehicles are brisk when reversing (5)

I (the clue-writer) mean that old vehicles (in this case TRAMS) are brisk (that is, SMART) when reversing, or when written in the reverse order. What is more, that is precisely what I have said in the clue, so I have said what I mean or, if you prefer it, what the answer means. However, if you innocently accept the clue at its face value as a simple statement, what I appear to be saying is that old vehicles are brisk when reversing, which is, to say the least, unlikely to be true. But, of course, I only *seem* to be saying that and I don't necessarily mean it. Thus I have said what I mean, but I need not mean what I say. Here's another example:

(e) This little bird was a great builder (4)

I mean that this word for a little bird (WREN) was also the name of the great builder of St Paul's Cathedral. I have said what I mean, but I don't honestly mean what I seem to be saying, namely that the wren was, or is, one of the great builders of ornithology.

Let's try another:

(f) Blades that decapitate swine (4)

I have said that there is a word for blades (OARS) which

removes the head (or first letter) from a word meaning swine (BOARS), and what I have said is true in that respect. On the other hand, OARS are not the kind of blades which decapitate anything, let alone swine—it was, in fact, just one of my little tricks to fool you!—so I don't mean at all what the reader thinks I am saying.

Look finally at this clue:

(g) You're sure to find a slattern in the tribe somewhere (5)

Once again, I mean that if you look inside the words 'triBE SOMewhere' you're sure to find BESOM, which means a slattern, among other things; I have said what I mean. This time, for a change, the clue's statement makes sense and is probably true also, so I do mean what I say on this occasion, as it happens, even though I needn't.

From these examples it will be seen that what we may call 'Afrit's Law', when put into a less epigrammatic form of words, really amounts to: 'You may not *necessarily* mean what you *appear to be saying*, but you must say what the *answer* (and its component parts also, if necessary) means.'

The clue-writer's duty

It follows from what we have discussed in this chapter that there are certain basic obligations which the deviser of cryptic clues must honour if he is to play fair and to satisfy even his most critical solvers. Firstly, he must be prepared to take infinite pains in revising his work so that careless slips and slovenly construction are eliminated. Only by a consistent policy of this kind can he hope over a period of time to construct a bridge of faith, as it were, which his solvers can cross again and again with complete trust.

Secondly, he must constantly remind himself that he is taking part in a game for entertainment only, and that his aim is not to concoct clues which will defy solution but those which will stimulate thought, challenge ingenuity and finally yield, if possible to the accompaniment of an appreciative chuckle by the solver. He must therefore seek to be genuinely helpful by supplying not merely an accurate definition but also some subsidiary indications of a more indirect nature.

Lastly, and perhaps of greatest importance, he must ensure that the information that he does give, however cleverly camouflaged for the purpose of misleading, is absolutely accurate and that he really does say with complete clarity what the answer means, so that the solver, once he has worked out the clue, can be certain that his answer is the unique one which satisfies all the conditions.

To sum up, he must give his solvers faith, help and clarity—and perhaps the greatest of these is clarity.

5 The art of cluemanship

The previous chapter has dealt with some of the basic principles which govern cryptic clues, and much emphasis has been laid upon the necessity of maintaining a judicious balance between misleading and being helpful, as well as upon the obligatory concomitants of accuracy and fairness. How are we to set about meeting these conditions in a typical clue, which offers the solver the twofold assistance of a definition and a subsidiary indication? The answer to that, briefly, is that there are numerous techniques, or combinations of techniques, available to the clue-writer, depending upon the shape, sound, sense, associations and so on of the word being clued, which will be fully considered in turn in the forthcoming chapters which form the remainder of this part of the book. Before we analyse the different methods separately, however, there are certain features of cluemanship which are common to all types of clue and which we must constantly bear in mind whether we are attempting to compose or to solve them.

Making sense

A fundamental requirement of a good clue is that it should mean something to the solver immediately upon impact, as it were, and not be an unintelligible collection of words, however correct they may be in relation to the answer. In other words, the writer's art lies in being correct and at the same time making sense, even if that sense is deliberately misleading. Some examples should make this point clear.

We want, let us say, to write a clue for the word LEGALLY, which means 'in a lawful manner'. One possible treatment which leaps to the eye is to split the word into two parts, LEG and ALLY. Now, a leg is a limb and an ally is an associate, so we could say, quite accurately, something like this:

A limb and an associate, in a lawful manner (7)

Nobody could accuse us of giving inaccurate indications for the subsidiary parts, LEG and ALLY, nor again of being in any way unfair. But what sense does the clue make? What mental picture is evoked as you read it? None at all, obviously. Then let's give it a little more thought and, while employing exactly the same method of clueing which resulted in the meaningless phraseology above, produce something more sensible and satisfying. What else can LEG be, besides a limb? A member: that's more promising, because then one thinks of a person rather than a thing, and now we have a member and also an associate, who is a confederate, or—yes, this sounds better—a partner. That leaves the word LEGALLY to be fitted into the idea we have in mind, which is 'member, partner, and in a lawful manner'. Here's a possible clue:

Member gets partner, in a lawful manner (7)

This makes sense and it conjures up a mental picture as one reads it. If you want to polish it up a little, you may alter the phrasing slightly and finish with:

A member should have a partner, according to law (7)

This is a perfectly adequate clue, which satisfies all the requirements: it gives the subsidiary information that a word for a member (LEG) should have (i.e. next to it) a word for a partner (ALLY); the definition of the answer LEGALLY is provided by the phrase 'according to law'; and it reads sensibly as an English sentence. What is more, it is fully cryptic because, even though each component part tells the truth about the word to be found, what the whole clue appears to say doesn't happen to be true, so that it misleads the solver, initially, into thinking along the wrong lines; nor is it obvious to him at first sight which is the definition and which the subsidiary indication.

Let us similarly consider a word like AMUSING, which will be seen to have quite a number of tempting possibilities in its literal make-up. We can separate it into (a) A + MUSING, (b) AM + USING, (c) the reverse of MA + USING, (d) AM + U + SING, (e) the word US inside A + MING, or (f) the words A + MUG about, or standing around, the word SIN—quite an embarrassment of riches for once! And we haven't fully exhausted all the potentialities of this word by any means. Let's see which treatment will yield the neatest and least complicated clue. What we are trying to achieve, remember, is a form of words which makes a superficial connection between the answer's meaning and the make-up of its letters; and we must also ensure that the complete clue can be assimilated by the solver as readily and as sensibly as if he were reading, for example, a novel, a newspaper article, a headline, a telegram or an item in a catalogue—anything, in short, which makes good sense in an easily imagined context.

We begin by deciding upon a workable definition of AMUSING. 'Capable of causing laughter' is a little long-winded, so we ought to reduce this phrase to a single word if possible, such as 'funny' or 'laughable'. Now what can we make funny or laughable about the various arrangements of the word's letters without straining credibility? We'll take them one at a time.

(a) A + MUSING means 'one' and 'pondering': nothing funny about that, at first sight. But A is also the indefinite article, so we can say that an article needs (to have with it) pondering. Why does an article, in the sense of a newspaper article, need pondering? Because it's complicated, difficult or possibly amusing in a subtle way. We can now produce this sensible-sounding clue:

(a) The article needs pondering—it's funny (7)

When analysed, this means that A needs MUSING next to it, and it (i.e. the answer) is AMUSING.

(b) AM + USING: not so promising, this. 'Am employing' isn't a funny idea. We can't say 'Am employing something funny', because 'something funny' indicates a noun, not an adjective, and we must be accurate in our definition. The best we can do is this:

(b) Am employing what's funny (7)

This means that AM and USING make what's funny, i.e. AMUSING. (We shan't employ this, though, because it isn't!) Let's look at the next treatment instead.

(c) Reverse of MA + USING. This isn't any real improvement on (b). We can say the following:

(c) Mother's back, employing what's funny (7)

That means that MA is written in reverse, followed by USING, but it isn't very sensible, so we'll shelve it, for use in emergency only.

(d) AM + U + SING. Thanks to the late Nancy Mitford, who helped to popularise Professor Alan Ross's original classification of people into 'U' and 'non-U' social grades, the letter U has become a boon to clue-writers, previously more or less confined to one of the categories of film censorship or the cramped quarters of German U-boats. In the case that we are considering here, we can avail ourselves of this meaning and imagine the following brief message about the school concert from the music teacher:

(d) Am getting upper class to give song—it's laughable (7)

Here we see AM getting (next to it) U (upper class) SING (to give song), and the answer is laughable (AMUSING).

(e) US in A + MING (A + Chinese dynasty). Well, that is funny according to one way of looking at it, and we can say so quite simply, as follows:

(e) Funny, including us in a Chinese dynasty (7)

We have here, precisely as we have said, AMUSING (funny), including US in A MING.

(f) A + MUG about SIN: not hilarious, it's true, but it has the elements of amusement. Since innocent or naïve adults are often regarded as figures of fun, a clue can be concocted on these lines from the words that we have here, as follows:

(f) A duffer about vice is laughable (7)

We have said that A MUG (a duffer), when placed about SIN (vice), becomes AMUSING (laughable).

We began by thinking that we were going to have a large number of equally good clues, but we find in practice that a couple of them are barely sensible as they stand, or at best either very weak or merely dull. Yet we are still left with (a), (d), (e) and (f) to choose from, all sensible and not difficult to solve, with perhaps (d) the most AMUSING! Readers, however, will naturally have their own preference and find something in one of the others which takes their fancy more; while the regular crossword-composer has a varied stock to choose from each time he includes the word AMUSING in his diagram.

Soundness and unsoundness in clues

It is most important to bear in mind in the course of excogitating a clue not only that it should make sense when completed but also that the normal rules of grammar and syntax must be observed. Failure to maintain these rules invariably results in an unsound clue which, however ingenious or witty, cannot be accepted as justifiable by the discriminating solver. Before we proceed, therefore, to bring into play any of the clueing devices described later, let us be quite sure that we understand what constitutes unsoundness, so that we may avoid being guilty of the same abuses of language, grammar and allied topics in our own work.

Use of language

A clear distinction must be made between a clue and its answer, and this is not always sufficiently appreciated. For example, if the answer to a clue is DEFORMED, the clue-writer may play with its letters in any way that he chooses: by splitting them up, jumbling them, reading them backwards, and so on. Let us suppose that he has chosen to treat it as the word FORM inside the word DEED. In that case his clue must say so, in correct English, with some subsidiary indication like 'Class caught in the act', from which the solver may work out FORM (class), which is caught, as it were, inside DEED (the act). This is perfectly fair; but what he must not say is something like 'The class *indeed*', and assume that the solver will eventually read it as the separate words 'in' and 'deed'. Just as one can't write 'Pure in thought and in deed' as 'Pure in thought and indeed', so the clue-writer must realise that when he is writing a clue he is giving information in words that must conform with the usages of the language.

Or, to take another example, imagine that he wishes to write a clue for the answer BAN, and he decides that it might be an idea to say that it is the word BAND minus the letter D. Should he be tempted to say, as part of the clue, 'it makes the orchestra nod', hoping that he is cleverly suggesting 'BAND, *no D*', that is to say 'without the letter D', let him firmly resist any such temptation, because in written or spoken English 'nod' does *not* mean 'no D' and we learned in the previous chapter that we must always say what we mean.

Linguistic accuracy must also govern the wording of definitions. It has already been stated that a definition must guide the solver, specifically or by strong implication, to the correct part of speech of the answer. It is quite unhelpful, as well as blatantly unfair, to clue TIMID, say, as 'He's afraid', which suggests a noun as the answer; that should now be clear. But another aspect of definitions needs to be mentioned here also: the fact that, contrary to mathematical law, if A = B and B = C, linguistically A does not therefore automatically equal C. For example, INTEND = MEAN (in one sense) and MEAN = AVERAGE (in another), because in each pair they are synonymous. We are not entitled to say that therefore 'Intend' is a fair clue to AVERAGE, leaving the solver to deduce the missing stage with its different meaning. Indeed, it is patently not a correct definition and cannot be justified.

A further example of this may be seen in the following *unsound* clue:

Fat man who carries luggage (5)

This clue has two definitions, one accurate, the other not. 'Fat' leads correctly to the answer STOUT, whereas 'man who carries luggage' gives us PORTER, which in one sense is a type of STOUT. It must be emphasised, however, that even though FAT = STOUT and PORTER = STOUT it is incorrect to infer that FAT = PORTER, as we are expected to do from this clue's wording. The plain fact is that a clue to PORTER in the human sense can in no way be transferred to mean PORTER in the STOUT sense.

A clue to a clue

Another device, in some ways similar to the one just mentioned, and which should be avoided by the clue-writer who wishes to be helpful, is the 'clue to a clue'. While this, unlike the previous examples, cannot be called inaccurate in any respect, it may be considered something of an imposition upon the innocent solver. Here is an example:

It's caused by having bedroom in a mess (5)

You are supposed to obtain from this answer ENNUI, by first realising that the phrase 'in a mess' is a way (and quite a fair one, incidentally) of indicating that the letters of 'bedroom' are mixed up to form the word 'boredom', and from 'boredom' you arrive at the five-letter answer ENNUI.

The element of unfairness here is this: that after you have worked out what you thought was the clue and now have the answer to the jumbled letters, you find that you haven't solved the problem after all, but merely presented yourself with a new clue; in other words, you have been given a clue, not to the required answer ENNUI, but to a clue, namely 'boredom', to the required answer. It is a way of saying to the solver, 'I'll give you a definition all right, but you'll have to work it out first'. It certainly makes a clue harder to solve, if that is what its perpetrator is aiming at, and it has a defensible logic about the stages of solution; but it is, in my opinion, rather like having run a mile, only to discover that the race is due to begin at the point where you thought it had finished.

Obsolete and foreign words etc.

A more debatable aspect of definitions, one which is more concerned with helpfulness than with soundness, must be left to each crossword-composer to consider thoroughly, after which he will doubtless base his future policy upon his conclusions. The question is: how much extra help should the solver be given when the answer is an obsolete, Scottish, foreign, or slang word or phrase? My own view is that it depends on the nature and standard of difficulty of the crossword concerned, and also upon whether the use of a named dictionary is recommended or specified. Let us consider this further.

Whatever one's opinion may be of either the ugliness or, it may be, the graphic appropriateness of certain slang words, they are part of the bloodstream of a living language which is constantly growing and adapting itself to a changing environment. Therefore, while bypassing, it is hoped, the crude and obscene, one is fully entitled to include, without the need for further explanation, any slang which has achieved dictionary status or is sufficiently current to be familiar to the majority of solvers.

(This latter consideration involves a question of judgment on which one may occasionally err. Some time ago I included in a crossword the answer UPTIGHT, which I had begun to hear increasingly on TV and see from time to time in print. Its use brought a mild rebuke from a friendly solver who had never heard of it and could not find it in any dictionary. However, when the new edition of *Chambers Dictionary* was published a few months later, I was immensely relieved to find the offending word now firmly established within its pages!)

As for the rest, one does not, generally speaking, expect to find obsolete words included in the normal daily crosswords, where recourse to a dictionary is not usually called for; and the same may be said of Scottish (or Irish or Welsh) and foreign words which are not likely to be immediately recognisable by a person of average education and reading. In the case of foreign words and phrases which have been incorporated into the English language, such as the French FAUX PAS and TÊTE-À-TÊTE or the Latin STATUS QUO and VICE VERSA, there is surely no need to shrink from using them in a popular crossword, nor should it be thought necessary to make special mention in the clues of their exotic origins. With some familiar Scottish words, however, which have a different meaning from English words of the same spelling, the clues would not be accurate unless both definitions were included. Two examples of these should suffice, as follows:

(a) English eager to lament in Scotland (4)

The answer is KEEN, which is English for 'eager', while in Scotland it also means 'to lament'.

(b) Band of roughs to go over the Border (4)

The word GANG, or a band of roughs, also means 'to go' in Scotland, or 'over the Border'.

In addition, if I found that I had used a word that was exclusively Scottish, such as AGLEY, in a 'non-dictionary' type of crossword, I should be inclined to indicate its Scottishness in the definition, on the ground that such words don't turn up very often, so that when they do it is perhaps fairest to draw the solver's attention to their unusual nature.

On the other hand, in the harder type of crossword like the former Ximenes and the present Azed in the *Observer*, Mephisto in the *Sunday Times* or those in the *Listener* composed by many different hands, it is understood from the outset that the possession of a dictionary is often a solver's essential prerequisite, since he knows that the setter feels free to include in his diagram any words which appear in the dictionary—be they foreign, obsolete, dialect, slang or whatever—as well as proper names drawn from other sources if he so desires (which means, usually, if he is unable to find a word in the dictionary that will fit in!). In these circumstances the solver should be prepared for anything, with the strict proviso that the clues must offer him sufficient accurate information to give him a fair chance of arriving at the answer. With rare and obsolete words and the like, the standard bipartite clue, consisting of an accurately worded definition and a subsidiary indication, should be more than adequate for the purpose. And when the author of a crossword further reveals that a specific dictionary has been used, then the answer will be found in that dictionary whether it is obsolete or not. Nevertheless, if the clue-writer feels that a word like 'old' or 'formerly' is likely to be of real help to his solver in cases of possible doubt on their part, by all means let him insert it in his clue (as in practice I frequently do myself) as an extra bonus; but I hope that it is now appreciated that, when a dictionary has been named, or implied over a long period, he is not obliged to do so.

Double duty

Undue haste or carelessness unrelieved by conscientious revision can sometimes lead one into grammatical or syntactical errors and so make an otherwise neat clue unsound. One such error consists in making one word do double duty: once as it is used in its real sense, and again as it is required in its apparent or misleading sense. See whether you can spot the incorrect 'double-duty' word as you read each of the following examples:

(a) Uproar in which one is disorderly (5)
(b) Tree in a rotten condition, but it's intact (6)
(c) To go back to her—that's different (5)

In (a) the answer is NOISE (uproar), and we are meant to find it by rearranging the letters of ONE IS, which we are told are in a disorderly state. But what the writer should have said, to be syntactically correct, is 'Uproar in which ONE IS *is* disorderly', but instead he has made the one word 'is' do double duty, both as part of the letters to be rearranged and as the verb in the sentence, which is impossible, and so the clue is unsound. A satisfactory version of this same idea might be:

(a) Uproar—one is disorderly (5)

This means what it says: NOISE (uproar), and ONE IS, out of order.

In (b) we have TREE IN *in* a rotten condition (i.e., by crossword licence, all out of order) to make ENTIRE (intact), and the word 'in' has been unfairly overworked. Correctly rewritten, it could be:

(b) Intact, in tree that's rotten (6)

This says that the phrase IN TREE that's rotten, or out of order, is ENTIRE (intact).

Finally, in (c), if you mean that the word TO has to go backwards to HER, making OT-HER (different), you can't say 'TO, go back...' and expect it to be read as 'Get TO *to* go back...'. A clue observing correct syntax might be:

(c) To back her—that's different (5)

There should be no difficulty in analysing this version, which says: TO back (i.e. backwards, which makes OT) HER—that's OTHER (different).

It will be discovered later (in Chapter 18) that there is one rather subtle technique by which every single word in a clue is made to do double duty: in other words, the entire clue has to be read twice over to achieve its full effect. That is quite different, of course, from omitting one essential word from a clue or a sentence and thus making it syntactically incorrect.

Redundant words

Whether your preference is for short and snappy clues or for more verbose ones which paint a clear mental picture—and most crosswords (apart from those in which brevity amounts almost to an obsession) tend to be an amalgam of both kinds—the result, if it is to be at all satisfactory, should make good sense. On this point the following warning is issued: however long or short the clue may be, every word in it must be relevant to the answer, and redundant words must not be introduced merely to make the *apparent* meaning sensible. This will require further elucidation.

Take the word GULL, which is a bird and also a person who is easily taken in or duped. A simple clue using the two separate definitions would be:

(a) Bird, one easily duped (4)

If you wish to be even more clear in indicating the two nouns, you can lengthen it to:

(b) A bird, one that is easily duped (4)

Now although three words have been added to the first clue, the new version is unexceptionable since everything in it is relevant to the two meanings of GULL.

Now examine the word REED, which is a type of grass and which also happens to form the animal DEER when read backwards (on the assumption that we are dealing with an Across clue). What we have, then, is the reverse of DEER, or 'The animal goes back', and also REED, clued as 'grass'. We want the whole clue to make sense, so we put both 'halves' together and (hoping that nobody will notice) add an inoffensive word to join them, thus:

(c) The animal goes back to the grass (4)

Are we justified? No, a thousand times no! Have we said what we mean? Well, we have indicated that DEER is to be written in reverse order, and we have defined REED as grass; but what information about the answer REED, or any aspect of it, does that redundant word 'to' give to the solver? None whatsoever; on the contrary, its very presence misleads the trusting solver into believing that it *is* an essential part of the real clue—but that type of misleading is illicit. Out it must go, together with all similar interlopers, to stand in a corner until required to perform a genuine rather than a spurious function.

What then, you may ask, of the definite and indefinite articles included in the above examples? Are they redundant too? In my view, their inclusion or exclusion is entirely at the discretion of the clue-writer, and considerations of space, neatness of wording, consistency within a clue and so on will be the determining factors. For example, one could clue the word AMOUNT (whole sum) by splitting it into A and MOUNT (horse), as follows:

(d) Whole sum will get a horse (6)

There's something not quite fluent about the sound of that clue, and it doesn't take long to see that what it needs is the definite article before 'whole' to balance the indefinite one before 'horse', giving:

(e) The whole sum will get a horse (6)

There is surely nothing irrelevant about that extra article, since a dictionary, under the word AMOUNT, gives the meaning '*the* whole sum'. Similarly, just as KING can be defined by the single word 'monarch', so it may be accepted with equal accuracy as either 'a monarch' or 'the monarch' (as in the expression 'to become king'). Since, therefore, brevity in clues—normally, within reason, a desirable objective—should never be achieved at the cost of clarity or good sense, it is sometimes preferable to lengthen a clue by adding either 'a' or 'the', if doing so will improve the appearance of a clue without committing any inaccuracy or redundancy.

It must be added that the use of the article, as indicated above, is best restricted to nouns to be fully justifiable; but on the same principle there is nothing wrong with prefacing a verb with the word 'to', if that will make better sense of the clue.

It is also reasonable at times to use a conjunction between the two 'halves' of a clue, without being guilty of introducing redundant wording. Three examples should make this clear, as follows:

(f) A sweet and lovely shot (5-3)

This is a concise way of saying that the answer consists of

two separate definitions, one meaning sweet *and* the other a lovely shot, leading to the answer BULL'S-EYE. The word 'and' is therefore performing a useful function.

(g) Sweet, but sour (4)

It is a fact worth exploiting that the word TART, as a noun, is a sweet that one has with a meal, while as an adjective it can mean acid or sour. Thus the extra word 'but' in this clue can be justified as follows: the answer means sweet, *but* (oddly, at the same time, also means) sour.

(b) Nick, or wound slightly (7)

The word 'or' need not be considered redundant here if the clue is analysed thus: the answer can be defined simply by 'Nick' *or* by 'wound slightly'. Whichever synonym is used, it should produce the same answer, SCRATCH, which is another name for the devil—as 'Nick' is—and which also means to wound slightly.

The letter I etc.

One of the most common grammatical errors perpetrated in crossword clues, even in some of the highest pedigree, is that which involves the letter I. Its prevalence vitiates many an otherwise attractive idea, and the pity of it all is that the error is so unnecessary; for once the point is clearly understood, the pitfall can quite easily be circumvented with no detriment whatsoever to the original thought.

The letter I, when printed as a capital letter, may be read either as a single letter in a longer word, or as the Roman numeral for the figure one or as the personal pronoun. In order not to confuse the functions of each of these, let us examine some examples.

In the word PLAIN, we find that the letter I is surrounded by, or is included in, the word PLAN. An *incorrect* clue for this word would be:

(a) I am included in the plan, it's obvious (5)

In this clue it is intended that the solver should say to himself that the letter I goes inside PLAN to make PLAIN, which means obvious. Quite so; but the wording employs incorrect grammar which will not successfully stand up to analysis. Just as in the word BEAT, for instance, E is in BAT or A is in BET, so in the word PLAIN, I is in PLAN; and therefore, since we shouldn't dream of saying that (the letter) E *am* in BAT or (the letter) A *am* in BET, so we must not say that (the letter) I—which is used here in the third person—*am* in PLAN. What is more, we need not be forced into this infraction of grammatical law at all, since the meaning that we are trying to convey can be achieved with equal clarity by only the slightest alteration to the original wording, as follows:

> **(b) I must (may/can/will/should) be included in the plan, it's obvious (5)**

This time the clue really does say what it means, for the solver is told that the letter I must be included in PLAN (or may be, can be, will be, should be, etc., as you please) to make the answer PLAIN (obvious).

(This device of introducing auxiliary verbs, incidentally, can often avoid awkwardness in a clue's wording when there is a clash between singular and plural. For example, in the word NEWEST, the word WE is in the word NEST. Now since 'WE *is* in the NEST' makes an accurate statement about the answer but is grammatically unacceptable, while 'WE *are* in the NEST' is correct English but not true of the answer, we can satisfy both requirements by using an auxiliary verb and saying 'WE *must* be in the NEST'. On a slightly different level, when the word US forms part of another word, as in ROUST, it would be entirely incorrect to say something like 'We are dumped in rubbish' and expect the solver to deduce US inside ROT, because WE is not the same as US at all. The correct procedure here would be to write a clue that included something on the lines of: 'See us surrounded by rubbish', which clearly indicates US surrounded by ROT, making ROUST.

It should be made clear that in these two examples we have been concerned only with the wording of the *subsidiary* parts of the clues. For complete clues to the words NEWEST and ROUST we should, of course, also require their definitions.)

To revert to the word PLAIN. If the clue-writer prefers to take the letter I as the Roman numeral instead of the pronoun, a similar clue can be devised as follows:

(c) One should be included in the plan, it's obvious (5)

The instruction to the solver is that the number one, identical as it is, when printed, with the letter I, should be written inside the word PLAN, making PLAIN.

Are we then debarred from ever using the letter I in its pronominal sense? Not at all; there are two situations in which its use is both natural and legitimate—despite the apparent contradiction in terms! Firstly, in a word like DIAMETER, you will notice that the words I AM are contained within the word DETER. Without working out here a complete clue for the answer, it will be sufficient to say that the subsidiary part of the clue could well be 'I am coming inside to deter . . .', meaning, as it says, that we have I AM coming inside DETER to make DIAMETER. Or, similarly, the word TIMED can be treated by the deviser of the clue as I'M with TED round it, from which he might concoct, as part of his clue, 'I'm embraced by Ted . . .', meaning that the letters IM are surrounded by TED, making TIMED.

Secondly, there is a useful convention in crosswords, having something in common with the game of spoken charades (as opposed to the mimed variety, which will be more fully described in Chapter 7), which permits the answer to speak to the solver. In this game, for instance, we might be presented with the following: 'My first is a team, my second a group of directors and my whole is a piece of furniture.' From this, after due deliberation, we discover that the first element is a SIDE, the second a BOARD and the whole a SIDEBOARD.

(I was once told the following clue, clearly inspired by this game, which appeared many years ago in, I believe, a crossword in *The Times*:

(d) My first is what my second is not (7)

If that was indeed the complete clue, then it lacked the essential definition which would have made it completely fair. But even as it stands, it is as brilliant an example of camouflaged simplicity as one could wish to meet. At first sight it appears to be fiendishly complicated, but in fact the answer (WHATNOT) is actually staring us in the face if we will only accept the evidence of our eyes—a thing which most of us (and with reason!) are often too suspicious to do when solving clues. A generous salute to the unnamed optical illusionist who devised this clue is not, I believe, out of place here.)

In the same way a crossword clue may be so phrased as to appear to be speaking directly to the solver, as in the following example:

(e) I worship images, I do, afterwards (8)

It will be seen here that the answer who is speaking is IDOLATER, and that the make-up of the word is I DO + LATER (afterwards). It is also worth pointing out that the first 'I' represents the complete answer, whereas the second one is merely one element in its literal constitution.

A further example is the following:

(f) I'm a fop, by the sound of it, and a beast, but I'm just a weed (9)

The answer is DANDELION (a weed), and it consists of DANDE, which is DANDY (a fop) by the sound of it, and LION (a beast). Note that this convention of making the clue speak in the first person is most suitable when the answer is in fact a person, as in example (e) above; makes perfectly good sense (as in example (f)) when it is any noun at all; and would be permissible, but perhaps rather less effective, if the answer were any other part of speech.

Different methods

Now that the basic principles and requirements of cryptic clues have been discussed in some detail in the two chapters now ending, with words of caution, advice and even admonition given on matters relating to their soundness, the accuracy of grammar and syntax, the precision of definitions, the necessary mixture of deception and helpfulness—all of which considerations affect clues using every type of approach—it is time to learn about the various methods available to us of clueing the words and phrases which crop up in our crossword diagrams. Some words lend themselves to one treatment more naturally than to another, while others have a make-up of letters which makes them most versatile and malleable. Some appear to call for a mixed approach, and others again prove very intractable and almost defy being forged into neat clues.

Lest there should be any confusion along the way, each of the succeeding techniques of clueing will be afforded the dignity of its own chapter, which will exhaustively deal with that technique alone so that the reader may have the opportunity of mastering it without any extraneous distractions. (An exception is Chapter 19, a round-up of miscellaneous techniques which do not require more than a brief mention each.) It should be borne in mind, however, that any word or phrase, particularly if it comprises many letters, may call for a combination of several different treatments in one and the same clue. It is in achieving a neat balance and variety in every complete crossword, without undue tortuousness or straining of the language, while at the same time injecting into the challenge a measure of enjoyment and genuine fun, that the art of cluemanship lies.

6 Two or more definitions

As has already been stated in Chapter 3, a single-definition clue which calls for a factual or synonymous answer, with no attempt at misleading the solver, is not in any sense cryptic. Faced with the clue 'A fruit (5)', we may be at a loss for a while before thinking of one which has exactly five letters, and even then we shall need the help of a letter or two from other words before we can confidently choose the right one from among APPLE, MELON, LEMON, GUAVA, etc. But we know from the outset precisely what we are looking for, and no hint of deception enters our minds, or that of the clue-writer.

Similarly, if in a puzzle of that type we are asked to name a flower, we immediately start thinking of roses and tulips and the like, as of course we are meant to do, and there is no danger that the setter is having us on and really means a river, or something that flows—*that* kind of flower!—as could well be the case if at least some of the puzzle's clues were cryptic.

We shall see later how it is possible to devise single-definition clues of the 'flower' type so as to set the solver off on the wrong foot, thus making them cryptic; but for our present purposes, one straightforward definition alone has no place in a cryptic crossword.

Curiously, however, as soon as two definitions are given in a clue for the same answer instead of one, the cryptic element begins to creep in. This is noticeable when the answer concerned has two different meanings (for example, DATE, which is a time and a fruit) or is used as two different parts of speech (such as SNAFFLE, which can be a noun meaning a bit that restrains a horse and a verb meaning to steal; or FAIR, an adjective meaning just and a noun for a bazaar). In each of these cases one has merely to put both meanings side by side in order to introduce a cryptic flavour into the clue, as follows:

(a) Fruit time (4)
(b) Steal a bit (7)
(c) Just a bazaar (4)

What makes these clues cryptic is the fact that, although each one consists of two straightforward, non-cryptic definitions, the resultant phrase or short sentence presents a different picture from that given by each definition separately, and that picture itself is deliberately misleading. 'Fruit time' in example (a) immediately suggests a stage in a meal, and if the solver pursues that idea he will find himself a fair distance down the garden path before he realises that he has been tricked and that he must think of the word DATE, which can mean both fruit and time. Similarly in clue (b), although 'steal' on its own or 'bit' on its own will clearly indicate the answer SNAFFLE, the sentence 'Steal a bit' gives the impression of an instruction to someone to commit theft in a small way, which is not precisely what the answer means. And again in clue (c), while the words 'just' and 'a bazaar' both mean FAIR, the combination of the two definitions makes the answer less obvious, especially since the solver will naturally read 'just' as if it meant 'only', which is a form of deception characteristic of cryptic but not of definition clues.

Here are a few further examples of two definitions in juxtaposition which produce a somewhat misleading picture:

(d) Drop the rent (4)

TEAR = a drop from one's eye, and a rip or rent.

(e) Squeeze a lot of rags (5)

PRESS = to squeeze, and a lot of newspapers or 'rags'.

(f) Army entertainer (4)

HOST = an army, and one who entertains guests.

It is also a common and perfectly legitimate practice to separate the two definitions, by the use of punctuation or by the insertion of extra words, provided that they are relevant, as in the following examples:

(g) A race calls for a violent effort (6)

This clue says that a word meaning a race (in the sense of a stock or breed) calls for, or demands from the solver, a word meaning a violent effort. The word STRAIN answers both these definitions.

(h) Rest and sit again (6)

This looks like a suggestion to someone to have a respite first and then take an exam a second time. In fact, though, we have to find some word, either a verb or a noun, which means rest, as well as (hence the word 'and' in the clue) to sit again. REPOSE is rest, and to RE-POSE is to sit (as a model) again.

(i) Slam—that's a square cut (4)

We are invited to think of a cricketer hitting a ball hard, but the clue really means nothing of the kind! Its writer has told us that there is a word for slam, and that when we have thought of the right one, that word is also a square cut. The answer proves to be BANG (another word for to slam), which can also mean a style of hair that is cut square across the brow, or in other words a square cut.

The principle of using more than one definition to make a clue cryptic can, of course, be extended to include any number of a word's meanings. It might be objected that any clue which contained, say, three different definitions side by side would positively scream the answer, since if the solver didn't recognise one meaning on sight he would be sure to know the second or, failing that, the third, and that therefore such clues must be suitable for only the simplest puzzles. Certainly, if it were made obvious from the start that three distinct definitions were being offered for the same word, this would be so; but oddly enough it does not necessarily work out that way. Indeed, if the clue is worded with sufficient skill or cunning, it will not be immediately apparent that it is a 'definition-only' type at all. For the very liberality of the information that is presented serves to disguise its true nature or, as was stated earlier (Chapter 4), makes it difficult for one to see the wood for the trees.

Let us remember, however, that the object of good clue-writing is primarily to entertain, not to concoct unsolvable clues. It may well be, therefore, that some clues with multiple definitions will turn out to be quite easy to solve after all, while others may prove more baffling, especially if the definitions chosen by the clue-writer, or the answer itself, are of the more recondite kind, suitable for a more difficult standard of puzzle. In either case, they can give as much pleasure by their neatness as any other type of clue that we shall be considering in the chapters ahead.

The following examples are mostly of an easier standard, but a few harder ones are included so as to show that this technique, although essentially uncomplicated, is capable of creating a broad range of very satisfying clues.

Here are several which contain three definitions.

(j) It's terribly valuable, yet apparently free—that's quite absurd (9)

The answer, PRICELESS, means very valuable, yet it can also be taken as meaning without a price, or free. Another meaning of this word, as in the expression 'a priceless remark', is 'quite absurd'.

(k) Drum and wind for the dance (4)

The apparent sense of this clue is that two kinds of musical instrument are available for use at a dance. But the real sense is that a word meaning a drum, and the same word meaning to wind, will also do for the name of a kind of dance. REEL satisfies all three requirements.

(l) The computer opposite the table (7)

A computer is something that counts, and so it is a COUNTER, which also means contrary or opposite, as well as a table over which customers are served.

(m) At liberty to deliver without payment (4)

Three different uses of the word FREE are involved here. A person who is free is at liberty; to deliver someone from trouble is to free him; and to get something free is to get it without payment.

To find as many as four different definitions for one word or its homonyms will almost certainly call for a study of the dictionary and the employment of little-known meanings such as delight the linguist or anyone who enjoys a more difficult challenge. How many solvers, for example, would be likely to know, unless it has cropped up previously in a hard crossword, that the word BEAR, in addition to its familiar meanings of a big furry animal and a verb with the sense of to carry or endure, has another couple of homonyms besides? One of these means barley, and the other a pillow-case. Thus we have four words, all of different derivations but all with the same spelling, which offer the clue-writer a wide choice of definitions, and he may sometimes attempt to join them together in one clue. Now while he is unlikely to convince his solvers that one can get a big furry animal to carry a pillow-case for barley, there will certainly be other occasions when he *can* devise a sensible-sounding clue by connecting four different definitions, and both dispense and derive enjoyment in the process.

Here are a few examples of four-definition clues which make good sense without, incidentally, having to depend on a large number of unknown meanings.

(n) Scold degree class producing rot (4)

To RATE is to scold; a certain RATE is a certain extent or degree; a RATE can mean a rank or class; and the word that stands for all these three meanings is also producing here the homonym RATE (also spelled RAIT or RET), which means to rot. This is a harder-than-average clue, despite its four straightforward definitions, because the synonyms used are not of the kind that leap to the mind, except perhaps the first.

(o) Hook is a scoundrel, utterly base (3)

The answer DOG is a hook for holding logs; a cur or scoundrel; utterly, in the sense that dog-tired means utterly tired; and spurious or base, as in dog-Latin. As a description of the notorious Captain Hook, the complete clue makes convincing reading and will probably mislead many solvers nicely for a while.

(p) A whole page for bank interest—that was long, long ago (4)

The answer to this nostalgic clue is SIDE, which is a whole page of a book; it also stands for a border or bank; it means an opinion or an interest; and in Shakespeare it is an adjective meaning long, so it was long, a long time ago.

(q) Rushed off once to flog a piece of land and lie low (4)

HIDE is the way Spenser used to spell HIED, so once it

meant the same as rushed off; to HIDE is to whip or flog; a HIDE is an area of land; and the only familiar meaning used in this clue is to conceal oneself or lie low.

Here finally are a couple of examples which will show how this technique can accommodate as many as five definitions within the compass of clues no more than average in length.

(r) Determined company of dancers decline to become rigid and formal (3)

Five meanings of the simple answer SET are: as adjectives, determined and formal; as a noun, a company of dancers; as verbs, to decline (like the sun) and to become rigid (like jelly).

(s) Secure a fish, save the shoal—a Scottish jest (3)

The answer is another small word, BAR, revealing some unexpected meanings. One is to fasten or secure; another is a type of fish; it can mean except or save (e.g. all bar one); it is a bank or shoal; and finally, it is a Scots word for a jest. This is a difficult clue too, especially because only two of the five definitions are at all familiar, and even they are so disguised by their context that the solver, when reading 'Secure', is bound to think of it in the sense of catch and will take 'save' to be a verb instead of the preposition that it is.

Once you have consulted your dictionary for the purpose of seeing how many meanings a word has, you quickly discover that in some cases, for instance with a common word like SIDE, used in example (p) above, its different synonyms are so numerous that even a ten-definition clue is not beyond the bounds of possibility. However, there is a practical limit to the number that a clue-writer needs in order to entertain and mislead his public. For the average popular cryptic, just as the solver ought to be given two parts to each clue, so he should be presented with two definitions, if it is that type of clue. Occasionally three definitions may help to round off the general sense, as in the quite easy example (m) above, but in practice it is rare to find more than two. When we consider harder crosswords, however, such as Azed's or those in the *Listener*, a multiplicity of definitions, skilfully but sparingly used in any one puzzle, can be most effective in contributing to the intriguing nature of a clue.

7 One after another

In the party-game of charades, the object is to work out a word or phrase from a series of hints, or clues. The normal practice is to split the required answer into its component syllables, each of which is acted in a little scene with the aid of mime, and finally to present the complete word or words, which must also be acted.

Thus, if the word to be discovered is SEESAW, the 'actor' may first raise his hand to shield his eyes and gaze into the distance, to suggest SEE. Next, he may rest his knee on a chair and go through the motions of cutting through a piece of wood, to indicate SAW. And finally, he will have to do his best to simulate the action of moving up and down; at which point, it is hoped, the word SEESAW will occur to the 'solvers'.

The same basic idea is often applied in crossword puzzles

to those words or phrases which lend themselves to this treatment. The obvious difference is that here the component parts are indicated by some written means instead of by mime and the complete word or phrase by a definition.

For example, the word BLOCKHEAD, meaning a fool, may be split into BLOCK, meaning to obstruct, and HEAD, which means principal. A clue for this word employing the charade principle could therefore be:

(a) Obstruct the principal, a fool (9)

In this clue the sequence of events is identical with that in a charade: a definition of the first syllable, a definition of the second syllable and finally a definition of the complete word.

Here is another example:

(b) Fellow gets permit for a garland (7)

A fellow is a CHAP; to permit is to LET; and together they make CHAPLET, a garland. Note, by the way, that the word 'permit' in the clue makes the solver think of *a* permit, whereas it really is meant to indicate *to* permit. This is all part of a clue-writer's legitimate deception.

Let us now see the same rules operating with words of three syllables, as follows:

(c) The role a sovereign is sharing (9)

PART (the role) + A + KING (sovereign) = PARTAKING (sharing).

(d) The way people, sound as a bell, are filling in potholes, etc. (4-7)

ROAD (the way) + MEN (people) + DING (to sound as a bell) = ROAD-MENDING (filling in potholes, etc.).

It will be seen from example (c) above that sometimes in crossword clues, although not in the game of charades itself, a syllable may be presented as a free gift to the solver instead of being disguised by a definition or other means. In this example the letter A has been given unchanged.

Just as there are, no doubt, other variations of the game

of charades, so too in its crossword adaptation the rules can be extended in several respects. Firstly, it is just as correct, in crossword terms, to *begin* with the complete word and then give the component parts afterwards, as follows:

(e) Serfs—the man has plenty (6)

HELOTS are serfs, consisting of HE (the man) and LOTS (plenty).

(f) Slightly bitten, writer lost blood (7)

NIBBLED (slightly bitten) comprises NIB (writer, or something that writes) and BLED (lost blood).

Secondly, the division of a word or phrase into its component syllables need not follow its real derivation, so long as it treats the letters in their correct order. Thus NIGHTRAIL may be treated as NIGH-TRAIL, GRAND-SON as GRANDS-ON or GOODS-TRAIN as GOOD-STRAIN. The following is an example:

(g) Revolutionary set of logs, a new version (2-5)

RED (revolutionary) + RAFT (set of logs) = RE-DRAFT (a new version).

Thirdly, the word to be treated need not be split into single syllables only. A word of three syllables, for instance, may be more suitably clued as a combination of a monosyllable and a disyllable, such as SUP-POSING; or *vice versa*, for example POPPY-COCK—and the same principle applies to words of more than three syllables, provided only that the component parts come one after another. Here are a couple of examples of the one- and two-syllable combination.

(h) The prophet, a mug, gets linen fabric (10)

SEER (the prophet) + SUCKER (a mug) = SEERSUCKER (a linen fabric).

(i) Threatened, the mischievous child stopped (8)

IMPENDED (threatened) is a combination of IMP (the mischievous child) and ENDED (stopped).

In conclusion, here are some typical examples of the one-after-another principle, in which words of more than two syllables are split according to any of the rules mentioned above, and with the complete word or phrase appearing either first or last.

Three syllables

(j) Wet weather causes reduction in corn (7,4)

FALLING RAIN (wet weather) = FALL (reduction) + IN + GRAIN (corn). Observe that once again one of the syllables (in this case IN) has been presented to the solver without any disguise.

Four syllables

(k) John gets the ring to drop deals—he's very versatile (4-2-3-6)

JACK (John) + O (the ring) + FALL (to drop) + TRADES (deals) = JACK-OF-ALL-TRADES (he's very versatile).

Five syllables

(l) Being frank, with nothing to write, listen to Edward, the head (4-11)

OPEN-HEARTEDNESS (being frank) is obtained with O (nothing) + PEN (to write) + HEAR (listen to) + TED (Edward) + NESS (the headland, or head).

Six syllables

(m) Assured one friend—strictly between ourselves (14)

CONFIDENT (assured) + I (one, Roman numeral) + ALLY (friend) = CONFIDENTIALLY (strictly between ourselves).

8 Inside and outside

We have just seen how the principle of the game of charades can be usefully applied to the wording of a crossword clue, in which the component parts of an answer are indicated in their correct order and the definition of the word itself either precedes all the parts or follows them to complete the clue.

Closely related to this device, although it is never practised in the parlour-game itself, is the method of splitting up a word in such a way that, instead of finding the component parts one after another, we are presented with one part inside another or, when looked at from a different standpoint, with one part encircling another.

For example, faced with the word MEANT, the clue-writer may choose to treat it as a charade consisting of the two words ME and ANT side by side, or he may see better possibilities in reading it as AN inside MET or MET around AN.

Similarly, HASSOCK may be clued as either HAS + SOCK (i.e. the charade) or H-ASS-OCK (i.e. ASS in HOCK or HOCK about ASS); BOASTED as BOAS + TED or B-OAST-ED; BELLOWED as BELL + OWED or B-ELL-OWED; and LEGATEE as LEG + A + TEE or LE-GATE-E. His final choice, as always, will be determined by the method that leads to what he considers the neatest clue in each case.

More often than not, however, words that can be split neatly into two or more components which happen to be complete words will lend themselves naturally to one or other of the above techniques, but not to both. Since the previous chapter has dealt with successive components, let us now examine some examples of the 'inside and outside' principle.

(a) One of the family puts us in the money (6)

Solving this clue should prove fairly easy, for it will quickly be realised that the only member of any family who can put US in COIN (money) is CO-US-IN.

(b) The pole, in the centre, shows rust (7)

If we put ROD (the pole) in CORE (the centre), it will show COR-ROD-E, which means to rust. The fact that we naturally read 'rust' as a noun, whereas it is intended as a verb, is due to the clue-writer's cunning wording of the sentence.

(c) Is trapped in burning lift (5)

This is a way of saying that the word IS is trapped inside the word HOT (burning), becoming HO-IS-T, which means to lift. Again, as in example (b) above, there is a deliberate ambiguity here to mislead the unwary solver, who is sure at first sight to read 'lift' as a noun meaning an elevator when it really is a verb. What is more, the use of 'trapped', to indicate that one word is stuck inside another, helps to make macabre sense of the clue as a whole, thus tending to sidetrack the solver away from its real and quite innocuous meaning.

This 'inside' treatment is no less effective when the answer is a hyphenated word, as in the following example:

(d) Canvas wrapper, ancient, seen in lobby (4-3)

The canvas wrapper we are looking for is a HOLD-ALL, which consists of OLD (ancient), which itself is seen in HALL (lobby).

And if hyphenated words can be so treated, why not also phrases and the like? Here are a couple of examples using two-word answers.

(e) Summon to the colours everyone in the vessel (4-2)

To summon to the colours is to CALL UP, and this answer comprises ALL (everyone) in CUP (the vessel).

(f) Limb found in river—my goodness! (4,2)

When ARM (limb) is found in DEE (river), the result is DEAR ME! (my goodness!)

Sometimes the clue-writer finds that it suits his misleading purpose better to take the outside word first and make it surround the inside one, or to mention the inside word and then put the outside one around it. In that event, we are likely to be offered clues containing significant words like 'outside', 'embraces' or 'embracing', 'hold', 'grasp' and so on. Here are a couple of the more straightforward kind.

(g) Slaughter the horse, and worry about it (7)

The answer, meaning slaughter, is CARNAGE, having in its make-up NAG (the horse) and CARE (worry) about it, thus: CAR-NAG-E.

(h) Wet at home, with a gleam of sunlight about (5)

Another word for wet is RAINY, which is IN (at home) with RAY (a gleam of sunlight) about, or around, it.

A slightly trickier example is the following:

(i) Imagined having great fear without me (7)

What makes this clue more difficult than the average is the word 'without', which in the majority of cases, in crossword clues as well as in normal speech, means lacking. A solver will therefore be tempted, on first reading this clue, to think that he must find a word for 'imagined' which has also the meaning of 'great fear' minus the letters ME. On this occasion, however, he must really place DREAD (great fear) without (in the less common sense of outside) ME to form DREA-ME-D (imagined).

Now for an example which shows that either the outside or inside section (in this case the inside) may consist of more than one word, thus:

> **(j) A collapsible shelter needs a fold outside, obviously (8)**

From this we discover that A TENT (a collapsible shelter) needs PLY (a fold) outside to make P-A TENT-LY, which means obviously.

And again, just as we had 'insider' clues leading to answers of two words—*viz*. CALL UP and DEAR ME in examples (e) and (f) above—here is an 'outsider' which also results in a two-word answer:

> **(k) Immediately becomes an expert about weight (2,4)**

A two-word phrase for immediately is AT ONCE, which becomes (when split up) ACE (an expert) about TON (weight), or A-TON-CE.

All the above examples, in employing the 'inside and outside' principle, have been confined to answers whose component parts are complete words. It must be added in conclusion that solvers are certain to meet many versions of this technique in which some, or even all, of the component parts are either incomplete words, anagrams, abbreviations or any of the many other legitimate devices available to the clue-writer. This may be made clear by one final example, typical of many, in which the part that is not a complete word happens to be an abbreviation:

> **(l) Stagger about quietly and drive off (5)**

'P' is familiar as a musical abbreviation of 'piano', meaning softly or quietly. In this clue we have REEL (stagger) about P (quietly), and that gives the answer REPEL (drive off).

9 Reversals

Centuries before the advent of crosswords, there were scholars who attached great importance to the letter arrangement of certain words; and in some instances they went to the lengths of investing those containing a particularly striking sequence of letters with mystic, magical or religious significance. They were the Cabbalists, mentioned in Chapter 1. This branch of scholarship is by no means without its serious devotees today, nor, of course, is it confined to the English language. In this chapter, however, our own concern will be limited to some English words which, to our constant delight, happen by sheer accident to be equally sensible whether we read them in their normal order or back-to-front.

One such type of word, which is identical whether spelled forwards or backwards, is called a palindrome (a word of Greek derivation meaning 'running back'), and a fair number of these crop up spasmodically in crosswords. Three-letter palindromes like BOB, DID, TOT and MUM are very common, as are such four-letter ones as DEED, PEEP, NOON and TOOT. Even five-letter examples are not difficult to find—one readily thinks, for instance, of MINIM, MADAM, RADAR and CIVIC. Longer palindromes are there in the dictionary for the finding, but less plentiful if we shy away from little-known words. A few that are familiar to everyone are REDDER, ROTATOR and REVIVER.

(It is also possible—to digress from crosswords for a moment—to compose a complete palindromic sentence, such as the melancholy remark which Napoleon might have made: ABLE WAS I ERE I SAW ELBA. Furthermore, on the unwarranted assumption that the first man on earth spoke English, he might well have formally introduced himself to Eve—herself the primordial example!—with the first palindromic sentence in the history of mankind: MADAM, I'M ADAM.)

Two typical clues to palindromes are the following:

(a) It turns in either direction (5)

This means that the answer ROTOR, which is something that turns, is the same word when written either way round.

(b) Part of a ship that's unaffected when overturned (4)

What the clue says is that a POOP (part of a ship) is still the same word POOP when you turn it over.

Easy though palindromes are to clue, crossword composers do not go out of their way to find them and work them into their diagrams, so that an average puzzle may have the odd one or, more likely, none at all. What we do find with great regularity, however, is an answer, or more frequently part of an answer, which when written backwards becomes a completely different word or combination of words. For example, the reverse of TAB is BAT, of LIAR is RAIL and of TENDER is RED-NET, while PARTAKE is the reverse of RAP plus TAKE and ALOOF is A plus the reverse of FOOL. Solvers will therefore often be presented with clues in which either the whole answers or parts of them have been indicated in reverse.

Those who employ this most useful technique should exercise particular care in choosing the significant words which are to indicate to the solvers that they must write certain groups of letters the wrong way round; for it is important to check in every instance whether the word being clued has to be written horizontally or vertically in that particular diagram. It is patently unfair, for instance, as well as totally inaccurate, to say that POT is 'sent up' (to make the word TOP) if it happens to be an Across clue; or that RAT 'goes back' (to give the answer TAR) if it is a Down. As always, the clue-writer must say what he means, and it simply isn't true that 'up' means 'back' or *vice versa*.

Some forms of words are equally suitable for both Across and Down clues, such as 'in the opposite direction', 'the other way', 'turned over' and 'reversed' (which can mean turned back or upside-down), and these will be used whenever they fit into the sense of the rest of the clue. Others, like 'climbing', 'turned up', 'upset' and the like, are clearly appropriate to Down clues only, whereas 'returning', 'sent back', 'backward', 'rejected', etc. immediately suggest a reverse action on a horizontal plane only.

Here are three examples showing how the reversal principle can be effectively employed for either Across or Down answers.

(c) Face set in the opposite direction (4)

The answer is DIAL (face), which is LAID (set) when written in the opposite direction, that is backwards if the answer goes across or upwards if it goes down.

(d) Game that's the reverse of a fiddle (5)

The game is DARTS, which is the reverse (or the opposite) of STRAD, the colloquial word for a Stradivarius violin or fiddle.

(e) Obscene talk makes kiddies' stomachs turn over (4)

The clue says that SMUT (obscene talk) makes TUMS (a childish word for stomachs) turn over, either vertically or horizontally.

Then there are clues that need only a slight adjustment according to the direction taken by the answer, as follows:

(f) Exchange prisoners on the way back (4)

The solver will quickly realise, from the revealing word 'back', that this is an Across clue for a word meaning exchange, which will come to mean prisoners when written backwards. The answer is SWOP (an alternative spelling of SWAP), which is POWS backwards. Had this been a Down clue, however, the words 'on the way up' could have replaced 'on the way back', without in any way affecting the sense of the clue.

(g) Like a king, having beer sent up (5)

This, with its word 'up', is just as obviously a Down clue, indicating that REGAL (like a king) has in its make-up the word LAGER (beer) sent, or written, upwards. For the same answer to be entered in the diagram horizontally, some rephrasing of the clue is necessary, such as:

(g) Like a king, knocking back beer (5)

Sometimes the word being clued will work quite nicely as an Across clue but not at all convincingly as a Down, even with a change of wording, and at other times it is the other way round, as the following examples will show:

(h) Pulls up the grass (5)

Here the word DRAWS (pulls), when written upwards, becomes the answer SWARD (the grass), and so this clue is suitable for a Down only. Since it would hardly make good sense if changed to 'pulls back', or something similar, for an Across clue to the same word, it might be advisable for the clue-writer not to attempt a reversal clue to SWARD except as a Down, unless he could hit on a credible form of words to indicate a backward movement.

(i) Gaudy witch embraces knight—both are taken aback (6)

A harder clue, this, to the word GARISH (gaudy), in which HAG (witch) embraces, or enfolds, SIR (knight) to make H-SIR-AG, after which the information is given that both parts of the word are to be taken backwards, with this result: GA-RIS-H. This time the clue fits only an Across answer, and a different technique might be necessary if this word appeared as a Down in another diagram.

It will be observed that in example (i) above, the reversal was not the complete exchange of one word in one direction for another word in the opposite direction that we have had in all the previous examples. Nor need it be so; for it is perfectly legitimate to split up the reversal in any way, so long as the clue accurately provides the necessary information for the solver. Examine, for instance, the following couple of clues.

(j) Dishes placed on mountain upside-down (6)

Dishes are PLATES, and they consist (if this is a Down clue) of SET (placed) on top of ALP (mountain) to make SET-ALP, which when written upside-down becomes PLATES.

(k) Communist party sent back more rum (5)

A word for Communist is RED, and a synonym for a party is a DO. Therefore RED-DO when 'sent back' in an Across clue (or 'sent up' in a Down clue) becomes ODDER, which means stranger, or more rum. (The reader will by now, of course, be getting quite used to the idea that when a clue-writer says 'more rum' he doesn't mean 'more liquor' at all but 'more odd'!)

In all the foregoing examples, the complete answers have been reversed, but it is also common to have clues in which only a part of the answer is reversed, with the remaining part clued by a different method. Here are three clues which have been treated in this way.

(l) American underground transport reverses with style (6)

The solver is required to pause after the first two words, which form the definition of the answer, SUBWAY. This consists of the reverse of BUS (clued as 'transport reverses') together with WAY (meaning manner or style).

(m) Abusive speeches help backward races (9)

Exactly as in (l) above, the first two words are the definition of the answer, in this case DIATRIBES. And again, the subsidiary indications comprise a reversal and a synonym, DIA being the reverse of AID (or help backward), and TRIBES meaning races.

(n) Mother takes murderer back—he's mad (6)

This time the sequence is different but the method identical. MA (Mother) takes the reverse of CAIN (indicated in an Across clue only as 'murderer back'), which is NIAC, giving the answer MANIAC (he's mad).

And finally, an example that uses a part-reversal in a two-word answer instead of in a single word, thus:

(o) Face raised, make a noise like an ox, felled (4,3)

This, suitable only for a Down clue, tells us that DIAL (face) must be raised, or written upwards in our diagram, giving LAID. Together with the word LOW (make a noise like an ox), it becomes the answer LAID LOW (felled).

It should now be evident that there is ample scope for employing this simple and pleasing device of reversing the spelling of syllables, part-words, whole words or parts of phrases. Whatever the standard of puzzle involved, it adds variety to the clueing and thus helps to keep the solver guessing all the time. In conclusion, however, it is perhaps worth stressing, yet again, that indications of reversals must always be linguistically fair, taking full account in particular of whether they are appearing in Across or Down clues.

10 Hidden

Probably the easiest type of cryptic clue to solve, not surprisingly, is one in which the answer is actually given, hidden inside the clue's wording, and simply has to be written in the diagram without alteration. Even the most inexperienced solver, if offered the clue 'Vehicle found in Scarborough (3)', would very quickly notice the three-lettered CAR in the town's name and move on to the next clue in record time.

Not that there is anything unsatisfactory or unfair about the above example. On the contrary; it makes an easily understood statement, it misleadingly suggests some vehicle supposed to be particularly associated with Scarborough (as trams are, for example, with Blackpool) and it has a completely accurate definition (vehicle) as well as the subsidiary indication that the answer is found in Scarborough, which is undeniable. Perhaps the only criticism that can be levelled at it, indeed, is that it is too easy. But for those setters who like to give their solvers a good start, especially in crosswords containing a fair proportion of tricky clues, this kind of almost-free gift serves the purpose as well as any.

Despite the fact that in all clues of this type the answer is literally under the solver's nose, there is still plenty of scope for ingenuity and artistry on the part of the clue-writer in his efforts to disguise the hiding-place in such a way as to make it protrude rather less prominently. Most of us, I imagine, if my own experience is any guide, have from time to time failed to solve a clue at first sight, realised only after a second attempt that it was one of these hidden answers and mentally kicked ourselves for missing it the first time. What we ought to do in such cases, however, is congratulate the clue-writer for having so skilfully camouflaged the obvious.

One method of preventing the answer from screaming at the solver is to hide it among words in such a way that it must be read with a different pronunciation from its own. That CAR of our previous example sounds just the same whether it is on its own or inside the word Scarborough. But if we alter that clue to 'In Quebec a racing vehicle (3)', suddenly it becomes a shade less obvious because, when the whole clue is read aloud, nowhere do we hear the sound of the word CAR, although it is still staring us in the face in 'QuebeC A Racing'.

Here are a few more examples, in which no answer is ever given its exact pronunciation in its clue, either because its vowels or consonants sound different or because of slight changes due to stress or accent in the hiding words.

(a) In Spring a periwinkle is open wide (4)

The answer GAPE (open wide) is hidden in the three consecutive words 'SprinG A PEriwinkle', with no sound in these words to suggest it.

(b) Part of camera found among stolen swag (4)

What is found among 'stoLEN Swag' is LENS (part of camera).

(c) Braid inserted in mitres sometimes (5)

The answer TRESS (braid) has been inserted in 'miTRES Sometimes'.

(d) Man who's invested in Chinese rice (4)

This clue shows how thoroughly the simple answer ERIC (invested, or enveloped, in 'ChinesE RICe') has been disguised, since only the letter R of its normal pronunciation has been preserved in its hidden form. The E, which is pronounced in the name, is silent in the final letter of 'Chinese'; the I has changed from a short to a long sound in 'rice'; and finally, in the word 'rice' again, the hard C of ERIC is pronounced as an S.

A study of these four examples above will reveal that there is nothing in each of them except the definition and the minimum number of other words necessary for containing its answer. The point is worth making here for those who wish to employ this type of clue, as well as for the guidance of solvers, that it is bordering on the unfair to add superfluous or irrelevant words to a clue merely to make the answer harder to find. For example, if that clue, 'Vehicle found in Scarborough', were extended to read 'Vehicle found in Scarborough and other Yorkshire towns', the answer would still be CAR, which is found somewhere in the clue after the word 'in', so that the clue's deviser could not be accused of inaccuracy. Yet those final four words are superfluous padding, contributing nothing whatever to the clue except extra length, thereby ignoring a basic principle, that every word used in a clue should be necessary for its solution.

It is strongly recommended, therefore, that if answers are to be hidden with some attempt at artistry, no unnecessary words should be added to the hiding-place, with the very reasonable exceptions of the definite and indefinite articles. The following couple of examples should make this clear.

(e) It contributes to a clever balance of words (6)

What contributes to the make-up of 'a cleVER BALance' is

VERBAL (of words). The inclusion of the word 'a' is not essential to the hiding process, but if it makes the clue read more naturally it is surely a harmless intruder.

(f) A feature of the Brahmin I must note (5)

This time the answer, MINIM (note), is a feature of the words 'BrahMIN I Must', and although strictly the word 'the' is superfluous it can be justified by the argument that in this clue it means 'the group of words'.

In addition, it is a perfectly legitimate practice to use a hyphenated word as part of the hide. For instance, if HERB can be found in 'anotHER Bed', it (or he) can surely just as fairly be put in 'anotHER Bed-sitter', if that suits the sense of the complete clue better, without any suggestion that superfluous wording has been introduced. Here is a full clue where a hyphenated word is involved:

(g) Move slowly in a dream, blear-eyed (5)

The answer is AMBLE (move slowly), which is hidden in 'a dreAM BLEar-eyed'. This clue also establishes the principle that, whenever a hidden answer is concerned, it is only the succession of letters that needs to be examined, and any incidental punctuation, such as a comma (as here), dash, apostrophe, inverted commas, etc., may be ignored as irrelevant. For this type of clue says, in effect, that the letters of the answer are to be found (in their correct order) inside certain words in that clue. Once it is accepted that parts of the answer can be separated by blank spaces between words, it is equally valid, in my view, to have punctuation marks there also.

The examples given so far serve to show, further, that clue-writers are not limited to the words 'in', 'among' or 'part of' when they wish to indicate that the answer is enclosed within another word or more than one word. Here is a further clutch of clues, by no means exhaustive, to demonstrate that variety in such indications, even if the standard of difficulty may scarcely be affected thereby, is in plentiful supply.

(h) Plea always employed by Bengali bishops (5)

An ALIBI (plea) is always employed whenever the two words 'BengALI BIshops' are written.

(i) Make enthusiastic? Enthusiastic is only part of it (4)

If we look at the phrase 'maKE ENthusiastic', we see that the word KEEN (enthusiastic) is only part of it. Note that this time the position of the words 'part of' at the end of the clue makes it less easy to recognise them as a 'hidden' indication.

(j) Language that needs translating, to some extent (5)

Writing the answer LATIN (language) needs a certain extent of the word 'transLATINg'. It will be seen that, even though the answer is accommodated here within a single word, the pronunciation of the longer word disguises it, at least temporarily.

(k) Even nuisances can show weariness (5)

ENNUI (weariness) can indeed be shown in the words 'evEN NUIsances'.

One more way to ring the changes with this clueing device is to hide the answer in reverse instead of forwards. There are some words, especially shortish ones, that do not readily lend themselves to other techniques like charades, anagrams, inside and outside, and so on, but will conveniently hide themselves in other words without altering their normal order of letters. Sometimes, however, a neater clue may emerge from reversing the order, in which case the usual care must be taken about whether it is an Across or Down clue in that particular crossword, as was emphasised in the previous chapter.

Our final examples, then, must be of these hidden reversals.

(l) Section of hotel dining-room's set back and unoccupied (4)

This tells us that ELDI (section of 'hotEL DIning-room') is set back—i.e. reversed in an Across clue—to make IDLE, which means unoccupied. The hyphenated dining-room is, of course, regarded as a single word.

(m) Class distinction gets accepted, partly, in retrospect (5)

ETSAC (which is 'gETS ACcepted', partly), when seen backwards in an Across clue, as indicated by 'in retrospect', gives us CASTE (class distinction).

(n) A piece caught up in the contraption (4)

The answer PART (a piece) is caught up, or contained when going upwards in a Down clue, in the word 'conTRAPtion'.

The clue-writer can now, it is hoped, confidently add this technique to his repertoire in the knowledge that many a pleasing clue may result from its use, and that at times it may even prove to be the only suitable method when all others, or inspiration, seem to fail. Although it has been demonstrated that it can temporarily mislead quite as well as any other type of clue, it still remains comparatively obvious to the seasoned solver at least. Because of this, it is recommended that it should be severely rationed to a maximum of two such clues per puzzle, with only a single appearance in any complete set of clues being the norm. It is also advisable, in a regular series of crosswords by the same setter, to have some of them with no hidden answers at all, so that the solver, no longer able to take it for granted that there must be at least one somewhere, will be obliged to tackle every clue strictly on its merits, which is exactly as it should be.

11 Puns

In other media, whether oral or literary, a fair amount of licence is allowed in the use of puns—in some quarters, indeed, the more outrageous the pun, the more merriment it arouses. A mild example of punning may be seen in the comment (which might be made after the introduction of a hefty new tax on wills) deploring the 'rise in the cost of leaving'. Such a quip is unlikely to fall flat simply because 'leaving' does not sound exactly like 'living'; for it is an accepted convention that a pun merely calls to mind a word or words with similar sounds.

Even when little more than a vague sound pattern is offered by the punster, it usually requires no great effort to recognise the allusion. For instance, when a man in fear of his life has been saved by being offered sanctuary, he may punningly express his gratitude by whispering 'Sanctuary much'!

Whether it is a matter for regret or relief, we cannot in fairness to the solver allow such excesses to creep into our crossword clues. Remembering that what a cryptic clue really says, as distinct from what it may appear to say, must in fact be correct, a clue-writer is never justified in indicating—to take the words involved in the first example above—that LIVING 'sounds like LEAVING', since plainly it does not. The two words may have an *approximate* similarity of sound, but unless that approximation is stated quite clearly in the clue's wording it is not accurate to claim that their pronunciation is identical, and therefore such an indication cannot be admitted.

This means that in crossword practice the use of puns in clues should strictly be limited to homophones—that is, words having the same sound as each other. In this connection it must be borne in mind that the way in which a word is normally pronounced in one region of the country may well differ slightly, or even substantially, from its pronunciation in other regions, so that a punning treatment of such a word is best avoided, certainly in any crossword intended for national readership. For example, while there can be no possible ambiguity in indicating that STEAK sounds like STAKE, SOUL like SOLE or BEET like BEAT, it is inviting trouble to state as a fact that WHICH sounds like WITCH, for many people pronounce these words differently, although many do not. Similarly, there are those for whom DOOR and DAW have identical sounds, but many others to whom they are very different; and the same is true of BEEN and BIN, and of other variations in the length of vowels, and so on, which are typical of certain geographical areas.

It is advisable, therefore, to play safe with this technique and to use it, as far as possible, only when the sounds concerned are accepted as standard throughout the British Isles, although one may be forgiven if occasionally the absolute accuracy of the pun is, as it were, on the Border-line. An example of the latter may be seen in the following:

(a) Grim man of action, by the sound of it (4)

The answer, DOUR, means grim. It sounds like DOER, a person who does things, or a man of action. Or does it? No doubt many Scots at least will insist, with complete justification, that DOUR is a monosyllable but DOER a disyllable, and that consequently they don't sound alike. The majority of English-speakers, however, including many Scots, would probably accept that in this case the two pronunciations are so close in practice as to obviate the risk of any misunderstanding.

A factor that reduces the number of punning clues in comparison with other types—one seldom finds more than a couple in any average cryptic crossword, and quite often there are none at all—is the difficulty of disguising them sufficiently to add real variety to the clueing. There are several methods, however, and here are four examples in which the indications are at least a little different from each other.

(b) A fine lot of drops—sounds like what butter-fingers did (4)

The clue clearly tells the solver that MIST (a fine lot of drops) sounds like MISSED (what butter-fingers did).

(c) Listened to the noise of cattle (5)

This time the answer is rather less obvious. The word HEARD (listened to) is the noise—i.e. the sound—of HERD (cattle) as this word is spoken.

(d) Character to carry out a revolution, so it's said (4)

The character that an actor plays is a ROLE, which, as it is spoken, sounds like ROLL (to revolve, or carry out a revolution).

(e) Audibly entranced, being embraced (7)

The answer is audibly RAPT (entranced), being in fact the word WRAPPED (embraced).

The opportunity sometimes occurs of injecting a little subtlety into such clues, despite the inclusion of a word so apparently obvious as 'sound'. Here are a couple of examples.

(f) The band sounded like a trumpet to an audience (5)

The answer is BRAID, which among other meanings can be a band (of fabric). This word, to an audience—i.e. as it is heard—is BRAYED (sounded like a trumpet). The deliberate deception in this clue is the inclusion of the words 'sounded like', which are designed to make the solver look initially in the wrong place for the homophone. In reality, of course, the pun is indicated by the less familiar formula 'to an audience'.

(g) Its sound may be found in it (5)

This looks more like a conundrum than a crossword clue, amounting in other words to: 'What word is there that may have its own sound in it?' The answer is CACHE, a hiding-place for treasure, which may have in it CASH, a word with the same pronunciation as itself.

The punning clue is not limited to single syllables but is freely available for use with any number, as in the following two examples.

(h) Attack by big guns gives clergyman help, we hear (9)

The answer CANNONADE (attack by big guns) gives us, as we hear when it is spoken, CANON (clergyman) AID (help).

(i) The pub appreciates, according to hearsay, what an insult does (8)

The answer is INCENSES (or enrages, which is what an insult does). According to the way in which we hear it pronounced, this word is INN (the pub) SENSES (appreciates).

Nor are single words only so treated. Here is an example leading to a two-word answer:

(j) Russian permitted, so people say—it's recited (4,5)

In this we begin with the sound of the answer and end with the definition. RED (Russian, as in 'Red Army') ALLOWED (permitted) are the sounds we hear when people say the answer READ ALOUD (recited).

Finally, as with most other clueing devices, we are also likely to find a version of this type in which a part of the answer is indicated by one method and another part by a pun. Our last two examples will demonstrate this point.

(k) Underground sprite soundly beating instrument (9)

To solve this clue it is necessary to tackle it in three stages. First there is METRO (Underground); then NOME (which 'soundly', or from the way that it sounds, is the word GNOME, a sprite); and lastly, the combination of the two parts produces the answer METRONOME (beating instrument).

(l) The sound of hags by the beach, perhaps, should be good for picnics (10)

What sounds like WITCHES (hags) is WICHES. When these letters are placed by, or beside, SAND (the beach, perhaps), the result is SANDWICHES (should be good for picnics). This wording, incidentally, suits an Across clue only.

It should become evident from a study of the above examples that, of any two elements treated as having the same sound, the element that appears in the answer need not be an actual English word at all, or a familiar foreign word either, but that the word that it sounds like must be. For instance, in example (h) above (CANNONADE), both CANNON and its homophone CANON do happen to be words, but of ADE and AID only the latter is a real word. And in the SANDWICHES of example (l) which we have just considered, SAND is clued by a definition, while WICHES, a non-existent word, is clued as a homophone of WITCHES, a genuine English word.

12 Anagrams

It has been alleged that the inclusion of an anagram in a clue is the last resort of an uninspired mind. One might with similar unkindness vilify it as the first resort of a lazy or hasty one. The conscientious clue-writer, however, is entitled to feel grossly maligned by either calumny; for a carefully contrived anagram can undoubtedly contribute towards as neat and satisfying a clue as any other legitimate device available to the crossword composer.

An anagram is the rearrangement of the letters of a word or phrase in such a way as to produce a different word or words. For example, the letters of HUSTLER can be shuffled about to become HURTLES; IDLENESS can be converted to DINE LESS; ADDING MACHINE to DID I CHANGE MEN?; and DISTURB THE PEACE to RIDE, TEST EACH PUB.

It must be categorically stated at once that, although the same letters are used in each case, the words and their anagrams are in no sense synonymous. It can never be correct to clue SAVE, for instance, as 'Rescue the vase' simply because VASE is an anagram of SAVE. 'Vase' is *not* equivalent to 'save' unless its letters are jumbled to make it so, and the clue-writer must make this jumbling clear in some way; otherwise he is being inaccurate and unfair. In the example just mentioned, the addition of a single word will convert an unsound to a sound clue, as follows:

(a) Rescue the broken vase (4)

This gives an unmistakable indication that the letters of VASE are broken up to make SAVE, which has been defined as 'rescue'.

We can say, then, that it is a primary essential of any clue containing an anagram that the solver must be given some indication that the letters of given words have to be rearranged. In the very early days of crosswords this was normally done by some such clue as 'Vase (anag.)': inartistic and dull, to be sure, but at least honest and true. In the more sophisticated puzzles of today solvers have grown to expect something less crude, and in many cases they are well served, but it must never be forgotten that the anagram indication must be visible and not left to be supplied by the solver himself by the aid of some telepathy.

There is an almost infinite variety of ways in which an anagram may be indicated. Any verb, adjective, adverb or phrase which, granted a little artistic licence, can reasonably suggest that letters have undergone some change from their original order (such as 'tortured', 'silly', 'in disarray', 'badly', 'dreadful', etc.) are fair guides to the solver. Here are several complete clues incorporating this technique, with the anagram indicators shown in italics.

(b) Imposing drain goes *bust* (9)

The answer GRANDIOSE means imposing. The word 'bust'

shows that the letters of DRAIN GOES have been broken up.

(c) For a jollification, *cook* beef with Santa (9)

The jollification is a BEANFEAST, for which the solver is invited to 'cook' BEEF and SANTA, or to tamper with these words, as one 'cooks' the books.

(d) *Rum* may propel taxi—just about (13)

The letters of MAY PROPEL TAXI, which are 'rum', or odd, will become APPROXIMATELY (just about).

(e) Quiet *variety of* lionesses (9)

The answer NOISELESS (quiet) is a 'variety', or different version, of LIONESSES.

(f) Joints that *upset* the bowels (6)

The joints meant here are ELBOWS, the letters of BOWELS being 'upset'.

(g) Behaved like a horse, *not properly* heeding (7)

One feature of horses' behaviour is neighing, so the answer here is NEIGHED. In this the word HEEDING is written 'not properly' but in a strange order.

(h) Our town *needs a new look*—it's old-fashioned (7)

We are told that the phrase OUR TOWN 'needs a new look', or different appearance, to make OUTWORN (old-fashioned).

There is also a type of clue which uses the same devices but for part of the word only, and which we may call a part-anagram. There are four main variations: (i) part-answer plus anagram; (ii) anagram plus part-answer; (iii) anagram inside part-answer; (iv) anagram outside part-answer. An example of each of these variations should make this clear.

(i) **(i) Petty officer has to be *swinging* lead (6)**

BEADLE, a petty officer of a church, needs BE + an anagram of LEAD, indicated by the word 'swinging'.

(ii) **(j) Here's the cub, *mangled* and bloody, cruelly killed (9)**

The letters of THE CUB have been 'mangled' to become BUTCHE; together with RED (bloody) it becomes BUTCHERED (cruelly killed).

(iii) **(k) Damage a *wagging* tail, but keep silent about it (8)**

To MUTILATE is to damage. It consists of an anagram of TAIL, which is 'wagging', about which you must keep MUTE (silent).

(iv) **(l) Neat drivers he found among *jostling* crowds (8)**

Drivers of neat, or cattle, are COWHERDS. HE is found among an anagram of CROWDS, indicated by the word 'jostling'.

In addition, especially in the case of longish words or phrases, one may find one or more part-anagrams contributing to the clues, with other features (such as abbreviations, reversed parts of words, etc.) interspersed among them. Here is an example of this 'multiple-feature' clue which is not too complicated:

(m) I shall *upset* Aunt, blushing, being peevish (3–7)

The answer is ILL-NATURED (peevish), the component parts being I'LL (I shall) + NATU (anag. of AUNT, the letters having been 'upset') + RED (blushing).

Some cautionary remarks on this topic need to be added. Firstly, since variety should always be the clue-writer's aim, he must not be seduced by the attractiveness of anagrams into indulging in a surfeit of them in any one set of clues. In a typical crossword of twenty-eight or thirty clues, four full anagrams and perhaps two or three part-anagrams should be regarded as a maximum, beyond which there is a danger of satiety. No doubt this may occasionally be exceeded slightly, at a pinch, but equally there will be many puzzles in which the full ration is not claimed.

For puzzles with more than thirty clues, the number of anagrams may be proportionately increased; nor need the clue-writer feel any sense of guilt if from time to time he exceeds this suggested optimum, especially if he considers that an extra anagram either makes for a neater clue, or avoids a particularly tortuous one, or is in some way of greater help to the solver. Nevertheless, since there is no doubt that anagrams have a habit of being over-represented in some crosswords, some restraint in their use ought to be kept constantly in mind.

Secondly, the solver presented with an anagram should be offered the actual letters to be arranged and not a synonym of them (or what is called an indirect anagram). If the answer to be found is AMPLE, for instance, it is practically useless, and therefore blatantly unfair to the solver, to clue it as 'a damaged *tree*'—there are scores to choose from! Nothing less than 'a damaged *maple*' will suffice if we really mean to be helpful.

This having been said, and the main principle established, we can qualify the rule in some small degree. Where the anagram includes, let us say, a Roman numeral, to which there is an obvious and unique answer, then that is virtually the same as giving the actual letters.

For example, if the word to be clued were SCREAM (which comprises the letters C MARES, in a different order), one could with complete fairness offer the following:

> **(n) Shrill cry produced by a hundred mares *in agony* (6)**

The answer SCREAM is a shrill cry, which is produced by C MARES twisted about, indicated by the phrase 'in agony'. The substitution by the solver of C for 'a hundred'—the only possible one-letter answer—is a simple process, far removed from the search for just one of innumerable possibilities such as trees. Similarly, the use of 'Northern', say, to indicate the letter N (but not, be it noted, 'compass-point' or 'direction', which would admit of several choices) would be admissible as part of an anagram.

Finally, it is only rarely accurate to use a single noun to indicate an anagram. It is true that a 'rain-storm' is a phenomenon involving the whirling about of rain, and in this spirit it may be accepted as suggesting an anagram of RANI; and a 'car crash' is clearly the damaging of a car, from which ARC can be fairly deduced. On the other hand, 'great confusion' does *not* mean the confusion of 'great' (leading to the answer GRATE), nor does 'much trouble' signify that there is trouble with the letters of 'much', from which the answer CHUM can be worked out. In such cases, extra thought is required until something more accurate emerges. For the word GRATE, one could use a verb instead and say 'great *riots*' (i.e. the word 'great' becomes riotous or disorderly); and for CHUM, what about 'much *troubled*' (i.e. the word 'much' is in a troubled or disturbed condition)? It will be apparent from all this that the occasions on which a noun can legitimately indicate an anagram are very few, so that such a device is best eschewed altogether.

As a footnote to this chapter it is perhaps necessary to mention a curious fact: of all the manifold techniques resorted to by clue-writers, the anagram is undoubtedly the one in which even elementary rules of fairness are most blatantly violated. It is more than likely, therefore, that solvers will be faced time and again with clues containing anagrams that are either not indicated at all or inadequately (and so, in my view, unfairly) indicated. Thus forewarned, they may still solve the offending clues and justifiably congratulate themselves on their acumen, but they would be striking a blow for fair standards if they expressed their strong disapproval!

13 Cryptic definitions

It has been stressed that the minimum requirement for every clue which aims to be accurate and fair is a definition of the answer. We have seen that there are numerous crosswords, enjoying a wide circulation and popularity, which consist exclusively of such definitions, but that in cryptic crosswords these are normally supplemented by further information designed to lead the solver, albeit by a roundabout route, to the correct answer. In one clueing method, described in Chapter 6, the juxtaposition of two plain definitions or more was shown to be capable of disguising the true meaning of the answer, by making the combination of the definitions conjure up a picture rather different from that suggested by each one separately.

It may come as a surprise, therefore, to discover that it is also possible to include in the range of cryptic techniques a type of clue which consists of one definition only, with no secondary indications, like anagrams, charades and the rest, to help the solver to build up an answer from such features as the arrangement of its letters or the sound of its syllables. This is sometimes referred to as a 'straight' clue, in the sense that it is not diluted by any subsidiary element; and in view of its effectiveness at its best, it could with equal aptness, if the same alcoholic metaphor were used, be named a 'neat' clue. However, since it will be seen that such clues, while apparently straight, are really deliberately deceptive, they may be better understood if we call them what in fact they are—cryptic definitions.

What makes a definition cryptic is the ambiguous wording used in it, even though, on analysis, it is found to be giving absolutely correct information. This may be shown by examining two clues to the same word, as follows. 'River in France (5)' is a straightforward, no-nonsense, definition clue to SEINE, such as will be found in countless crosswords all over the world. But 'French flower (5)', as a clue to the same word, is deliberately misleading, for it appears to be asking the unsuspecting solver to think of a plant indigenous to France, whereas in fact it is saying that he must look for something that flows in France. The unexpected use here of the word 'flower', therefore, gives the clue a cryptic flavour which makes it unacceptable for inclusion in a crossword comprising plain definitions only but perfectly suitable for use in a cryptic crossword, in which the solver is prepared to be tricked at every turn.

Let it be clearly stated, however, that a definition's cryptic nature is not necessarily sufficient to justify its presentation as a complete clue. It is true that 'French flower' is a cryptic definition and that it may give pleasure to the solver when the penny eventually drops. But even so, what real help has he been given towards the answer? He now knows that he must find a French river of five letters, but the choice is still a very wide one and he is entitled to ask for more information to enable him to narrow it down to the precise one intended by the deviser of the clue. This clue therefore will serve as an example of a cryptic definition which requires the addition of a subsidiary part before it can be considered complete.

What we need, then, if we are looking for a cryptic definition capable of standing alone, is one which is ambiguous enough not to expose the answer too soon but which, once the disguise has been penetrated, defines more or less unambiguously an answer that fits the given number of letters. The following clue—or something very like it—which I understand was written by Torquemada many years ago, is a good example:

(a) He makes Father late (9)

This will defy solution unless the solver tears himself away from the most natural reading of the sentence, which is to the effect that someone, in some way, delays Father's arrival. But once it is remembered that 'late' can also mean dead, the answer can only be a person who kills his own father, that is a PATRICIDE. It should be clear from this that the brilliant deceptiveness of the superficially simple wording amply justifies its use as a complete cryptic clue, even though it consists of nothing more than a plain definition, artfully disguised by the ambiguous word 'late'.

Another cunning use of a familiar word for cryptic purposes may be seen in the following clue, several versions of which have been concocted by many setters:

(b) A number of persons (11)

There is no guarantee that everyone, even after being told that the answer is ANAESTHETIC, will immediately appreciate why. That is because it is virtually impossible to read this clue except as meaning 'A certain quantity of people'. To spot the deception, however, we are required to interpret the second word not as 'num-ber' but as 'numb-er', that is to say something that numbs our persons. It should be pointed out that this clue's understanding depends on a coined word which, while perfectly reasonable by analogy with lots of similar words ending in '-er', is nevertheless not normally used by anyone. Other coined words can be used to equally good effect, as in the following quartet of clues.

(c) A wicked thing (6)

At first sight, something evil is brought to mind. But no; what is meant is an article that has a wick and is therefore 'wicked', just as a person who has land may be called 'landed'. The answer is CANDLE.

(d) A period noted for old crockery (6,9)

Not an extract from the history of ancient earthenware, but a cryptic allusion to the time of life that brings decrepitude, turning people into 'old crocks'—a state, the clue suggests, knows as 'old crockery'. This period must, of course, be SECOND CHILDHOOD.

(e) What Mother had when she was missed (6,4)

The verb 'missed' here is intended to mean 'called Miss'; and what Mother had at that time, before she became a Mrs, was her MAIDEN NAME.

(f) Desired, as it were (10)

If 'debagged' can mean deprived of one's trousers, then theoretically 'desired' can mean deprived of one's sire, leading to the answer FATHERLESS. The coinage this time is so fanciful, however, despite the analogy, that the words 'as it were' are added to warn the solver that the definition is not to be taken at face value.

It should be evident from the above examples that a complete set of clues of this type would be too baffling for most solvers as they stood, so that no more than a couple is recommended for any average crossword. In practice, those involving coinages are comparatively rare, and one can solve a dozen consecutive crosswords without meeting a single example. More common, however, and in general less difficult to solve, is the milder form of cryptic definition, more on the lines of example (a) above, which relies not on coinages but on the ambiguous meanings of very familiar words, whether used in the clues singly, as phrases or as whole sentences.

Here are some examples, designed to demonstrate that, once the solver has fathomed the clue's real meaning, as distinct from the meaning artfully suggested at first sight, there is really only one possible answer, and that answer is almost invariably a word or phrase in common currency.

(g) A stiff examination (4-6)

There seems almost no room in these three words for any double meaning, the sense being evidently a difficult ordeal for candidates. But deception there certainly is, for the answer is POST-MORTEM, or, to put it indelicately, an examination of a stiff, a slang word for a corpse.

(h) Replace the receiver (9)

The apparent meaning is to put the telephone receiver back on its cradle. The real sense is to relocate the (intended) receiver (of a letter, say), who has moved from his original address. READDRESS answers this meaning.

(i) Its pages are used for drawing on (6-4)

The misleading words here are 'drawing on', which are intended to convey not a sketch-book, as they naturally suggest, but a CHEQUE-BOOK, on each page of which people draw money.

(j) They arrive after the milk and stay for countless meals (9,5)

Who are these early-morning visitors who more than outstay their welcome? Not mothers-in-law after all, it will be discovered, but our PERMANENT TEETH, which are welcome to stay indefinitely after the departure of our milk ones!

And here, finally, is a version of the cryptic definition in which there is an allusion to a well-known story:

(k) Spirit produced by action of rubber (5,2,3,4)

Both the first and last words are the revealing ones here. We are not concerned with alcohol mysteriously distilled from rubber but with the story of Aladdin and his magic lamp, whose action of rubbing, or being a rubber, produced the genie. The clue's answer then is GENIE OF THE LAMP.

Clues of this last type, to be fair, should be limited to stories or other literary references which really are familiar to the majority of solvers; otherwise, like the quotation clues disapproved of earlier in this book, they will be impossible to work out on the merits of the clue's wording alone. In fact, it is worth concluding this chapter with a strong recommendation that the cryptic definition be restricted to words and phrases in common use. Its great virtue is that it affords the solver a moment of sheer delight when the penny drops. If the answer then fails to materialise, either because there are too many possibilities or because it is a little-known word, the pleasure will surely turn to dissatisfaction; and that is precisely what every well-constructed cryptic clue, of whatever type, is designed to prevent.

14 Addition and subtraction

We have seen that many English words are so accommodating or flexible that we can split them into two or more parts, each part being a word in its own right, or find several different definitions for the same answers, or rearrange their letters to form other words, and so on. A vast number of words, however, are less than completely obliging in these respects, so that the clue-writer is sometimes driven to perform surgical operations on them, making good a deficiency here by external grafting or removing excess matter there by excisions of one kind or another. And even when a word does admit of being clued by any of the methods already discussed, a setter may wish, especially if he has used the more obvious technique on it previously, to give it the surgical treatment this time for the sake of variety.

Suppose, for example, that the word HEARS is in the

diagram. One clue-writer may decide to treat it as an anagram of, say, HARES or SHARE, according to which one suits his clue better. Another may see it as SHEARS, which has lost its initial letter, or perhaps EARS, after the answer's first letter has been removed. A different composer may notice that this word HEARS is HEARSE minus its last letter, and yet another that, if the central letter were cut out, it would become HERS. This gives the deviser of a clue for HEARS considerable variety of choice, but he must be careful to phrase it so that the solver is given a clear indication of whether he is expected to add or subtract, and whether he must do so at the beginning, middle or end of the word he is manipulating. The examples which follow will, it is hoped, give ample guidance on each aspect of these matters and suggest a variety of significant words with which to indicate the appropriate treatment in each case.

We shall start with several removals of heads.

(a) Put in a vessel and roasted, decapitated (5)

The clue has cunningly invited us to think of some fowl being prepared for dinner, but the equally cunning solver will examine the wording more carefully and discover that he has been offered two clues: the definition, 'Put in a vessel', leading to the answer URNED; and 'roasted' (BURNED), which has been decapitated, or lost its initial letter, to give the same answer as perfectly satisfactory corroboration.

(b) Possess a topless dress (3)

The answer OWN (possess) is GOWN (a dress) without the top (the letter G). Note that words like 'top', 'crown', 'lid', etc. are suitable, as in this example, for Down clues only.

(c) I'm flexible, but more inquisitive with leader absent (5)

The answer, which is addressing the solver, is OSIER, a flexible plant, which is NOSIER (more inquisitive) without the leading letter.

(d) Confident fool, decoyed, losing head (7)

This example shows how a decapitation can be made to apply to one part only of a subsidiary clue. The answer ASSURED (confident) consists of ASS (fool) + LURED (decoyed) minus its head. It should be mentioned in passing that while words like 'top' should be restricted to Down clues, as shown in example (b), this is not necessarily true of 'head'. A person who heads a procession is at the front of it, as is one who stands at the head of a queue, and so an Across clue can be just as 'headless' without its initial letter as a Down. Likewise, the word 'tail' can indicate the final letter of an Across or Down word, whereas 'bottom' is suitable for Down clues only.

The next group of clues concerns words that are to be curtailed.

(e) The head cuts short the prank (4)

The head intended here is not the principal of a school but a geographical head, or CAPE. To obtain this answer we must cut short the word CAPER (prank) by removing its final letter.

(f) Take a bit off the score—it's hardly credible (4)

If we do as we are asked, and take a bit off TALLY (the score), we are left with TALL, which, as used in the phrase 'a tall story', means hardly credible.

(g) Pulse badly reduced after period of fasting (6)

If we think here of the pulse taken by the doctor we have fallen for the deception, for the answer is the pulse of the vegetable kingdom, the LENTIL. This word comprises ILL (badly), reduced in length to the letters IL, after LENT (period of fasting). As in example (d) above, the removal of a letter, this time from the end, affects only part of the subsidiary clue.

A further example of this, in a different sequence, is seen

in the following:

(h) Cut almost all and sundry (7)

This time the subsidiary indications come first, with SEVER (cut) followed by AL (almost the word ALL) to form the answer SEVERAL (sundry).

Now something rather different:

(i) Ration excerpts from authors? Not half (5)

This is a more drastic 'curtailment' than the normal one, which by accepted crossword convention means the removal of the final letter only, unless clear indications are given to the contrary, such as 'ends', 'final part', etc. (Nor should 'head' ever be understood as anything but the single initial letter; if more letters are intended, words like 'heads', 'early stages' and the like are required.) In the present case the clue-writer is quite clearly asking a question about the answer QUOTA (ration). Is it, he asks, the word QUOTATIONS, meaning excerpts from authors? Not half of it, he replies; so we obediently detach TIONS, the half that makes no sense, and thus are left with the half that does.

It may be appropriate here to explain more fully the meaning of 'half' in subsidiary indications. In the word FATHER, for example, it is of course undeniable that THE is just as correctly half of it as are FAT and HER—and so, for that matter, are the letters F, A and R, even though they do not run consecutively. Nevertheless, we must once again remind ourselves that a subsidiary clue is meant in the final analysis to give the solver the kind of corroboration on which he can confidently depend, especially when there is some doubt about possible alternative answers or where vital letters are unchecked. If he can never be certain which letters of a word are involved in this kind of surgical treatment, then such a clue is lacking in positive help. It should therefore be regarded as normal practice that when a clue says that only half a word is required, it must be either the first or the second half (either FAT or HER in the above example), and never any other half of the word's total number of letters, however mathematically accurate that half may be.

Now for a trio of clues that tell the solver to cut out the middle letters of words.

(j) Heartless remarks—they are not in favour (4)

The word 'remarks' is ambiguously used here, for it looks like a noun but is really a verb meaning 'notices'—in fact, NOTES. When this word is heartless, or loses its central letter, it becomes NOES, those voters who are not in favour of a motion. It must be pointed out that whenever a word like 'heart' is used it must indicate the exact centre of the word or words involved. For instance, the heart of LONDON must be ND or, at a pinch, ONDO—a rather large heart, but the complete centre nonetheless; merely O or N or D, each of which is *somewhere* inside the word, would be far too imprecise to be of any real help to a solver, and therefore unacceptable. Similarly, the heart, or core, or centre, of a phrase like NEAR EAST must be RE or AREA (or, less convincingly, EAREAS), leaving always an equal number of letters on either side of the centre.

(k) Those who falter, lacking guts, cause conflicts (4)

This is another way of indicating that a word's innards, or guts, are to be removed. In this example the word WAVERERS (those who falter), when lacking its middle section, VERE, is left with its four external letters to form WARS (conflicts).

(l) Still sang at dances, not disheartened (8)

The removal of the heart this time affects only part of the answer STAGNANT (still). The subsidiary clue gives, first, an anagram of SANG AT (indicated by 'dances', which suggests moving about), making STAGNA; then NT, which is the word NOT disheartened, or minus its heart.

Yet another method of subtraction is to take a complete word away from a longer one to leave the required answer.

Here are three examples.

(m) A cutter can't get on in this swell (5)

The use of 'this' makes it clear that the answer is a word meaning swell in some sense, but that answer may not strike us at once. From the rest of the clue we can work out that SURGEON (a cutter) can't get ON, which means that only SURGE (swell) is available to us, and that is the answer.

(n) Miss a cake that's lost at home (4)

To miss an easy catch is to MUFF it. This answer is formed from MUFFIN (a cake) that has lost IN (at home). Notice that, as this clue is read, we are meant to interpret 'that's' as 'that is', whereas in fact it means 'that has'.

(o) Men ejected from dwelling will give opinion (5)

If MEN are thrown out of TENEMENT (dwelling), what will be given us is TENET (opinion).

Finally, there is a variation of this method whereby, instead of subtracting, we can add a complete word to our answer to make another word or phrase, as these last two examples will show.

(p) Swellings that will cause no despair when you have a couple (5)

The swellings are NODES, which, when you have PAIR (a couple) added on, will make NO DESPAIR.

(q) This girl wants city to show truthfulness (4)

We are looking for a girl in four letters—either a word like MISS or an actual name—who will have to have CITY added on to her in order to show a word meaning truthfulness. A synonym for truthfulness is VERACITY, which means therefore that this girl who wants CITY after her name is VERA.

15 Bits and pieces

When a word in a crossword diagram happens to have in its make-up another complete word, with one letter or more left over as a fragment at either end or somewhere inside, it does not always suit the clue-writer's purpose to have such a word beheaded, curtailed or disheartened, as happened with the examples of the previous chapter. He need not despair, however, for he still has a few devices in reserve which he has not yet called to his aid. One very useful and common method of dealing with odd letters is to treat them as abbreviations of familiar words, such as N for North, ST for street, AB for sailor, etc.; and this method will be discussed in detail in the next chapter. For the present, let us follow some other hitherto untrodden ways.

Short combinations of letters, while making no sense in English, may nevertheless be foreign words sufficiently familiar to be admitted into our crosswords, provided always that their nationality is properly indicated. While it would be wrong to be dogmatic about what words are familiar and to give an exhaustive list on that basis, the principle involved may be simply stated thus: that only the most elementary foreign words should be included, such as will certainly be known by those who either have never learnt the language concerned or have never used it since their schooldays. This applies just as much to difficult crosswords as to those of an easier standard, since it is patently absurd to assume that anyone who can solve the most subtle or tough English clues must therefore necessarily be a linguist also. My own practice, whatever the standard of puzzle, is to restrict foreign indications to the minimum in the interests of fairness, and rarely to include anything more advanced than the following: in French, the words LE, LA and LES, UN and UNE, DE, DU and DES, MON, MA and MES, and IL, ILS, ELLE and ELLES; in Spanish, EL; in Italian, IL; in German, DER; and in Latin (or French) TU and EST. The following quartet of fairly easy examples may be regarded as typical.

(a) Ruin of French achievement (6)

The answer DEFEAT (ruin) consists of DE (of, French) and FEAT (achievement).

(b) Crowd following the Parisian ambassador (6)

This time the French word is LE (the, Parisian version), which when followed by GATE (the crowd at, for instance, a football match) gives LEGATE (ambassador).

(c) Very warm, the Spanish inn (5)

HOT (very warm) and EL (the, Spanish) make HOTEL (inn).

(d) Paintings, etc., returned by the German merchant (6)

ART (paintings, etc.) when returned, or written in reverse order, becomes TRA. When this is put by, or beside, DER (the, German) we have TRADER (merchant).

Much more often, however, the odd remnant will not be a simple foreign word; and, in any case, recourse to anything other than English should be very much the exception in normal crosswords. How, then, do we cope with odd letters without having to resort to abbreviations and without deviating from English? This can best be answered by the following example. Let us assume that we wish to clue the word BARGE, and it occurs to us that its make-up is BARE around the letter G. 'Move clumsily with nothing on' nicely accounts for the definition of the answer and also for most of its letters, but we are still left with that G to dispose of. One way out of the difficulty is to clue G as part of another word, whether as that word's first, middle or last letter—or, indeed, any letter so long as it is unmistakably indicated; for instance, since G is the third letter of August, we could do our barging 'with nothing on around the third of August' (i.e. BARE around G).

More often, though, such precision can be achieved only by reference to a beginning, middle or end, as in the following three versions of this same clue.

(e) Move clumsily, with nothing on, around middle of night (5)

Here BARGE (move clumsily) consists of BARE (with nothing on) around G (middle of the word night). As was mentioned in the previous chapter, this use of the word 'middle' must be taken, if it is to be of any real assistance to the solver, to mean the exact centre of the word indicated.

(f) Move clumsily, with nothing on, around end of evening (5)

This is identical in principle with (e), but here the letter G is obtainable by taking the end, which must be the last letter only, of the word evening.

(g) Move clumsily, with nothing on, around capital of Greece (5)

This too is like (e), but the reference to the capital of Greece, intended to mislead solvers into thinking at first of Athens, is really doing no more than pointing to that country's capital letter, which is G.

The technique, then, of dealing with odd bits and pieces consists of treating such fragments as parts of other words—words that the clue-writer chooses for their appropriateness to the context of the clue, as will be evident from the remaining examples in this chapter. Before they are set down, however, some cautionary remarks about the method of indicating these bits and pieces may be found useful.

To indicate a single letter at the beginning of a word, phrases like 'start of', 'head of', 'capital of', 'initially' and the like are absolutely clear and accurate. The use of 'head' and 'start' to mean a couple of letters at the beginning of a word, while not actually inaccurate, is not recommended, since a solver is likely to find himself uncertain on this point, and a confused solver is not being helped by the clue as much as, ideally, he should be. But to indicate, say, GERM as 'head of German' is downright unfair, because in no reasonable sense can the head of anything be as much as four-sixths of its total length. The same considerations apply to the words 'end', 'finish', 'conclusion', 'finally', 'tail', etc., all of which should indicate the last letter only. It must be realised that solvers are not normally thinking of creatures like snakes and tadpoles in these matters!

Care should also be taken about the correct syntactical wording of clues in which heads and tails of words are involved. For example, 'mouth of river', or even 'river mouth', can fairly be said to indicate R, the first letter of river; but 'Portsmouth', written as one word without an apostrophe, is *not*, regardless of the derivation of its name, the same as 'port's mouth' as an indication of the letter P. Similarly, while 'school's head' really does mean the head of school (and so, in crossword terms, the letter S), the name 'Gateshead' does not mean the head of gate to give G, nor can 'redhead', in any sense, convey the meaning 'head of red' (i.e. R). Again, any reader of the phrase 'lane end' or 'lane's end' will naturally understand it to mean 'end of lane' (i.e. the letter E), just as 'week-end' is the end of the week (i.e. K); but that is certainly not to imply that therefore 'Gravesend' means 'end of grave' (= E) or 'end of graves' (= S). Nor, what is even worse, can 'West End' possibly be construed in English as 'end of West' (i.e. the letter T).

It follows, therefore, that in clues of this type, as in all others, it should always be the setter's aim to offer correct syntactical information to the solver as he reads the clue. Even where there is a choice—for instance, in a phrase like 'school principal', which is perfectly acceptable as meaning the principal of a school—it is better to be consistent and to prefer 'school's principal', which not only reads quite naturally to give the same meaning but also clearly points to the first letter of school.

As in the case of words that are used to indicate anagrams, a certain amount of artistic licence may be regarded as reasonable for beginnings and endings. 'A spot of gin' might be accepted as not too far-fetched for the letter G, 'a dash of soda' for S, or 'lake's edge' for either L or E. One frequently used phrase, however, which is somewhat less clear-cut than these, is 'a bit of'. It can be argued, simply and irrefutably, that 'a bit of trouble' can equally correctly be any one of the seven letters of 'trouble', or any pair of successive letters of the word, or even a slice of three letters together, just as 'a bit of cake' can be any piece, not too large, taken from any part of it. Nevertheless, since to say to a solver that he must find one letter, or possibly more, *somewhere* within the length of the word 'trouble' would be worse than useless, it may be safely taken as a crossword convention that most clue-writers use 'a bit of' only to mean the word's first letter.

The following examples are designed to show how bits and pieces of required answers can be treated, with some variety of phraseology, in accordance with the principles propounded above.

The first group uses these oddments as beginnings of other words.

(h) Head of household has a little custom (5)

It should now be apparent that the 'head' of the word household is the letter H. When this has A BIT (a little) next to it, it becomes HABIT (custom).

(i) Grating top of soil with fork (8)

'Top of' is suitable only for a Down clue, which we must therefore imagine this to be. So the letter S (top of soil) with TRIDENT (fork) gives us as the answer the adjective STRIDENT (grating), which has been misleadingly written in the clue to suggest a verb.

(j) Books that inject a touch of madness into extreme members (5)

The letter M, clued with a little licence as 'a touch of madness' to suggest a very small amount of the word, when injected into TOES (extreme members of the body) makes TOMES (books).

(k) Make expiation about first of crimes without delay (2,4)

The fact that the answer is a two-word phrase instead of a single word in no way affects this type of clue, as we see here. To make expiation is to ATONE. If these letters are placed about C (the first letter of crimes), we have AT ONCE (without delay). (See example (k) in Chapter 8 for a different clue to this phrase.)

(l) Loathe opening stages of defector's trial (6)

This time the odd piece has more than one letter, as is made clear by the words 'opening stages of'. Thus DE (the opening stages of defector's) and TEST (trial) combine to make DETEST (loathe). Note that this same word might have been clued, still on the 'bits and pieces' principle, by presenting DE as the French word for 'of' and TEST as an exam, and by slightly changing the definition to 'dislike', to give 'Dislike of French exam (6)'—a clue very similar to example (a).

(m) Here's a carriage, and inside a certain amount of laughter (6)

'A certain amount of', while not exactly specifying the number of letters required, suggests that several letters of the word laughter are to be used. If the clue to this six-letter answer is read correctly, it will be seen that AND is inside, and that therefore the remaining fragment consists of three letters, i.e. LAU. Put AND inside LAU and you have LANDAU (a carriage).

The next pair of examples will show how exactly half of a word's letters, taken from either end, can be incorporated in this kind of clueing.

(n) Invisible man shows trick, swallowing half of éclair (7)

A person whom nobody sees, and so in a sense an 'invisible' man, is a RECLUSE. This answer shows us RUSE (trick) swallowing ECL (half of éclair).

(o) Bank's principal, by latter half of August, is broke (4)

We have here a double dose of the treatment. B is the principal, or leading letter, of the word bank, and it appears by, or beside, UST, which is the latter half of August, to form the answer BUST (broke). It should be observed that half of a word may be either the first or the second half, without the need for such a generous indication as is given here. There is, after all, a very limited choice, for if one half doesn't work the other will. Note also that correct syntax demands such phrases as, say, 'half of book' or 'book's (first or second) half', whereas, for instance, 'better half' (as an attempted indication of BET or TER) will not do, since it does not and cannot mean 'half of better'. To make it syntactically correct, one would have to say 'better's half'; but that phrase makes no sense at all, and so the whole idea must be abandoned in that case.

Now for a few examples in which endings of words are involved.

(p) Layabout finally having to seek a job (4)

The word layabout, finally, provides us with the letter T. Having ASK (to seek) next to it, it becomes TASK (a job).

(q) Ask advice of old Republican leader before closure of court (7)

The answer CONSULT (ask advice of) has CONSUL (leader of the old Roman Republic) before T (closure, or end, of the word court).

(r) Spectators, around finish of game, exulted (6)

CROWD (spectators at a sporting event) around E (finish of the word game) becomes CROWDED (exulted).

(s) Quote it in concluding parts of service (4)

The answer CITE (quote) consists of IT inside CE (concluding parts of the word service, the plural indicating more than one letter).

A piece amounting to more than half of another word can also be accommodated in this technique. Here is a tricky-looking clue in which two such pieces appear:

(t) ⅔ of 1 + ⅔ of 1—what kind of sign is that? (4)

This is not as difficult as it may seem at first sight, particularly if the figures are converted into words. Two-thirds of ONE must be either ON or NE. In fact, both are used here, the latter two-thirds coming first, to make NE + ON, the answer being a NEON sign.

Finally, what can be done when the fragment consists of a couple of letters which do not conveniently form two successive letters of an appropriate word? Suppose, for instance, that when clueing the word CROWD we want to say that it has ROW inside CD—what shall we do with the awkward CD fragment? No word comes readily to mind which has CD in the middle of it, and none, surely, has this pair of letters as its beginning or end. We could, of course, employ a different method of clueing this word, such as CROW + D, C + ROWD(Y), C + anagram of WORD and so on; but actually there is a way of treating it within the rules of this chapter, as follows:

(u) Multitude makes din, gripped by extremes of cold (5)

We have said that CROWD (multitude) makes ROW (din) gripped by CD (the extremes, or the first and last letters, of cold).

Here are two further examples in conclusion, to demonstrate that this combination of the initial and final letters of a word can be used as a change from other devices.

(v) Learner taking transport to the limits of endurance (7)

Our learner is a TRAINEE, who takes TRAIN (transport) to join EE (the limits at either end of the word endurance).

(w) Avaricious rush in the outskirts of Germany (6)

A synonym of avaricious is GREEDY. It consists of REED (a plant also known as a rush) inside GY, which are the first and last letters, or outskirts as it were, of Germany.

16 Abbreviations

In an age in which the PM, or another MP, has discussions with the TUC and CBI, addresses a UN debate in the USA about the influence of NATO and SEATO, attends the FA Cup Final, shown on BBC TV, or OKs the menu for a dinner at No. 10 for foreign VIPs, there is no need to seek to justify the inclusion of abbreviations of all kinds in the language of crosswords. Indeed, the only real problem that faces a setter is which ones to adopt and which it would be fairest to reject. In this connection a few observations may be helpful.

In a crossword of a difficult standard, containing a fair proportion of recondite words, for which the solver knows that he must have a dictionary at his elbow throughout the solving period, it is fair to use any abbreviation, whether familiar or largely unknown, which is included in an accessible dictionary—patently so if it happens to be the dictionary recommended by the setter for that puzzle. What is not reasonable is to introduce an unfamiliar abbreviation which is missing from the recommended dictionary, or from those of a similar size, and which can be disinterred only from some technical book of reference not readily available. Any cluewriter who has to resort to such extremes must be desperately short of inspiration!

For the average type of crossword, however, it is advisable to be more selective and to avoid anything too technical, specialised or esoteric. This is not to suggest that all abbreviations of a specialised nature should be abjured, but only those which are quite likely to be unfamiliar to the layman. For example, one does not need to have had military training to recognise on sight the RA as the Royal Artillery and the RE as the Royal Engineers; but few of us, surely, are equally familiar with, say, RMA (Royal Military Academy) or RCT (Royal Corps of Transport)—two abbreviations that would therefore be out of place in a popular puzzle. Again, while we all know about dates accompanied by the letters BC and AD, probably all but those with classical backgrounds will be baffled by the initials AUC (*ab urbe condita*), corresponding to 753 BC, the date of the founding of Rome. And although no setter would have any qualms about using MA, BSc., DD and similar indications of degrees and qualifications, one could hardly expect solvers to be acquainted with SCL (Student of Civil Law), an abbreviation suitable only for a harder crossword or, for instance, one appearing in an exclusively legal publication.

There are two other forms of abbreviation which, although not normally found in the special list at the back of a dictionary, are nevertheless perfectly legitimate and fair in crossword clues: Roman numerals and shortened versions of names. With these it is for the setter to exercise his judgment as to the extent of his solvers' familiarity with those that he wishes to include; but in both kinds it is always wisest to avoid anything obscure. The Roman numerals from one to twelve, so familiar from clock-faces, L for fifty, C for a hundred, D for five hundred and M for a thousand, with an extra I tacked on here and there (e.g. CI for 101), or a double letter (e.g. CC for 200), are ample for our purposes and ought not to be exceeded. As for names, not only are diminutives like Peg, Pat, Sal, Bert, Lou and Abe, etc. suitable for clueing by the appropriate full names, but also genuine abbreviations like Chas., Jas., Hy., Geo., etc., such as are seen on name-plates and shop signs or in some reference books.

Since abbreviations are so normal a part of our lives in both written and conversational contexts—who would ever refer to ITV or the CID, for instance, by anything but their initials?—the question of clueing them raises no special problems. If the word BASIN, say, were being clued as a combination of BA and SIN, it would no doubt accord with strict pedantry to indicate BA as 'a bachelor, in short' or something similar. But as in practice one refers in speech or writing to one sort of graduate or bachelor as 'a BA' rather than as 'a Bachelor of Arts', the extra indication that it is abbreviated, while sometimes given as an extra bonus, should not be regarded as being obligatory upon the setter.

A further point of interest in this connection is the increasing tendency, in the press as well as in most of the information provided by computers, to omit punctuation of any kind in abbreviations. This trend has led many original abbreviations—for example, MATHS, RADAR, ERNIE, LOG—to develop into words in their own right, their abbreviated nature in some cases almost forgotten; and it also makes it likely that within another generation or so many solvers may even be unaware that words like FLU and PHONE started life as abbreviations, complete with apostrophes to draw attention to the omission of some letters. Even today one rarely thinks of such things as BUS and PLANE as anything other than complete words, so that any indication in clues of the shortness of their forms would be more likely to confuse than to help a solver.

It would serve no useful purpose to compile here a comprehensive list of recommended abbreviations: that is, those to which a setter may safely refer when clueing words in popular cryptic crosswords. The reason is that some of the items included might quite quickly become obsolescent and others, non-existent at this moment, could soon be clamouring for admittance on the score of universal currency. For example, no list in a dictionary of a generation ago could possibly have contained the abbreviated jargon of the space-age; but, on the other hand, some of the entries in that list, particularly the initials of various taxes, have now been superseded.

One can, however, suggest certain categories of abbreviations which are likely to be of regular use to clue-writers and solvers, as follows: days and months (e.g. Sun., Dec.); some points of the compass (e.g. N, NE, W, SW); regiments, units and ranks of the fighting services (e.g. RASC, RN, Lt.); familiar musical indications (e.g. p, pp, op., f, ff); the better-known chemical symbols (e.g. Au, Cu, Fe); Roman numerals (e.g. V, L, C, M); monarchs (e.g. GR, ER); abbreviated names (e.g. Hy., Wm.); commercial terms (e.g. inst., ult., Co., Inc.); money (e.g. £., p; but former currency like s. and d. should have their obsoleteness indicated); weights (e.g. lb, oz, cwt); organisations and institutions (e.g. BR, RADA, ITA, RAC); styles, titles, degrees, etc. (e.g. Kt, Rev, Mrs, SRN, MD, Prof.); abbreviations commonly used in notes and indices (e.g. vol., i.e., etc., PTO); countries, counties and states (e.g. USA, SA, Beds, NY); film classifications (e.g. A, U, X); thoroughfares (e.g. Rd, St, Ave); units of length (e.g. yd, ft, cm); and numerous shorter lists and single items, such as a.m. and p.m.; rly., or ry.; OK; KO; SS; and so on. The scope is manifestly very wide, but the decisions about which abbreviations can be counted on as being familiar to the majority of solvers, as well as considerations of obsolescence, will depend, as has been stated earlier, entirely on the clue-writer's judgment. In cases of doubt he would be well advised to learn, by trying it out on a friend, whether an abbreviation to which he intends to refer is really as well known as he supposes it to be.

The examples that follow are intended to demonstrate how to deal with odd letters of an answer by a different method from the 'bits and pieces' technique described in the previous chapter. As will be seen, it is possible to devise a neat clue by using an abbreviation either as a small part of the answer or as most of it, or perhaps by finding more than one abbreviation in the same word.

More unusually still, here, to begin with, is a clue to a word which is also entirely an abbreviation:

(a) Resistance units on Government service (4)

This is not the war-time underground movement that the clue's wording deliberately suggests but the electrical units of resistance called OHMS, which may also be read as the familiar abbreviation for On Her Majesty's Service which is printed on all envelopes sent out by Government departments.

The next group of clues also depends entirely on abbreviations for the solution of each of them.

(b) There's not one left—let's have the same again, twice (4)

We are looking for something that is extinct, and that ought to suggest the answer, DODO. The subsidiary clue says to the solver that we ought to have DO (short for ditto, or the same thing again) twice, making DO-DO, and thus confirming the answer defined in the first part of the clue.

(c) Eat out, and so on, taking an hour (4)

To eat out, with acid rather than gastronomically, is to ETCH, which is formed by ETC. (and so on) taking H (an hour).

(d) Pendants that are loud and antiquated (4)

The pendants intended here are FOBS, which are made of F (loud, musically) and OBS. (obsolete, or antiquated).

(e) The last carriage that is used in the railways (4)

The last carriage for anyone is a BIER. Look at the letters

of this word and you will find I.E. (that is) used in BR (British Rail, or the railways).

(f) Henry left the dining-room (4)

This is very slightly different from those above, comprising a diminutive name and an abbreviation, one of the diminutives of Henry being HAL, and L standing for left. Together they form the answer HALL (the dining-room in a college, for instance).

Another example involving the diminutive form of a name is the following:

(g) The painter, Diana and I got together, and more than one spoke (5)

A frequent visitor to crosswords is the RA, clued variously as a painter, artist or academician. When he and DI (Diana) and I are got (or obtained) together they finished as RADII (the plural of radius, a spoke, and hence more than one spoke).

Now for an example which manages to find as many as three abbreviations in one five-letter word:

(h) See the doctor duck work and grow weak (5)

What we see is DR (the doctor), O (a symbol on a score-card for no runs at cricket, otherwise known as a duck) and OP. (opus or musical work); and the combination thus produced, which is DROOP (grow weak).

The letters ST form one of the most commonly used abbreviations in crosswords, appearing with equal regularity as a street or a saint. One of each will be found in the following two clues.

(i) The street before you is an eyesore (4)

The letters ST (street) in front of YE (you) give us STYE (a sore on the eye, or an eyesore).

(j) The good man was in debt, getting put away (6)

This time ST is the good man or saint. With OWED (was

in debt) it gives us STOWED (put away).

The next example may take a little longer to solve, as we shall see.

(k) Row the ship around the Lake (6)

Features of this clue which are likely to delay a solver are: firstly, his initial uncertainty whether the 'row' mentioned here is meant as a din or a line or rank; and secondly, the possibility that he may think of L. as the abbreviation of Lake, as it is in atlases etc., with a word for a ship around it. In fact, it is the line or SERIES that is required, which consists of SS (the ship) around ERIE (the name of an actual lake).

Phrases also lend themselves to this treatment as much as they do to others, as may be seen in the following:

(l) A whole bunch of detectives falls for sweets (4,5)

This leads to A + CID (whole bunch of detectives) + DROPS (falls), and the resultant ACID DROPS are a suitable answer for the definition 'sweets'.

The inclusion of common abbreviations, then, can often help out a clue-writer when he is left with an odd letter or two of a word or phrase to indicate, and it can also be a boon to a struggling solver by giving him a useful start to the answer of a difficult clue. Abbreviations of some kind are to be found, if needed, in part of every word in a puzzle's diagram, but not all of them will be familiar enough for use in a popular crossword, while many of those that are may not lead to a satisfactory clue. For quite short words, however, for which the number of possible treatments is much more limited than for longer words and phrases, recourse to abbreviations can produce quite effective results. Let us conclude with a handful of clues which many solvers will find fairly easy but which may nevertheless give pleasure by the clear and sensible pictures that they bring to the mind, or by their neatness and economy of words. See how quickly you can solve them before looking at the answers, which appear below.

(m) Engineers given a brace to mend (6)
(n) This animal gets me about all right (4)
(o) Gather about a piano (4)
(p) The king's in the little house, injured (4)
(q) Well, give us back the Member (4)

The answers to these five clues are as follows:

(m) REPAIR (to mend), formed when RE (Engineers) are given PAIR (a couple or brace); (n) MOKE (animal) gets ME about OK (all right); (o) REAP (gather), comprising RE (concerning or about) + A + P (softly or piano); (p) HURT (injured), a word in which R (the king) is in HUT (the little house); (q) SUMP (a well), to obtain which the solver is asked to give to SU (US, back) the letters MP (the Member).

17 Punctuation

Although, as in other forms of written English, the punctuation of clues admits of many acceptable variations, nevertheless the discussion of certain theories and techniques may help to develop a policy consistent with fairness.

Omission of punctuation

It is a familiar convention that a comma, dash or any other method of signifying some pause or break in a clue may be left for the solver to supply for himself.

For example, the word PRIOR as an adjective means former; as a noun it means a monk. Put these two definitions together and they will form a neat clue which makes sense, as follows: 'Former monk'. Solvers will quickly realise that there are two clues here, not one, and will mentally insert a comma or dash between the two different definitions.

A slightly more subtle example may be devised. The TAIL is the stern, and to TAIL is to shadow or dog. A clue such as 'Stern dog' presents the two definitions together, with the comma once more understood; but this time the solver can't help being sidetracked at first into thinking of an adjective plus a noun, whereas in fact a noun plus a verb have been used—a legitimate deception because both definitions, though not immediately apparent, are perfectly correct.

This practice of omission can equally be applied to clues which contain a definition and a subsidiary indication. For example:

(a) Spare a young devil in heaven (6)

The answer SKIMPY (spare) is made up of IMP (a young devil) inside SKY (heaven). A pause is required after 'Spare'.

(b) Types of riddle awful cads hear (8)

The types of riddle are CHARADES, an anagram of CADS HEAR. We must pause after 'riddle'.

In this chapter we must also consider the situation in which punctuation is present but may legitimately be ignored; but let it be stressed in passing that there is no justification for deliberately introducing inappropriate punctuation—just to make things harder for the solver but easier for the setter—and then blithely saying, in the preamble to the puzzle, 'Punctuation may be misleading'.

There are certain 'novelty' crosswords in which the clues do not employ the familiar principles that operate in 'plain' puzzles. One such type of clue, known as 'DLM', or 'definition-and-letter-mixture', contains a definition of the required answer and also the letters of the answer in a jumbled-up form, often beginning in the middle of one word and carrying on to the next. For example:

(c) Watch over me and don't delay (4)

(d) What's an igloo-dweller like? Somewhat frigid (6)

In (c) the definition, 'Watch over', leads to the answer TEND, which is found jumbled as NTDE in the words 'doN'T DElay'. In (d) the definition is 'igloo-dweller', and the answer, ESKIMO, comes from 'lIKE? SOMewhat', after the consecutive letters IKESOM have been unjumbled.

Now obviously we are concerned here solely with the particular task of rearranging letters, and any intrusive punctuation, such as the apostrophe or question mark in these two examples, is irrelevant to this—as it is also in genuine anagrams, as distinct from meaningless jumbles, and in hidden answers, as explained in Chapter 19 (p. 109). It is therefore a perfectly reasonable convention for the setter to say, in his introductory remarks explaining what the solver has to do in that novelty puzzle, that punctuation in the clues should be ignored.

The apostrophe

A simple method of saving precious space—and this is often an important factor in published crosswords—is to shorten words by the use of an apostrophe. 'We'll' for 'we shall' and 'I'd' for 'I had' or 'I would' are obvious examples. Particularly valuable to the clue-writer is one use of the apostrophe which serves rather to disguise his meaning than to save space. Consider the following;

(a) The girl's failure to hit the mark (4)
(b) Make known the girl's weight (8)
(c) The girl's ring, given by brave man (4)

It will be discovered that, although at first sight identical, the meaning of 'the girl's' is different in each case.

(a) must be read as 'The girl *is* (i.e. is the same as) failure to hit the mark' (answer, MISS, for which there are two different definitions); in (b) 'the girl's weight' stands for 'the girl *has* weight', i.e. ANN has (or possesses) OUNCE (answer, ANNOUNCE, meaning to make known); and in (c) 'The girl's (= HER) ring (= O), given by a brave man' leads to the answer HERO.

The question mark

This is a conveniently brief way of saying to the solver, 'What I have written isn't necessarily true, but isn't is possible to imagine it in that light?' The following examples will illustrate this.

> **(a) Agreeing, like peeping Toms at both sides of keyhole? (6,3,2,3)**

The phrase SEEING EYE TO EYE means 'agreeing'. It doesn't mean two people spying simultaneously from opposite sides of a door, but part of the clue asks whether one might not humorously visualise it in this way.

> **(b) To retain one's skill, make one's workman stay after hours? (4,4,4,2)**

To KEEP ONE'S HAND IN is to retain one's skill. Can't the same words conjure up a mental picture of making one's workman, or hand, stay behind?

> **(c) I don't believe it—as the child said, still awake after one bedtime story? (4,2,7)**

TELL ME ANOTHER really means 'I don't believe it'. Might it not also be thought of as the words of a child asking for a second bedtime story?

In addition, the question mark may be used to give one example of a whole class of people or things. If an answer to be discovered is LANCASTRIAN, it is perfectly correct to clue him as an 'Englishman', for that is what he is and the solver has been instructed to look for someone who is English.

But if the *answer* is ENGLISHMAN, it is *not* correct to define him as a 'Lancastrian' because he may not be a Lancastrian at all, so we must not say, as a definite statement, that he is. The addition of a question mark here, however, makes all the difference. The clue 'A Lancastrian?' says, in effect, 'Might the answer to this clue be a Lancastrian?' An ENGLISHMAN certainly *might* be a Lancastrian, but it would be quite wrong to assert as a fact that he *is* one. There are, as it happens, other ways of thus defining ENGLISHMAN without employing the question mark; equally correct would be 'A Lancastrian, perhaps', or 'A Lancastrian, for example'.

The exclamation mark

The temptation to overwork the exclamation mark should be resisted, lest it should cease to have any real point. The mere fact that a clue happens to read amusingly is not a sufficient excuse for this extra emphasis, since the wording itself should achieve the desired effect.

Strictly speaking, the only times when its use is not only fully justified but also necessary are when an interjection or an imperative is involved and where it would naturally occur in writing—for example:

(a) A blow will make the bachelor shut up! (4)

The answer is BASH, made from BA (the bachelor) and SH! (shut up!).

(b) The grain-store is overturned—look! (4)

IS, when overturned, gives SI; LO! means look! The answer is SILO, a grain-store.

Even when one wishes to underline, as it were, some liberty taken with the English language, such as a coined word or a familiar word used with a coined meaning, it is on the whole advisable to refrain and not to give the game away too easily. The description of a meandering stream as 'windy' (because it winds), of a goat as 'butter' (i.e. something that butts) or a landlord who lets houses as a 'letter' might appear to call for an exclamation. To supply one, however, could well nullify the effect of a pleasant surprise in the solver when the penny eventually drops.

On the other hand, a device that could be called a 'trick clue', such as 'Wolf!' for EBB (because it is another way of saying 'Flow, backwards') or a neat example of a 'read it again' clue (discussed in Chapter 18) might, in its author's opinion, qualify for the additional flourish of an exclamation mark. Ximenes has written that he himself ceased this practice after it was pointed out to him that such punctuation was merely a form of patting oneself on the back and saying, 'That was rather good, wasn't it?' The point is a fair one, yet its occasional retention may still be condoned on the ground that it could equally be a way of saying to the solver, 'Do be careful—there's something unusual here!'

Very experienced solvers, of course, will seldom require this additional prodding; but if it is felt that the majority would otherwise miss a subtlety or a witticism, then a little harmless vanity (if it should be so construed) on the clue-writer's part is perhaps forgivable in the larger interest of extra helpfulness. Nevertheless, it must be borne in mind that the use of the exclamation mark in clues should be judiciously limited to special cases.

The dash

There are three kinds of dash used in crossword clues, each of a different length. The hyphen is used exactly as in any other form of English writing whenever it is appropriate. The other two we may call simply 'the dash' and 'the long dash'.

The dash may begin and end a parenthesis, just as brackets do. In addition, it is commonly used in order to separate the two 'halves' of a clue, and performs more or less the same function as a comma, colon or semicolon. Here are three identically worded clues.

(a) The reigning champion, e.g. Lord So-and-So (5-6)
(b) The reigning champion: e.g. Lord So-and-So (5-6)
(c) The reigning champion—e.g. Lord So-and-So (5-6)

Each of these three clues is equally acceptable for the answer TITLE-HOLDER, which applies to both a reigning champion and a man with a title, for instance a lord.

Similarly, there is no practical difference between the two following clues:

(d) Wild animal; therefore kept in a receptacle (5)
(e) Wild animal—therefore kept in a receptacle (5)

The answer is BISON, SO (therefore) being kept inside BIN (a receptacle).

A clear distinction should be made between the kind of dash just mentioned and the hyphen, which is shorter in length when printed. Suppose, for instance, that you wish to clue the word MAID, a term that may be defined as 'domestic help'. You notice that it consists of the letter A inside MID, so you want to say two things: that A is in MID, and that it is a term for domestic help. It might then be very tempting to put the two parts together to produce the following:

(f) One is needed in mid-term for domestic help (4)

What you have said is that A (one) is needed in MID, and that the answer, MAID, is a term for domestic help. There should therefore be a pause between 'mid' and 'term'. It is possible to put no punctuation there at all and write 'mid term', leaving it to the solver to supply his own punctuation, as explained in the opening paragraphs of this chapter. Or you may indicate the pause by a comma or a dash. But what you shouldn't do is put in a hyphen and hope that it will be read as a dash, because, to be honest, 'mid-hyphen-term' is *not* the same as 'mid-dash-term', and if you punctuate with a hyphen here, while elsewhere in the same puzzle the dash is longer, you are being unfair.

The long dash noticeably occupies more space than either of the two previously mentioned forms. This is used to replace a missing word which the solver is required to find. One obvious example is the missing word from a quotation: for instance, the answer ROMANS from

> **(g) 'Friends,——, countrymen, lend me your ears.' (6)**

(Although this is a purely factual clue, depending on knowledge and memory, and is in no sense cryptic, readers will find many crosswords, cryptic in all other respects, that insist on including their apparently statutory quotation or two.)

This same long dash has a cryptic function also and, as in a quotation, it replaces a missing word—the difference being that the answer has to be worked out from hints in the clue as well as from the obligatory definition. A fairly easy example is the following:

> **(h) Rummages for food: some tribes have done so—— (7)**

The answer, FORAGES, means rummages for food. The same answer, when the letters are treated as two consecutive words, can be deduced so as to form the missing part of the complete sentence, 'some tribes have done so FOR AGES'.

Here is another example, which may raise a smile:

> **(i) Nevertheless, trouser-seats get shiny,——! (15)**

The answer is NOTWITHSTANDING (nevertheless). And it is certainly NOT WITH STANDING that the seats of people's trousers get shiny!

Three dots

From time to time when concocting the clues of a crossword

one is suddenly struck by the curious accident that two successive answers in the diagram have some superficial connection, either in their meanings, or in the make-up of their letters, or perhaps in some allusive respect. In such cases the clue-writer is apt to draw attention to this by making the first clue appear unfinished and by so phrasing the second clue as to make it continue straight on from the first.

Suppose, for instance, that the answer at 1 Down happens to be PARIS, and that at 2 Down to be PAIRS. You see that one is an anagram of the other, and begin to wonder how to connect the clues to both these answers. Here is one possible treatment:

1 Dn Equality is shown in a foreign capital (5)...
2 Dn...which is rather awkward for couples (5)

The answer to 1 Down is PARIS, shown by PAR (equality) + IS, the whole being a foreign capital; and normally this would be the end of that clue. However, since we want to say in the succeeding clue, 'Paris is rather awkward for couples' (meaning that the letters of PARIS, when written rather awkwardly, or slightly out of order make PAIRS = couples), it is perhaps neater and more intriguing to ask the solver to use the previous answer as part of the new clue. The conventional method of indicating this connection is to add three dots to the first clue and to preface the second one with three further dots. It must be remembered that solvers often tackle clues out of their order and might therefore attempt the second of this pair of clues first. In that case, they would have no inkling of the reference to its predecessor if there were no dots at the beginning to draw their attention to it.

Let us now examine a slightly different example. We notice that two successive answers are ANNA and CENT—both coins, both of small value—and the coincidence is too tempting to miss. So we need a pair of clues run together, such as:

(a) There's little change out East for a girl (4)...
(b) ...little change in cinematic entertainment (4)

In (a) there are two different meanings of ANNA: a girl, and little or small change out East. In (b) CENT (little change) is hidden inside 'cinematiC ENTertainment'.

Note that there is really no need to connect these two clues at all, and they can just as easily be tackled independently without any cross-references to each other. Yet since this device adds variety and, as some believe, attractiveness to clues, it is worth using, albeit sparingly, when circumstances permit.

There may be times, indeed, when a particularly neat pairing of answers occurs to one before, or possibly in the course of, composing the diagram and is then worked in deliberately.

Here is an example that involves different meanings of the word 'mater', which may be used in the sense of a mother or of one who mates people. This might lead a setter to include in his diagram MOTHER SUPERIOR, which has fourteen letters, and immediately below it MARRIAGE BROKER, which by happy chance has the same number of letters and will balance it exactly in the symmetry of the diagram. To round things off, a suitable pair of clues might be:

(c) Mater, spiritual (6,8)...
(d) ...Mater, temporal (8,6)

Although short, and comprising definitions only, these clues are sufficiently teasing to qualify as cryptic definitions (see Chapter 13) and to delay a solver long enough to cause a chuckle when the solution at last occurs to him.

Finally, it is not always the two successive answers that have a superficial connection but rather something in the wording of one clue which leads naturally to the succeeding answer. For example, suppose that by sheer chance we have the word MISSILE in the diagram, followed by the golfing phrase GOOD LIE (which means that your ball is lying in a good position after you have made a shot). Without at first being aware of any connection, we might clue MISSILE as 'Weapon produced by girl—bad lie (7)', by which we mean that the word for a weapon (MISSILE) is produced by having a word for a girl (MISS) followed by an anagram of LIE

(ILE). Then it strikes us that the very next item for clueing is GOOD LIE; and since such coincidences are too rare to ignore, we make a connected pair of clues, as follows:

> **(e) Weapon produced by girl—bad lie (7)...**
> **(f) ...Just the opposite! It's what a golfer hopes for (4,3)**

The use of the dots at the beginning of the second clue of the pair makes it certain that the solver will immediately examine the preceding clue in order to discover to what the word 'opposite' refers; and since the opposite of 'bad lie' is clearly 'good lie', the answer is simplicity itself—provided that the solver looks at the correct words in the first clue!

Capital letters

Closely connected with the subject of punctuation is the matter of capital letters. In general, the same rules that govern their use in normal writing apply equally to the wording of clues: proper names beginning with capitals (e.g. Romans, the French, etc.), others doing so or not according to the context (e.g. King, Father, etc.). The position may be summed up as follows: it is admissible to give a capital letter to any noun at will, but less convincing to treat adjectives, verbs or adverbs in this way. Exceptionally, if a clue were presented in the form of, say, an advertisement, one could justifiably begin every word in it with a capital letter, whatever parts of speech were involved.

The converse, however, is never true. Any word that demands a capital letter by right must not lose it simply because it happens to suit the clue-writer's purpose; he must change his purpose, not the rules. Let us imagine that the word LUTON is being clued, and one wishes to indicate that it is in Bedfordshire, or Beds, for short. Any wording which contains 'in beds' (with a small 'b') is quite unacceptable, since only 'in Beds' is correct as a definition of this town. In these circumstances, if the word 'beds' (in its dormitory sense) is required by the nature of the clue, it must be made to appear as the first word in the clue, which has the capital letter naturally, and the rest of the clue must be adapted to fit in with that.

Likewise, if an abbreviation is used which is incorrect without a full stop (e.g. act. for active voice in grammar or Brig. for Brigadier), it is cheating to omit the full stop and use 'act' in the sense of deed, and doubly cheating to write 'brig' in the sense of ship, with neither capital letter nor full stop. The remedy here, if the idea is too attractive to discard, is to try to make such a word the last one in the clue, where the full stop (which must still be included to indicate the abbreviation) will not be so obvious—even though clues do not normally end with full stops—or where an exclamation or question mark, if justified, will disguise it altogether. However, as has been pointed out in the previous chapter, if the present trend towards omitting full stops from many familiar abbreviations continues, the clue-writer's freedom in this matter at least may gradually become less restricted.

18 Read it again

One of the fascinations of playing with words is the occasional, unexpected discovery of something in their make-up which enables us to devise unusually neat and apt clues, as we shall shortly see. However, since the process is a more subtle one than any other clueing technique, and there is a danger of innacuracy or unsoundness if it is imperfectly understood or carelessly executed, we must resolve not to attempt it unless or until the principles are clear in our minds.

This type of clue, used to some extent by Afrit, more regularly by Ximenes, and sporadically by several more recent setters trained, as it were, in the same 'school', is usually referred to as an 'and lit.' clue. That very title is far from illuminating, which may possibly explain why some versions of it prove less than satisfactory after analysis. The idea is, briefly, that the wording of such a clue gives accurate indications from which the answer can be worked out, and also that *the same wording*, exactly as it stands, is literally a definition of that answer. In other words, the solver must read the clue once to discover what kind of answer he is supposed to be looking for, and then he must read it again in order to see the instructions for working it out. A different solver may tackle the clue the opposite way round: that is to say, he may read the clue as an indication of how to arrive at the answer and then read it again, whereupon he will realise that the whole clue as it stands is a definition of the answer in itself. It seems to me, therefore, that we shall appreciate its purpose and its subtlety better if from the outset we think of this type as a 'read it again' clue.

Let us examine how it works. The first thing we discover is that it may be constructed in one of two slightly different forms, as will be seen if we consider, for example, the word ENRAGED. This means made angry, or ANGERED, which by one of those happy coincidences is also an anagram of the answer itself. We could therefore concoct the following apt clue:

(a) Angered—angered, terribly (7)

Any solver of moderate skill and experience will quickly realise that he has been given the usual two parts of a cryptic clue: the definition, 'angered', and also an anagram of angered, indicated by the word 'terribly'. By either or both routes he will arrive at the answer ENRAGED, and may even pause for a moment to reflect that it looks rather neat, having those same two words in both halves of the clue. But actually there is more to it than that: for in addition to being given a normal clue in two parts, if he cares to read it again in its entirety he will discover that he has been offered a more informative definition of the answer than that supplied by the one word 'angered'. That, then, is one form of a 'read it again' clue.

If we now take this same clue one stage further, we can dispense with the repetition of the word 'angered', as follows:

(b) Angered, terribly (7)

There seems to be here, at first sight, a clue devised by a lazy or hurried setter, who has not taken the trouble to present the usual two parts. Some will read it as a plain definition and nothing else, quickly thinking of ENRAGED and pass on, disappointed by its ordinariness, to the next clue. Others will see it as purely an anagram, work out the correct answer from it and mentally castigate the clue's author for omitting the essential definition. But the shrewd solver who reads it twice and realises that one reading gives the definition and the other the method of solution will appreciate the subtlety of this, perhaps the more perfect of the two forms.

It should be evident from the above examples that there is a strong possibility that a sizeable proportion of solvers may very easily find the answer to this type of clue without even being aware of the extra subtlety inherent in it. In view of the fact that only a small number of words in any crossword—and quite often none at all—readily lend themselves to this treatment, it is a pity to think that a particularly neat version, with which its deviser is justifiably pleased, may be largely wasted. For that reason, more in the hope of encouraging the solver to share in the pleasure than for the self-gratification of the composer, I would advocate in most such cases the use of the exclamation mark, this:

(b) Angered, terribly! (7)

If that kind of punctuation is resorted to by a clue-writer who is otherwise very sparing in its use, it may perhaps serve to draw the solver's attention to the fact that something rather special is going on (see Chapter 17, p. 157). If he then inspects the clue a second time, his enjoyment of it may prove to be a fitting reward. Of course, a setter who frequently features clues of this type in his crosswords may come to feel, after some time, that his regular solvers have become sufficiently familiar with their incidence for him to dispense with the extra nudge of the exclamation mark.

A good deal of practice is necessary with this type of clue before its mechanics can be mastered. Let us therefore analyse a fair number of clues, some following the principles of example (a) and others of example (b), and see in addition whether any of them can be made more intriguing by slight adjustments. We shall start with a quartet of the first kind.

(c) Chap who helps to cause bother—a scallywag! (6)

The answer required is clearly a person (defined by 'chap'), and he helps to cause 'botheR A SCALlywag' because he is an essential part of these words. This will be enough to satisfy any solver, since it contains both a definition and a hidden subsidiary clue. However, the fact that the whole clue, if read over again, will be seen as a fuller definition of RASCAL adds a pleasant bonus for those perceptive enough to spot it, perhaps prompted to do so by the exclamation mark.

(d) You'd find this man among the baser fellows! (4)

If we could solve (c) above, this will be plain sailing, since it is identical in method. 'This man' makes it clear what kind of answer we are looking for, and he is to be found hidden among 'baSER Fellows'. Furthermore, the whole sentence is a helpful indication of SERF. Note, incidentally, that since serfs belong to the past, the clue's first words need to be read in the sense of 'you used to find . . .'.

(e) Farewell to the French, about to depart! (5)

A word meaning farewell is ADIEU, and it consists of AU (to the, French) about DIE (to depart). The clue therefore very aptly defines a word which to the French, when about to depart, signifies farewell.

(f) Covering which surmounts small church? (6)

Once again we have a definition to show that the answer is a noun, and that it means a covering. Next, for extra help, we are told that THAT (which) surmounts (i.e. stands above—and therefore this wording can be used only in a

Down clue) the letters CH (an abbreviation for, *inter alia*, church), forming THATCH, something which, as the entire clue indicates, may possibly cover a small church. Since it would not be correct to state that all small churches have thatched roofs, the question mark is there merely to suggest the possibility.

The next three examples will demonstrate how it is possible, if extra subtlety is aimed at, particularly in a puzzle of a harder standard, to reduce clues like those above to shorter versions.

(g) Play in which one may get custard-pies right in the mug! (5)

This is an easy clue, because the definition occupies all but the clue's last four words and leads fairly obviously to the answer FARCE. This is reinforced by the subsidiary indication of R (abbreviation of right) in FACE (the mug). It is perhaps pertinent at this point to say that even easy clues, of whatever type, can provide entertainment and are not to be sneered at. This clue, especially when read a second time as it is intended to be, perfectly describes the answer and can hardly fail to raise a smile despite its easy solution. We can, if we wish, make this clue a shade less obvious by removing the most revealing of the definition words, as follows:

(h) Where one may get custard-pies right in the mug! (5)

The answer should not be long in coming, even in this shorter version, because the information and method in both are identical.

(i) An idler—one who's thrustful about nothing! (7)

Let us examine this clue in the opposite sequence for a change, starting with the complete clue, which is a definition and a further description of some lazy person who never shows any initiative. The answer may not immediately occur to us, so we read it again and notice that it is a perfectly normal cryptic clue in two parts: an idler as the definition and LUNGER (one who makes a thrust in fencing, or who's thrustful) about O (nothing, as in a football score), resulting in LOUNGER.

Although this has all the elements of a 'read it again' clue and is quite difficult enough for an average puzzle as it stands, setters and solvers who prefer a tougher challenge would probably derive an extra kick from a shorter version of the more subtle kind, as follows:

(j) One who's thrustful about nothing! (7)

In this we are reduced to the subsidiary indication only, namely LUNGER about O, and then if we want a definition of the answer we must read it all again.

(k) A place where you can display a vice among company! (6)

Such a place is a CASINO, in which you (the solver) can display (by writing down the answer) A SIN (a vice) among CO. (abbreviation of company). A second reading reveals a reasonably accurate description of a casino as a place where the vice of gambling is displayed among company. A shorter version of this clue would omit the first two words, as follows:

(l) Where you can display a vice among company! (6)

It should be observed that the word 'where' is to be taken in two ways: as part of the full definition it means 'a place where', but as the subsidiary indication it means 'a word in which'.

Our final group consists of clues devised on the principle of example (b), that is to say those which are 'read it again' clues in the purest form. For the sake of clarity I shall present only those which do not involve difficult words, and which are in the main fairly easy to solve. Nevertheless, because of the solver's need to read them twice before savouring them to the full, I do not recommend the inclusion of most of them in average cryptic crosswords except on rare occasions.

(m) I'm a leader of Mohammedans! (4)

One of the easiest of its kind, this clue virtually solves itself. The answer, following a common convention of crosswords and other word-games, is speaking directly to the solver, so that he knows whom he is required to find. The second reading gives the necessary information literally in the component parts I'M, A and M (leader, or first letter, of Mohammedans), which when joined together yield IMAM, who is a leader of Mohammedans.

(n) People having ill-disposed hearts! (6)

The clue as a definition makes us think of enemies and the like, but no single answer of six letters leaps to the mind. We can narrow down the choice, however, when we realise that the only people who can be formed by having HEARTS mixed up as an anagram (as indicated by 'ill-disposed', i.e. badly arranged) are HATERS, people whose hearts are indeed ill-disposed.

(o) Holds about half the dead! (5)

A synonym of holds is HAS. When that is placed about DE, which is half of the word 'dead', the result is HADES. We now look at the clue again and find that it is a reasonable—if fanciful—description of the answer, the assumption being that if there are two places available, roughly half of us are destined ultimately for heaven and the rest for the nether regions.

(p) There's still one to be seen! (4)

What can we think of which is alleged to exist but which nobody has set eyes on as yet? If our thoughts should turn to mountaineering, and to Everest expeditions in particular, we might think of the 'abominable snowman', known as the YETI. This is undoubtedly the answer for which we are searching, and we receive confirmation of this as we analyse the clue's wording and find that there is YET (still) I (one, as a Roman numeral) to be seen in the answer.

(q) Salt? (6)

I have included this final example, although it is a fairly tough one, partly because readers may enjoy it when it has been explained but chiefly in order to demonstrate that it is just occasionally possible to concoct a cryptic clue, containing both a definition and a subsidiary indication, as well as an extra bit of subtlety, within the confines of a single word.

This clue might be solved by the following method. The word salt immediately suggests three thoughts: a condiment as a noun, to sprinkle food with salt as a verb, and a sailor. If we concentrate on the culinary verb we may hit on the answer SEASON, which means to flavour with something such as salt, pepper, etc. Since seasoning need not involve the use of salt, there must be a question mark after the clue to suggest it as a possibility rather than state it as a fact. But what has SEASON to do with either of the other meanings of salt? Well, sailors are often referred to as sons of the sea, so one salt is a son of the sea, or a SEA-SON! Here a slight liberty has been taken with the English language, which has led the clue-writer to ask the solver whether it is reasonable to interpret SEASON as sea-son—hence the question mark—instead of presenting it as a straightforward definition about which there is no doubt. Thus we have in this one-word clue two definitions, to be read in two different ways in succession. The same effect could have been achieved by dispensing with the query and using two words instead as follows:

(r) Salt, perhaps! (6)

This version is preferable in some respects, since it clearly states that the answer may, not must, mean salt—which is true of to season—and it also leaves room for the exclamation mark, which I believe to be justified by the extra subtlety involved in reading the answer perhaps as a salt. However, it must be admitted that the temptation to include all these features in a one-word clue is a very strong one!

We cannot regard this topic as exhausted until we have disposed of a couple of misconceptions about it which persist among some setters and solvers. Firstly, it must be repeated, if necessary *ad nauseam*, that there is only one sure means of judging whether a clue is genuinely a 'read it again' type or not: that is, quite simply, by reading it again. If, after doing so, no matter whether it is constructed like example (a) or like example (b), we are convinced that *the entire clue* constitutes a definition or accurate description of the answer, and that there are no superfluous words anywhere which do not belong to that definition or description, then it does satisfy the exacting requirements of this type of clue. Nothing short of these conditions will suffice.

Secondly, there are those who seem to believe that any clue whose wording happens to present a true statement is one of this type. If they do, they are mistaken, although to some extent they may be excused for thinking along these lines because of the misleading name of 'and lit.' by which it has been known for so long and which naturally suggests the meaning: 'and this is literally true'. The rule is, however, that even if what a clue says does happen to be literally true, it must be true not of life in general but of *that clue's answer* in particular in order to qualify under this heading. The two following examples will, I hope, clarify this point beyond doubt.

(s) Putting people in the wrong causes distress (7)

The clue says, in crossword terms, that putting MEN (people) in TORT (legal wrong) causes TORMENT (distress). A solver—or the author himself—reading this sentence again may well be struck by the fact that the statement it makes is undoubtedly true, quite apart from its complete accuracy as a cryptic clue. But neither setter nor solver should be misled thereby into believing that it is anything more than a very neat and satisfying clue to the word TORMENT. The acid test is this: can one accurately define TORMENT as 'Putting people in the wrong causes distress'? Obviously not; the only acceptable definition of the answer in all this sentence is the final word 'distress'.

(t) To be backward in speed is a drawback (6)

If you are an aspiring sprinter, you will find this statement all too true. It is not, however, in any sense true of the answer REBATE (an amount of money that one draws back, and hence 'a drawback'), which is made of EB (= BE written backward, in an Across clue only) in RATE (speed).

We have been discussing in this chapter a clueing technique of some subtlety, which can often inject into crosswords of more difficult standards than average a measure of rare enjoyment but which also, in its more easily solvable forms, is capable of being appreciated to the full when it is used in popular cryptic puzzles. It will be found by experience, however, that only a small minority of words in any crossword will prove to be naturally adaptable to this treatment. This being so, those would-be practitioners who are stimulated by its attractiveness to experiment with this type of clue are strongly urged never to force words to conform with this method, lest the results turn out to be so tortuous as to nullify their apparent neatness. Nor should anyone embark on this exercise without first fully understanding the principles involved. To those who are not quite sure that they have got it right, I can do no better than conclude by offering the sound advice given by the heading of this chapter: READ IT AGAIN!

19 Miscellaneous

In addition to the clueing techniques already explained and exemplified separately in each of the foregoing chapters, there are several others which, although no less legitimate, are either resorted to comparatively seldom, are vaguely related to some of the previous devices or have an almost unique quality which does not readily admit of classification. Some of them call for an extra stage of reasoning not normally required in the solution of clues. Most, however, rely for their effect on certain peculiarities of speech—due, it may be, to regional pronunciations, to drunkenness, to a lisp and so on. This chapter, which concludes that part of the book which is devoted to cryptic cluemanship, is perhaps the most suitable place in which to put a selection of such unclassified clues on display for inspection.

In Chapter 14 we were introduced to the type of clue which

treats the required answer as a decapitated form of a different word—for instance, OWN was clued as a topless GOWN. A less drastic way of removing a word's initial letter, but one which is limited this time to those that are aspirated, is to imagine that it is being spoken by a person who habitually drops his aitches. This method may be seen in practice, affecting the words concerned in different places, in the following three examples.

(a) 'E gets one to warble, relaxing (6)

To solve this clue we must first write down the letter E, which has been given. This gets (next to it) A (one) and SING (to warble), and the result is EASING (relaxing).

(b) A yellowish colour—a doctor should be with 'er (5)

Despite appearances deliberately contrived by the clue-writer, there is nothing jaundiced about the real meaning here. In the answer AMBER (a yellowish colour), the letters A and MB (doctor) should be with 'ER—and so they are.

(c) What's up with 'im? Oh dear—it's the sausage (6)

This phraseology is suitable for a Down clue only, as the word 'up' makes clear. What is up (or written upwards) with 'IM is ALAS (Oh dear), to form IMALAS, which when read downwards in the normal way is SALAMI (the sausage).

These three clues, it will be observed, follow in all respects the familiar 'charade' principal discussed in Chapter 7, except that one of the elements in the make-up of each of them suffers from a dropped letter H.

Some people's trouble with aspirates, on the other hand, is a tendency to supply them when they are not required, as in the case of the politician who declared his slogan to be 'Hever honward, hever hupward!' An occasional clue based on this idiosyncrasy may turn out neatly, thus:

(d) Farming implements used by the Harchers? (7)

It should not take too long to run through a mental list of well-known farming implements and arrive at HARROWS. Since arrows are used by archers, the subsidiary clue quite reasonably asks whether this answer, which is an aspirated spelling of ARROWS, could therefore be used by aspirated ARCHERS. A further point of topical interest is the fact that the Archers are a farming family featured in a long-running BBC radio series. But even when the topicality has faded, this clue will still make good sense about any kind of archers, though preferably without the capital letter in the last word.

Failure to pronounce the final letter in words like hunting, shooting and fishing is an affectation in certain types and a form of slovenly speech in others. Whatever the cause, the phenomenon is one that can be exploited by setters on suitable occasions, as illustrated in the following example:

(e) A bird smokin' a pipe? (6)

The definition leads us to a bird, the answer here being a PUFFIN. Since PUFFING can mean smoking (for example, a pipe), then it is fair to suggest that PUFFIN' is equivalent to smokin'. The question mark asks, in effect, whether it is a pipe which is being puffed rather than the equally possible cigarette or cigar.

There are times also when the appearance of a stammer may be achieved in clues by way of innocent fun. There are two slightly different techniques for this, as will be seen in the two examples which follow.

(f) Loud prolonged noise made by h-hooter (4)

The answer is HOWL (loud prolonged noise), which is made by the letter H and OWL (hooter).

(g) Eastern s-schoolboy, upset, makes blunder (5)

When E (eastern) F-FAG (s-schoolboy) is upset, or written upwards in a Down clue, it makes GAFFE (blunder). Note that the answer to the stammering part of this clue is arrived at differently from that in (f) above. In that clue, HOWL was formed from the given letter H and a carefully selected synonym of OWL beginning with the same letter. In the present clue, the result is achieved by drawing a parallel: by saying, in effect, that if FAG is stammered in the answer to become F-FAG, then its synonym (schoolboy) should logically be so treated in the clue to become 's-schoolboy'.

The next example takes advantage of the sound produced by a lisp.

(h) What a dull pupil is—indithpothed? (5)

One word that describes a dull pupil is THICK. The clue-writer has realised that this is how someone with a lisp would pronounce the word SICK. He has therefore thought of a synonym of SICK—indisposed—in which sibilants appear, and presented it in lisped form in the clue.

There is a conventional way of indicating, in strip cartoons or on the stage for instance, that a character is under the influence of alcohol. The same convention makes it appear in the following clue:

(i) Disgrace that is identical, according to a drunkard? (5)

The answer here is SHAME, which means disgrace. Now if our caricature of a drunk were attempting to enunciate the word SAME (identical), he would probably be made to produce a sound that was indistinguishable from the word SHAME. Therefore the clue asks whether disgrace (SHAME) is identical (SAME), according to a drunkard.

Another mild speech defect, sufficiently common for the clue-writer to seize upon when the opportunity occurs, is the mispronunciation of the letter R as W. We see this at work in the following:

(j) Stwuck by a car, we hear, and brought round? (3,4)

The answer is WON OVER (brought round—to an opposing point of view, for example). If we imagine a person who has difficulty with the letter R trying to say RUN OVER (struck by a car), the result would *sound* like WON OVER—hence the words 'we hear'. Note that this particular impediment must be indicated to the solver by changing the R of the significant word 'struck' to a W (even if it leads to some inconsistency with any other Rs in the rest of the clue, as here), from which he can deduce that he must do the same to the one R in his answer which is pronounced—that is, in the word RUN.

Turning aside from actual impediments of speech, we find that regional dialect may sometimes provide a setter with a credible-looking clue where otherwise he might find himself awkwardly stuck with an odd letter. Here is a representative example:

(k) T'chap who repents is more sincere (5)

There will be nothing unusual in the appearance of this sentence to anyone familiar with, say, a typical Yorkshire accent. To solve the clue, however, we must ignore the superficial sense and see what information we are really being given. First we find the letter T, and next RUER (chap who repents), the combination yielding the answer TRUER, which is more sincere.

Abandoning Yorkshire and moving southwards to London, we may be grateful to a particular characteristic of Cockney pronunciation for inspiring an occasional clue, such as the following:

(l) Something that adds piquancy—a Cockney's room? (5)

This looks like a normal clue containing two different definitions, examples of which are given in Chapter 6. And so it is, except that one is a straightforward definition, while the other is based on an assumption of the likely pronunciation of a word instead of its meaning. The answer SPICE is something that adds piquancy; and it is also the spelling that a novelist would use if one of his Cockney characters were saying SPACE (room). Hence the clue is asking whether the answer to this clue could be regarded as a Cockney's version of a word meaning room.

There are those who, whatever their social or regional origins, studiously nurture pretensions to gentility, developing in the process a mode of speech which would describe, say, a pleasant experience as 'quate nace' and which might conveniently be termed 'refaned'. Determined as such folk are to attract notice, they must also be prepared to be mildly satirised in crossword clues, as in the following example:

(m) A 'refaned' vehicle for cook? (4)

The word cook defined here stands not for the noun, a chef, but for the verb, to BAKE. Now if the word BIKE (vehicle) were uttered by a 'refaned' type of voice, it would no doubt strike the hearer's ear as BAKE.

One slip of the tongue which affects most of us at one time or another is the Spoonerism; but since it is apt to arise more from conversational remarks (e.g. by saying 'a fit bat' instead of 'a bit fat') than from the words and phrases with which crosswords abound, it is not a device much encountered in clues. Should the odd chance present itself, however, the alert clue-writer, ever on the look-out for variety of clue presentation, will pounce upon it with alacrity. Here is a not too complicated example:

(n) Restrain the Rev. Spooner's courageous horse? (4,4)

The answer is HOLD BACK (restrain). If the celebrated Rev. W. A. Spooner, who was notorious for transposing initial sounds or letters of spoken words, had uttered this phrase, would his version of it, asks the clue, have been BOLD HACK (courageous horse)?

Finally, mention must be made of a type of clue which asks rather more of the solver than the replacement of one synonym by another, or the rearrangement of the letters of an anagram, or any of those other procedures which have been explained earlier. Although this type of clue *need* not be fiendishly difficult, there is certainly a danger that too much deduction may be expected of the solver unless a corresponding amount of information is supplied, or implied, to assist him in the mental exercise. Take, for instance, this clue: 'III (9)'. Most solvers would find this extremely hard, if not downright impossible, without some extra help. But what if the only help available is that supplied by letters of other answers which cross this one? If enough letters are thus formed to show the likely answer, then the reason for it may be worked out: but if not, then we must fall back on our powers of deduction, on the following lines: What is it? A Roman numeral. What numeral? Three. A Roman three—can that be rephrased? Yes, three in Rome. What's significant about 'three in Rome'? Ah yes, that period (60 BC) when Rome was governed by the powerful trio of Pompey, Crassus and Caesar. What were they called? TRIUMVIRS—that's it!

Needless to say, an entire crossword consisting of clues like that would defeat even the most brilliant solvers. Logically, it is completely sound; but the level of deduction and factual knowledge required for its solution places it in a category beyond the average ability, as it stands.

Deduction of a less demanding standard, however, can be incorporated in the occasional clue of a popular cryptic puzzle, as will be seen in the concluding three clues.

(o) What makes ghi, as it were, a strong influence in India? (6)

Many solvers will fairly quick think of GANDHI (particularly Mahatma Gandhi, but alternatively Mrs Gandhi) as having been a strong influence in India. But what has that name to do with ghi, the kind of butter that many Indians eat? An examination of its letters will reveal that it is made up of *G and HI*, which together form the name GANDHI. Something very similar can now be seen in the next example:

(p) The boy's extremities are, you might say, crooked (5)

Ask anyone to say what the extremities, or outer edges, of BOY are, and the answer will surely be B and Y. Write that down in the diagram as it has been given and you have BANDY (crooked).

(q) Strips off, as bats do! (5)

A synonym of strips off is PEELS, but no immediate connection is visible between that answer and the rest of the clue. We notice incidentally that it is a Down clue, and we wonder what special trick the clue-writer has perpetrated that has led him to finish with an exclamation mark. Then we spot that PEELS is *SLEEP upside-down*—which is exactly what bats do!

A vital point in these last three clues which is worth stressing is this: that despite their extra degree of difficulty caused by the need to insert an intermediate stage of reasoning into each of them, the one essential feature of every sound clue, namely an accurate definition, has been faithfully supplied in every case.

Readers will possibly derive some amusement from attempting to add to the above examples, either by searching for unusual angles in a word's make-up, or by widening their nets to take in further regional or national variations of speech—such as those associated with Somerset, Wales, Ireland, a Frenchman's English pronunciation and so on—or by suggesting the effect of a cold in the head on the letter N by turning it into a D. Any and all of these tricky formations or well-known features of speech are the legitimate prey of those who hunt for amusing and unusual twists in the course of devising cryptic clues.

Part III

Crossword Composition

20 A quick crossword

Having now been presented, as it were, with a brand-new recipe book, and with a larder—crammed with the necessary ingredients in the form of his own vocabulary and his dictionary—waiting to be raided, the reader is no doubt bursting with an urgent desire to bake the richest and most ambitious cake imaginable.

Without wishing to dampen his enthusiasm, however, I would suggest that a more modest sponge or madeira might be more suitable for a first attempt, and if that proves satisfactory he might then aspire to higher endeavours. In other words, before we rush to tackle a completely cryptic crossword, let us be sure that we fully understand how to construct a symmetrical diagram efficiently, where to insert the clue-numbers, how to fit in the words and what snags to avoid; and for this purpose we might best be served by postponing for the time being any thoughts of great subtlety and by concentrating instead on a typical 'quickie'—that is to say, a smaller crossword of 13 × 13 squares in size with straightforward clues of a non-cryptic nature.

Diagrams made-to-measure or off-the-peg

The composer of a crossword, of whatever size, description or standard, will be faced with one of two different types of diagram: a virgin square drawn on a blank paper or a grid with the blocks and clue-numbers already filled in. The latter, which might be called the 'off-the-peg' variety, is due to the fact that many publications have a set collection of up to a couple of dozen grids, each with a different arrangement of blocks, which for reasons of economy, convenience or efficiency of production they retain for many years. Any contributor to such a publication, therefore, would have to confine himself to its standard set of patterns and make his words fit into the available blank spaces. Similarly, anyone wishing to construct a crossword for his own amusement can, and usually does, use a ready-made diagram from his newspaper or magazine and supply his own words and clues for it. For those who are apt to find the task of arranging their own blocks too much of a complication, there are distinct advantages in having set designs available, despite some obvious limitations imposed by the immovable block arrangement; but those preferring and able to have a freer hand, and to adapt the symmetry to their own words rather than *vice versa*, will start from the blank square on each occasion and tailor the design progressively to fit the words as they are inserted.

In this chapter we shall see what an 'off-the-peg' block pattern looks like and how to fill its small squares with words; and then in the next we shall allow ourselves complete freedom to construct a full-size crossword, starting from scratch and arranging the position of the blocks stage by stage until we have a symmetrical diagram filled with words and phrases. Only when that ambition has been efficiently achieved shall we be able to move on and, in the subsequent chapter, bring into play many of the principles and techniques which we have learned, by devising a complete set of cryptic clues.

Arrangement of blocks

Within the comparatively narrow confines of a crossword square there is room for enormous variety in block distribution, even when symmetry is insisted upon, as is the almost universal convention. One has only to examine the patterns formed by the blocks in the crossword in one's newspaper on several successive days to realise this, and also to begin to have preferences for one pattern, or kind of pattern, over another, without quite knowing why, as well as to discover that certain designs tend to be associated with harder crosswords and others with easier ones. There are, in fact, good reasons for such impressions, which are worth discussing here.

Just as there are principles of fairness and helpfulness in the various clueing techniques, as already explained, so the same may be said to apply to the block arrangement of a diagram. For instance, if you had to solve a clue to a word of five letters, and on glancing at the diagram, discovered that only one of its letters was checked by another word and that the other four letters were hidden behind blocks—that is to say, unchecked—it should go without saying that you would consider yourself badly served and the victim of blatant unfairness. That, of course, is an extreme hypothetical example, which no self-respecting setter would be guilty of perpetrating. If we agree on that point, then do we also agree that it would be *almost* as unfair to 'show' the solver only two letters out of five? I fancy that at this point the discussion becomes less placidly unanimous and more heatedly argumentative! For there is no doubt that many crosswords today do regularly contain some five-letter words of which only two are checked and the other three unchecked, a balance which I myself would regard as unfairly tilted against the solver and in favour of the setter. Of course, if it happened that the answer were a word that appeared in the diagram as –B–Y–, then it wouldn't take the solver long to discover the answer OBEYS—even without reading the clue! Or at least he would know that, in a similar example, the first letter must be a vowel and therefore his search would be limited. But unfortunately it more often turns out that what we are faced with, just when for the moment we haven't been able to solve the clue, is something like –A–E–. No doubt a computer can calculate how many well-known English nouns and verbs, to say nothing of adjectives, can be made to fit that literal set-up: there must be hundreds, making the solver despair of ever finding the answer by going through the alphabet.

Many other examples will prove to be just as unhelpful, and therefore to some extent unfair; and experience teaches us that the exposure of very common letters such as vowels in such cases, with the consequent concealment of the 'helpful' letters, is far more usual than the type which gave us OBEYS above. It is fair to add, however, that as a word becomes longer such difficulties for the solver correspondingly lessen, so that having three checked letters out of seven, though still sometimes making the answer elusive, does not usually present so intractable a problem, and a cross-checking of four out of nine letters and *pro rata* for longer words would not normally be regarded as placing an insurmountable stumbling-block in the solver's path.

From this it may with some justification be recommended as a desirable aim that, if symmetry is to be allied with fairness, it should be such that the number of checked and unchecked letters in any word should either be equal or else favour the solver in preference to the setter. In a diagram containing blocks this means that in a four-letter word the ratio should be 2 checked to 2 unchecked; in a five-letter word, 3:2; for six letters, 3:3; for seven letters, 4:3; for eight letters, 4:4; for nine letters, 5:4; and so on. But we can at the same time accept that, in practice, no real harm is likely to be caused if in words of (occasionally) seven letters, and (at any time) of nine letters or more, the ratio suggested above is reversed.

(There are still many crosswords in Britain, and the majority of those in America and on the continent, that favour patterns in which the cross-checking is so generous that a good many words in each diagram are completely cross-checked. This is fine for the solver who likes things easy but is apt to be very inhibiting for the setter, who will find the same words unavoidably forming themselves again and again in his diagrams, whereas ideally he ought to be in control and to have a reasonable amount of choice about which words he includes.

In crosswords whose diagrams have an arrangement of bars instead of blocks, however, and which tend to comprise more unfamiliar words and harder clues, the proportion of checked letters in any answer is usually quite high, and in some answers, indeed, every single letter is checked. Even in a stiff puzzle, if it is a 'plain' one, such complete cross-checking ought not to be overdone, and as a rule at least one letter in every answer should be unchecked, just to make the solver work out the answer to his satisfaction instead of being presented with a free gift—except in the case of three-letter words, which the setter may be inclined to 'give away'. On the other hand, in the case of novelty puzzles, especially those in which there are complicated rules or certain clues are withheld—puzzles, in short, in which a difficult problem is added to the basic crossword—the setter may feel, as I do, that a certain amount of very generous cross-checking as a form of compensation is fully justified.)

In addition to the actual number of blocks that should be inserted in a diagram in order to 'uncheck' some of the letters of every answer, we must consider their location in relation to each other, conscious as we must constantly be of the need to play fair with the solver. Opinions and tastes will inevitably vary in this matter since justice, like beauty, so often depends on one's point of view. I propose, therefore, to make my own preference clear and to leave it to others to conclude, after due reflection, whether their own practices are, as they may well be, of equal or superior merit.

The most conventional type of crossword is one in which the alternate letters of each answer are checked or, to put it another way, unchecked. Such is the nature of English words that this arrangement hints strongly at their literal constitution and gives the solver ample scope for finding the answer in each instance. Not only is this 'half-exposure, half-concealment' formula fair, but it is also, with the scales of justice as evenly balanced as possible according to the best British legal traditions, seen to be fair. The setter should therefore attempt, provided that he has a free hand in constructing his diagrams, to offer the solver precisely that: an arrangement of blocks which results, whatever the pattern, in the exposure or concealment of every alternate letter of every word in them. We are speaking here of plain crosswords involving no special theme or other novelty, considerations that often force the setter to depart from standard procedure.

Let us examine some other methods of achieving the balance of checked and unchecked letters that we thought desirable in the interests of fairness. Suppose that we were given the definition clue 'Principal (4)'. Which of the following arrangements would give the solver most help, and which most trouble: HE––, H–A–, –E–D, –EA– or ––AD? It may be argued that it is such an easy clue that none of them would cause any difficulty, but even so, it is fairly obvious that the first is easiest, since we have the answer's first two letters to work on; the second is quite helpful, with the first letter as a start; the third is marginally easier than the fourth since the word's 'shape' is more readily discernible; while the last is very unhelpful, having the first half missing and unobtainable from any other words in the diagram. Now in all these cases half the letters are offered and half withheld, so that some may claim that they are all equally fair. What is more, it may be suggested, the first example (HE––) is the easiest of all and therefore an arrangement of two successive checked followed by two successive unchecked letters is most helpful. So it is; but remember this: symmetry demands that every time there is a word like HE–– in the diagram it must be balanced, in the opposite quarter, by one like ––AD, which is most unhelpful. And a solver who can complete most of a crossword but finds himself stuck because of a few words that lack their first couple of letters is going to be a disgruntled solver indeed. For these reasons it is on the whole preferable to avoid any pattern that results in two (or, what is worse, three) successive letters being unchecked.

Accepting, then, that we shall be doing our best for the solver by alternating the blocks, is it better to start with the blocks on the outer edges of the grid, or with the outer edges free of alternate blocks and the next row or column containing them? Practice varies; but since, as will shortly be demonstrated, putting blocks on the periphery more readily tends towards having more than half the letters of some words unchecked, my preference is for any pattern based on alternate blocks beginning on the second row. On pp. 192 and 193 are three miniature diagrams exemplifying the points that have been discussed in this chapter. (We can best identify the small squares of the diagrams by using the row letters and column figures as co-ordinates: e.g. in diagram **A** the first square at the top left—or what is often called the NW corner—is A1; the last at the bottom right—or SE corner—is I9; the block in the middle of the top row is A5; etc.)

In diagram **A** you will see that the first Down word will have its last two letters unchecked at D1 and E1—not too terrible; but notice that in its balancing word on the opposite side the first two letters will be unchecked at E9 and F9, imposing a formidable handicap. Also in this diagram the central Across word of three letters has only one checked letter at E5, and the remaining two unchecked; and similarly, the central Down word of seven letters has three checked and four unchecked, which is not desirable.

In diagram **B**, with the blocks alternating on the outer edges, even though the rest of the diagram continues to alternate symmetrically, it will quickly be apparent that every single word in the diagram has more unchecked than checked letters. This is an extreme case devised for demonstration purposes, and it need not all be so in a larger square; in fact, it could be partly avoided here too by moving the block at D6 one space to the left to D5 and the block at F4 one to the right to F5. Nevertheless, the tendency is there, and a proportion of words in such a diagram would rarely escape this imbalance.

Diagram **B** also demonstrates one further snag which the

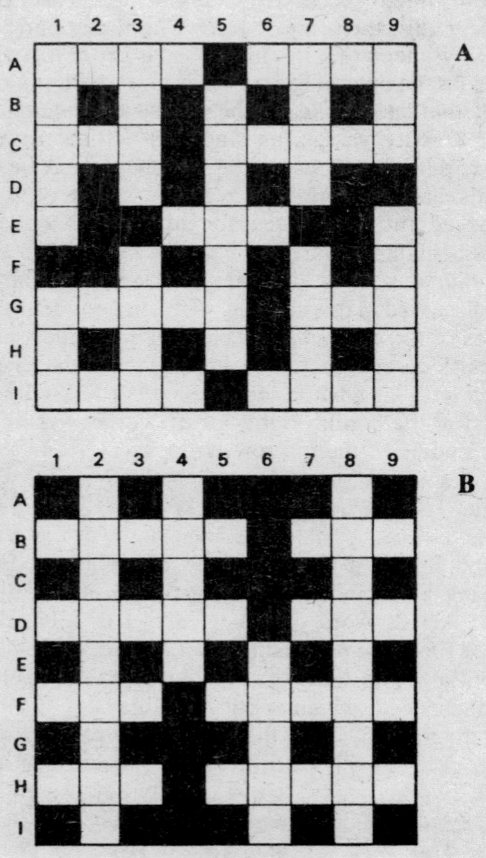

beginner (and, indeed, the expert) must be careful to avoid. One of the essential features of a crossword is that the solution of one clue should contribute at least one letter to the solution of another, so that answers may be woven progressively through the diagram by a sort of continuous thread. We must therefore ensure that our diagram arrangement does not produce—to change the metaphor—four walled quarters with no doorways from one to the next, or, what is almost as unsatisfactory if one should fail to find the key, one door only. In diagram **B** we see that the left half of the grid is completely cut off from the right, and if we were to insert other blocks at E2 and E8 all four quarters would be inaccessible to each other, whereas in fairness they ought to be interconnecting.

Diagram **C** is an example of the over-generous cross-checking that one is apt to associate with the definition type of crossword prevalent abroad but also common enough in this country. It will be seen that all the three-letter words in this particular diagram would be fully checked, as would the five-letter words going down at A7 and E3; and even the nine-letter words beginning at C1 and G1 would have only one letter each unchecked. To appreciate the restrictions that such a pattern places on the composer, try filling it in with words (beginning, I would suggest, with the longest ones). You will be lucky if you complete several full-size diagrams of this kind without meeting, for example, your old zoological friends GNU and EMU or your favourite priest ELI!

Composing a diagram

We should now be able to construct a great variety of symmetrical diagrams, each 13 × 13 squares in size, for use as quick crosswords. We should leave the outer edges free of blocks at the outset, and also observe two main cautions: not to put any word under the disadvantage of having two or more successively unchecked letters, and to be sure that there is an adequate passageway from one section of the diagram to another. (Furthermore, in most crosswords of this size or larger, three-letter words are in the minority and two-letter words or abbreviations are quite inadmissible.) Here, then, is our first stage:

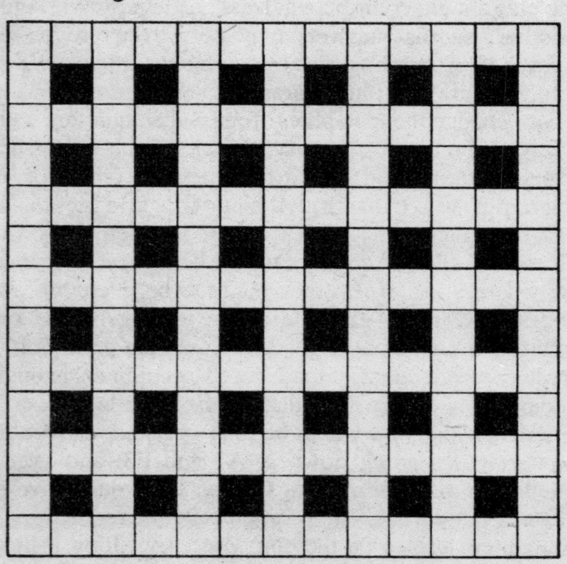

We have in this grid, to start with, seven thirteen-letter spaces across and another seven going down. The simplest arrangement is to insert the blocks in such a way that we have two words on each line, making fourteen words across and another fourteen down.

A rather more artistic method, and one that ensures an interconnection between one quarter of the diagram and the next, is to have four longer words (or phrases), two going across and two down, and then splitting up the rest, as suggested, into two words per line. An example is shown below.

If this is a set pattern taken from the newspaper, it will have the clue numbers already printed on the diagram, as above; but if it is a design that you have devised yourself, you will also need to write in the figures. Care is essential here, for it is only too easy, through haste, to miss entering a number.

The correct method is to begin at the top left-hand corner and move to the right along the row, inserting figures in sequence in every square that is the first letter of a word going either across or down. In this diagram the top row gives us 1 Across, 2 Down, 3 Down, 4 Down and 5 Down. Then the process is continued on the second row, where we insert 6, 7 and 8 Down; on to the third row, which gives us 9 and 10 Across; and so on to the bottom row, until the last number (in this case 23 Across) is inscribed. It often happens that the same figure indicates the first letter of an Across word and also of a Down word, although in this diagram this occurs once only, with the figure 18. In referring to any number as we fill in the words of this diagram, I shall add the word 'Across' or 'Down' only in the case of No. 18. Notice also that the design is such that every word has the same number of checked and unchecked letters if the total is an even number, and one more checked than unchecked if uneven, which is fairest to the solver; and also that solving the clues in any one corner will contribute some letters to another quarter of the diagram.

Initial and final letters

The diagram shown on p. 195 can be used over and over again, each time with different contents; and if a hundred people were invited to fill it with words of their own choice, the chances are that very few words would be heavily duplicated in the hundred different crosswords thus produced. We shall shortly attempt our own version, but first let us consider some useful hints about which letters are most helpful to us at the beginnings and ends of words.

Generally speaking, it is easier to begin a word with a consonant than with a vowel: consonants can begin innumerable words of any length, whereas vowels are less good as starters of short words, especially I and U, which are all right for longish words beginning with IN- and UN- but not for much else. Of the consonants too, perhaps surprisingly, L and N are not good beginners: we soon run out of the common words that they initiate and have to start repeating ourselves. Needless to say, X, Y and Z are not recommended as the first letters of words at any time, although if they are forced upon us there is no need to panic, since some usable words do exist.

As for the ends of words, D, E, R, S and T are commonest, with C, L and N useful for adjectives ending in –IC, –AL, –EN or –AN; Y for adverbs ending in –LY; and G best reserved for words ending in –ING. We shall, of course, avoid J, Q, V and Z for final letters as we would the plague; look considerably askance at H, K and X as consonantal endings; and offer less than a welcoming smile to terminal vowels I, O and U, but not feel so embarrassed by the arrival of A. Such is the versatility of the English language, aided by the adoption of a large immigrant vocabulary, that, with the atlas as a standby, we can if need be accept all the literary lepers held at arm's length above, while reserving the right to refuse them admittance so long as more suitable applicants are available.

Putting in the words

The first thing to discover when filling in a diagram is the location of the longest words, because we must keep an eye on them from the start. When short words are involved, one can often find something to fit even if a couple of the letters have already been fixed by other words; but once allow, say, a twelve-letter space to begin filling up with several immovable letters and the task of finding a suitable word or phrase to accommodate them becomes virtually impossible except by a sheer fluke, or perhaps by having to resort to 'dictionary' words unsuited to the desired standard.

In our diagram we can actually start at 1 Across, but had the longer words going across been on lower rows, for instance at 11 and 18 Across, we would have started at 11. Let's put in a word with mostly consonants showing: STOCKING will do, with I the only initial vowel (at 4), and we'll build on that.

At 2, which now begins with the letter T, the only space to watch carefully is its third letter, which will end the word at 9, so let's try the 'safe' letter D and insert TIDINGS. We're now working our way towards the twelve-letter word at 7, so we shall first do 9, to give us something to build on. We have ––––D, and the first and third letters are both the second letters of the other words. Vowels are most useful as second letters, because we then have a wide choice of consonants for their first letters; so we're looking for 'vowel, blank, vowel, blank, D': what about AMEND?

We must now think about the twelve-letter word at 7 while it has only the second letter fixed and before we are faced with any awkwardness. Awkwardness? That suggests PERVERSENESS, which by happy chance has twelve letters, with E as the second one. We accept it gratefully, put it in and look around to see if it's likely to cause any trouble elsewhere. A quick glance shows innocuous letters crossing other words, except for the V at 11, which now consists of ––V–N–– so far. We must deal with this at once before another letter makes it difficult, if not impossible. Not many words leap to the mind, but luckily REVENGE fits (or REVENUE; or, come to think of it, ADVANCE), leaving only 6 and 13 to complete the NW corner. It's best to tackle these together to ensure that the word at 6 doesn't spoil the possibilities at 13. If we have CARROT at 6 (or PARROT), we can have THRUSH (or THRUST) at 13. Let's sit back for a moment, see where we've got to and decide where to go next.

The obvious area in which to continue is the SW corner, where we find three words already supplied with a letter each; and those letters—E, E and S—are so versatile that we have a plentiful choice. So let's put in the first word we can think of at 18 Across: DRESS, which gives us a four-letter word at 18 Down beginning with D—try DUCK. Now a seven-letter word at 21 beginning with C–E; what about CHEROOT? That leaves 19 with S–O––; but before we commit ourselves here we must make sure that we can cope with the longer word at 23, in which every alternate letter is going to be the end of a word going down—at 19, 17 and 15. Let's start with the useful letter D as 23's third letter: this gives a good final letter for 19, making it STOOD or, better still, SWORD, and we must think of an eight-letter word at 23 beginning with S–D.

■	■	■	1 S	2 T	O	3 C	K	4 I	N	5 G	■	■
6 C	■	7 P	■	I	■		■		■		■	8
9 A	M	E	N	D	■	10						
R	■	R	■	I	■		■		■		■	
11 R	E	V	E	N	G	E	■	12				
O	■	E	■	G	■		■	■	■		■	■
13 T	H	R	U	S	H	■	14	15				16
■	■	S	■	■	■	17	■		■		■	
18		E		19	■	20						
	■	N	■		■		■		■		■	
21		E					■	22				
	■	S	■		■		■		■		■	
■	■	23 S								■	■	■

Things have gone very well so far because we haven't taken any risks with less popular letters, so let's be a little bolder for once and try SEDIMENT, which means that the M needs watching very carefully, though the N may be all right. What have we got now at 17? –––T–M. We daren't leave that to collect another letter, so we must think. Yes, I've thought of something—have you? I'm putting in BANTAM, with a sigh of relief! Of course, it may still lead to trouble later and we may have to discard it, as well as remove the SEDIMENT, but meanwhile we are entitled to be hopeful. Our diagram is taking shape, and so far it looks like this:

Now for the NE corner, and again the obvious word to think about is the one at 5, while we have no awkward letters to complicate matters. A twelve-letter word beginning with G? GRANDFATHERS looks reasonable, with the exposed letters all useful for other words, except that H inside 20. We'd better see if that's going to work, because if it doesn't we'll have to kill off our GRANDFATHERS and try again. At 20 we are going to have A–––H––: ABASHED is one word that fits—is there another? Yes, ANOTHER! We put it in, breathe again and return to the NE corner.

Short familiar words beginning with I are not too plentiful, so let's do 4 while there are no other letters in it: IDLER looks all right, and it fixes two letters in the word at 10, which we shall now examine, realising that its final letter will be the second letter of 8 and that therefore it had better be an E. We must also make sure that its first letter will work at 3. On the basis of ––L–A–E, it's best to go through the alphabet mentally and see what pairings we can make with 10 and 3. COLLATE and CYCLED is a possible combination; then not much else seems to suggest itself until we reach the letter P, which provides PILLAGE and COPPER, both well-known words, so let's use them. Another pair in this corner are 12 and 8, which share their final letters. Starting with the R–D at 12, we'll go through the vowels in turn and see what they offer us: RADIO/HERO, RIDGE/MERE, RODEO/ZERO—any of these will do, and the final letter O causes no trouble this time, so let's insert the first pair and check that the NE corner is satisfactory. Here it is:

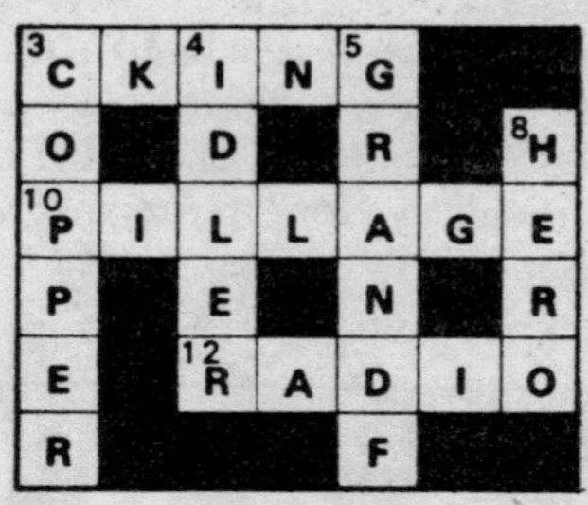

Finally, we set off on a trip to the South-east, where we find that 15 has two letters already written in (the O from ANOTHER and the N from SEDIMENT) and the other words-to-be have one letter each. Two fixed letters are quite enough to cope with in any new word, so we must tackle it now. Notice once more that its first letter is the second letter of a word at 14, so we'd better not start with J, V or Z! A quick mental run through the alphabet shows that there isn't a great deal of choice here: FLODDEN is a place-name and so best avoided except in an emergency; SPORRAN gives an awkward S as 14's second letter, more or less restricting us to ESSAYS there, but it's not to be sneezed at; TRODDEN is the best so far, and that will give, say, STRAND at 14, DARED at 22 and lastly DERIDE at 16. Well, why not? TRODDEN it is then, and we're home and dry.

Because it is the only quarter in which we must constantly

be watching our word-endings for both Across and Down words, the SE corner is always potentially the trickiest part of a diagram to complete. You will have noticed that, although we weren't really in difficulties on this occasion, our choice of words in this corner was more limited than anywhere else.

If we attempt to put words into a diagram containing bars instead of blocks, the same general principle of filling in one corner at a time will apply as a rule, after the longest word in any quarter has been accounted for first. The difference in filling in the two types of diagram is chiefly one of concentration, because with far more letters checked than the alternate ones that we have encountered in the present diagram we need to have our eyes all over the place at once, and must be prepared to do a fair amount of erasing and rethinking as we proceed—particularly, for the reasons just mentioned, in the SE corner. Let us now see the result of our efforts in the shape of the completed diagram:

			1 S	2 T	O	3 C	K	4 I	N	5 G		
6 C		7 P		I		O		D		R		8 H
9 A	M	E	N	D		10 P	I	L	L	A	G	E
R		R		I		P		E		N		R
11 R	E	V	E	N	G	E		12 R	A	D	I	O
O		E		G		R				F		
13 T	H	R	U	S	H		14 S	15 T	R	A	N	16 D
		S				17 B		R		T		E
18 D	R	E	S	19 S		20 A	N	O	T	H	E	R
U		N		W		N		D		E		I
21 C	H	E	R	O	O	T		22 D	A	R	E	D
K		S		R		A		E		S		E
		23 S	E	D	I	M	E	N	T			

The clues

We can now treat this diagram in any way that we please, presenting it as a 'quickie' with definition clues only, as a cryptic crossword of an easy or difficult standard, or as part-definition, part-cryptic. The answers, as we have seen, are all familiar words, but their solvability will depend on the quality of the clues provided. Since we shall soon be attempting a full-scale cryptic crossword, let us concentrate here instead on clues that are straight definitions, with no tricks, and bear in mind that, however simple it may prove to be, the 'ten-minute' crossword gives pleasure to countless solvers and we must not diminish their satisfaction by offering them vague, shoddy or inaccurate clues. Here is a suggested list for our recently completed diagram.

ACROSS

1 Item of hosiery (8)
9 Correct (5)
10 Plunder (7)
11 Retribution (7)
12 Means of communication (5)
13 Bird (6)
14 Thread (6)
18 Clothing (5)
20 Someone else (7)
21 Cigar (7)
22 Ventured (5)
23 Dregs (8)

DOWN

2 News (7)
3 Metal (6)
4 Lounger (5)
5 Relatives (12)
6 Vegetable (6)
7 Obstinacy (12)
8 Brave man (4)
15 Trampled (7)
16 Mock (6)
17 Small fowl (6)
18 Lower the head (4)
19 Weapon (5)

Now for some practice. Using the same diagram, let's start again and fill it with words entirely different from those that we've just clued. My own second version, complete with clues, will appear in Part IV, and you may be interested and amused to discover whether any of the words that I have included have also turned up in your diagrams.

21 A cryptic crossword—words and blocks

In our composition so far, we have restricted ourselves to the exercise of filling in a ready-made diagram and of providing clues for the words in the grid, in the form of plain definitions. We are ready and eager now to cast off such restraints and to give ambition a freer rein. Imagine that we have been presented with an empty grid, 15 × 15 squares in size, and been invited to extend our virtuosity by composing a cryptic crossword of average standard for popular consumption. Where do we begin? Are we still limited in any way? Do we think of some clues and then work the answers into the diagram, or put the words in and then write the clues?

To answer the last question first: we put in the words and think of the clues afterwards; otherwise we may spend much of our time devising beautiful clues only to discover that we can't fit the answers into the diagram, and then we shall have to reserve them for later puzzles in which they do fit. Let us consider before we put our words in, then, what vocabulary we shall have at our disposal.

Words and phrases

If a crossword is aimed at solvers who normally tackle it on the train or bus, in bed, or during the lunch-break, vocabulary should consist as far as possible of familiar words and phrases, so that recourse to a dictionary should be unnecessary. On the other hand, if it sets a much harder standard and is clearly intended for the more tigerish solver, who doesn't feel that his intellectual powers have been sufficiently challenged if it is completed in less than a couple of hours of concentrated cerebration, then the setter is at liberty to comb the dictionary and other works of reference for his diagram's contents. In either case, however, it should go without saying that the words employed will neither overstep the bounds of decency and good taste nor gratuitously insult minority groups: will not be, in a word, offensive. (In practice it is noticeable that in reputable papers and periodicals the standard of crossword vocabulary and clues is consistently higher than that of some other features and language appearing in those same publications, so that it may be truly claimed that, even in these permissive times, to crossworders at least the most familiar four-letter words are PURE and GOOD!) Subject to these considerations, words may be used in any grammatical form that suits the number of spaces available or which the setter considers will inspire the neatest clue. All parts of speech are equally eligible for inclusion as being essential features of the language.

The matter of phrases is rather more subtle and calls for separate consideration here, since it is not always easy to determine what constitutes a familiar phrase. In the previous chapter we confined ourselves to single words as answers of our quick crossword; but we could have included (and we shall do so in future as the occasion arises) recognised phrases here and there instead. What do we understand by a familiar phrase? At either extreme there is no difficulty of recognition:

for example, PRIME MINISTER is a two-word phrase as familiar to all as the single word PRESIDENT, and as such it has every right to appear in a crossword; whereas HARD EXERCISE, although making sense, is not a self-contained expression with an automatic familiarity, as would be, say, HARD LABOUR, which is a set formula with prison connections.

Between these extremes there lies a vast number of phrases—some admissible, others unsatisfactory—and it takes experience, as well as judgment, to decide in each case. One of the things we can do is adapt recognised phrases to our needs, according to the number of letters available to us. For instance, WALK THE PLANK is a well-known expression, which contains twelve letters. Should we happen to have thirteen spaces to fill, we could change it to WALKS THE PLANK; if fourteen spaces, WALKED; and if fifteen, WALKING—all reasonable versions of one familiar phrase.

Another way to adapt a phrase to the number of letters required, or to accommodate a letter that has already been fixed in the diagram, is to alter the person involved. For example, CHANGE ONE'S TUNE will be just as acceptable if presented as CHANGE THEIR TUNE or CHANGE MY/HIS/HER/OUR TUNE. Care is required here too, however, because sometimes the change of person doesn't work, as in the following example. Although a polite reply to a word of thanks is DON'T MENTION IT, which justifies its inclusion in a diagram as a familiar idiom, it won't do at all to change it to something like DOESN'T MENTION IT, which is far from being a recognised expression. Similarly, while MY SAINTED AUNT is a well-known exclamation, YOUR SAINTED AUNT would be meaningless.

It would take a complete book of phrases to give anything like a comprehensive list, but as a guide here the most reliable phrases to use are the following: significant parts of proverbs (like REPENT AT LEISURE, HE WHO HESITATES) or of nursery-rhymes (e.g. RAN UP THE CLOCK, HAD A GREAT FALL); idiomatic expressions with or without minor adaptations (e.g. SAVES ONE'S/HIS/HER BACON); stock phrases (e.g. FAST AND FURIOUS, IN COLD BLOOD); common associations of adjectives and nouns (e.g. SCRAMBLED EGGS, CHRISTMAS CARD); literary titles (e.g. TREASURE ISLAND, JULIUS CAESAR); and place-names (e.g. PICCADILLY CIRCUS, NEW YORK). All these and their like are phrases that one recognises on sight; indeed, many of them are unique and are therefore eminently suitable for our purposes. Contrast any of them with something like HE WAS YAWNING—a perfectly sensible part of a longer sentence, no doubt, but quite hopeless and not self-contained when out of context—and the distinction between permissible and unacceptable phrases should become clearer.

Each of the phrases mentioned above contains many letters and therefore when used will occupy a full line (or most of one) of the diagram. It is worth bearing in mind during composition, however, that the inclusion of shorter phrases is just as legitimate and that such expressions as ON EDGE, AT LAST, CLOSE SHAVE, NO ENTRY, etc. may get the setter out of a difficulty when no single word seems to fit the conditions, and can even give rise to clues as neat and amusing as those for longer phrases or single words.

One small restriction in the use of phrases, long or short, is advisable: it is not regarded as good practice simply to add the definite or indefinite article unless it is an essential part of the phrase. For example, THE GONDOLIERS, being the title of a musical work, not only requires the article but also would strictly be incorrect without it; but ODD MAN OUT is perfectly clear and adequate without being preceded by a superfluous THE. Similarly, CUP OF TEA does not need A in front of it (if an extra letter is required, CUPS OF TEA will be better), whereas in the expression A BIT THICK the A is vital to the sense while merely BIT THICK is patently incomplete.

Filling a diagram

We now come to our pleasant task of constructing a diagram

for a cryptic crossword. Each new crossword has a habit of presenting its own peculiar problems, so we shan't hope to become expert after one attempt; nevertheless, all crosswords of this type cover a fair amount of common ground which, once trodden, should be more familiar on each successive expedition. As we set off together, then, this first time, please allow me to be your guide, and to point out *en route* the features worth noticing as well as those that it is best to avoid.

What kind of a diagram are we trying to produce? It will measure 15 squares by 15, with every alternate square on alternate lines already blocked in. When completed, the block arrangement will form a symmetrical pattern, and the words and phrases will all be, as far as possible, familiar ones, as will any names of people or places which may clamour for admittance.

We could aim to have two words per line going across and two per line going down, making a total of thirty-two words—sixteen across and sixteen down. (Some crosswords have as many as three words in some lines, as they may if the composer so wishes, but this inevitably leads to a lot of short words.) More artistic, as well as more helpful to the solver, is an arrangement of two full-line words or phrases going across, with the remaining rows having two words each, and the same with the columns going down, making twenty-eight clues in all. This can cause some headaches for the composer, as will be seen, but the solver who successfully works out a couple of the long phrases will have given himself a good start in many other words spread over the grid.

As we saw in the last chapter, it is most important to work the longest words or phrases into the diagram before anything else. In that example their location was already fixed by the ready-made pattern. Now we have the freedom to place them where we wish, but this must be done before any squares begin to be filled in from shorter words, thus making our task impossible. We begin, therefore, by thinking of a couple of phrases consisting of twelve, thirteen, fourteen or fifteen letters: say, BELOW THE AVERAGE (15) and CARDINAL VIRTUE (14). (It is, of course, also possible to use phrases of nine, ten or eleven letters, but this will mean committing ourselves to several fixed blocks immediately and restricting our freedom of manoeuvre at too early a stage. We may likewise avail ourselves of phrases that exceed fifteen letters, such as COME TO A PRETTY PASS. The most satisfactory way to deal with this is to split the phrase into two parts, with COME at the end of one row and the rest occupying the following row, or COME TO A PRETTY in the first row and PASS the first word of the next. But here again, when we have made provision in the diagram for the words which must balance these because of symmetry, we shall be committed to several blocks from the start. For our present purposes, therefore, let's give ourselves as much elbow-room as we can while we have the choice.)

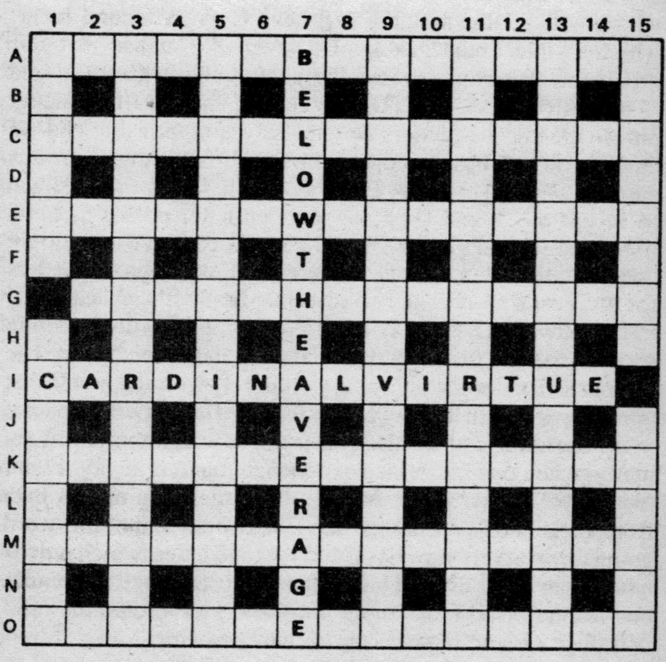

Next we see whether these two phrases can cross each other anywhere in the diagram, preferably towards the left-hand side of it so that we can work our way eventually from north-west to south-east. Let us experiment with the fourteen-letter phrase, to discover which of the two possible sets of exposed, or checked, letters will serve us the better. If we put CARDINAL VIRTUE in row I (see diagram on p. 209), starting at the extreme left at I1, the checked letters will be C, R, I, A, V, R and U. We then put a block in the remaining space at I15 and, to balance it symmetrically, a corresponding block at G1. It will now be possible to put BELOW THE AVERAGE in column 7, because its letter A at 17 is also the second A of CARDINAL. In the diagram we see the two phrases interlocked.

This seems fairly satisfactory, for we notice that the word which will go down at H1 will have C as its second letter, which is quite manageable. However, we realise that this arrangement leaves exposed the potentially awkward V and U of CARDINAL VIRTUE. When we have a fifteen-letter phrase the checked letters fix themselves immovably and we have to do our best to cope with any difficult ones—in this case the W and H in rows E and G. But before we are obliged to accept the V and U of the fourteen-letter phrase as inevitable also, let us give the whole phrase one move to the right and see if the newly revealed alternate letters improve matters for us. Yes, they do—in two respects: firstly, the checked letters are now A, D, N, L, I, T and E, a far more accommodating set than the one that included V and U; and secondly, we can put our fifteen-letter phrase in column 3, with the result that when we deal with the NW corner the fixed letters will be nearer to the beginnings of words. This is not of vital importance, actually, when one has gained experience, but it is always easier to think of words when working from their beginnings than from their ends. We notice too, incidentally, that the word going down at H15 now has E as its second letter, which is even better than the C that we had before at I1. So since on balance our second effort looks more promising, let's scrap the original diagram and replace it with the following:

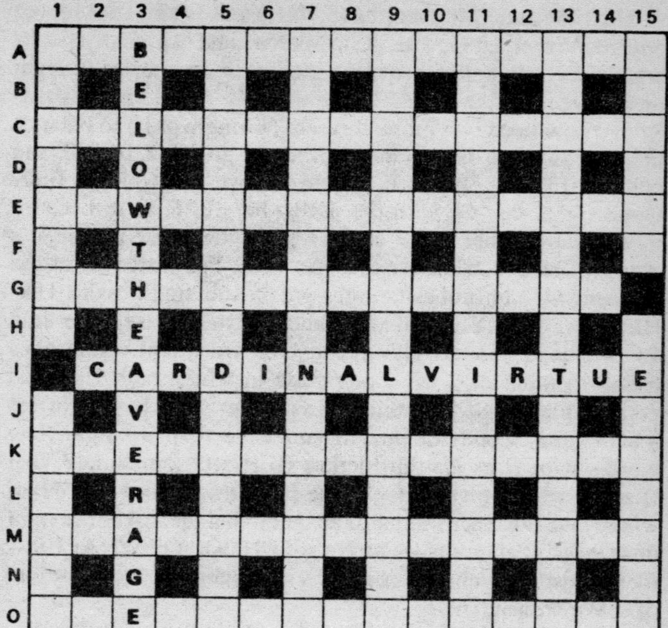

(All very well, you say, but what if our two original phrases don't happen to coincide at any point in the diagram? This indeed is often so, and in that case we must use another phrase which we've previously made a note of and try that, or else make do with one phrase to start with and then see if we can think of something else to cross it. In the latter case, where shall we put CARDINAL VIRTUE as a starter? Whether we decide to begin it in column 1 or 2, it is not happiest in row A, where it will cause several Down words to start with vowels or with L and N; nor in row O, because I, A and U are bad for last letters of words, and V is hopeless. A fourteen-letter word is not normally suitable for rows C and M, because it would mean putting in three blocks at once at A1, B1 and C1—or A15, B15 and C15, depending on where we begin writing it in—and another three to balance at M1, N1 and O1, or at M15, N15 and O15. That leaves any row from E, G, I or K available, and we shall choose whichever one happens to interlock with our newly thought of phrase.)

• We now need two more phrases (or long words) to balance the two that we have, and they must go in at row G and column 13. Can you see which one we must tackle first? Quite right: row G, with the not-so-helpful H in it; because if we add another letter at G13 from the other phrase it's going to be much harder to cope with. For instance, at the moment we can unhesitatingly put in the single word UNHESITATINGLY, but if we found that the phrase in column 13 produced another H, say, at G13 we might spend ages trying to think of a word or phrase in which both Hs fitted at those places. So let's think of a phrase—which often offers much more scope for an amusing clue than a single long word—with H as the third letter. BEHIND something? That B as the penultimate letter of the first Down word in column 1 may be a nuisance; better to abandon that idea. After several unsuccessful attempts we arrive at SCHOOL OF WHALES—there must be a chance here of some reference to the sound of a Welsh academy!

How does that affect our fourth and final long phrase? We now have E–T in the middle of it, which should offer us some choice. The T suggests THE, followed by four letters, and the E perhaps a verb ending in –ED: 'somethinged the something'. What about CROSSED THE LINE? No, a letter short: a pity, because we could have had the double meaning of a person sailing over the equator and an athlete finishing a race. We'll make a note of it for use in a later puzzle and try again. What was that about an athlete? We needn't discard him after all, because as he crossed the finishing-line he also BREASTED THE TAPE, thus obligingly providing us with our fourth phrase.

(Don't be deceived by the apparently casual ease with which that last phrase formed itself for our benefit. Would that it were always so! In practice we can usually come up with some useful phrase, and even on occasion pick and choose from several possibilities, so long as one letter only is already fixed. But the moment we reach the fourth phrase, which now has two letters fixed, and these often separated from each other by several spaces, we can stare at the diagram and mentally run through the alphabet over and over again before anything even remotely sensible occurs to us. In such circumstances we should not be stubborn, but rather delete a phrase and replace it by another which might prove to be more helpful all round. I wish that I took this very sound advice more often myself! The fact is, however, that from time to time, in a diagram that has taken me perhaps four hours altogether to compose, fully half that time has been occupied in filling in the four long phrases.)

Let's see what the diagram looks like now.

	1	2	3	4	5	6	7	8	9	10	11	12	13	14	15
A			B										B		
B		■	E	■		■		■		■		■	R	■	
C			L										E		
D		■	O	■		■		■		■		■	A	■	
E			W										S		
F		■	T	■		■		■		■		■	T	■	
G	S	C	H	O	O	L	O	F	W	H	A	L	E	S	■
H		■	E	■		■		■		■		■	D	■	
I	■	C	A	R	D	I	N	A	L	V	I	R	T	U	E
J		■	V	■		■		■		■		■	H	■	
K			E										E		
L		■	R	■		■		■		■		■	T	■	
M			A										A		
N		■	G	■		■		■		■		■	P	■	
O			E										E		

Our four phrases have provided us with a framework on which we can build the rest of the diagram. They have already ensured that the solver has at least one gang-plank from each of them to another quarter of the grid, and as we now think about the disposition of blocks and the symmetry we must try to improve on that situation if possible.

Let us start from the central area and see where to put our next blocks in columns 7 and 9, which need some. Placing them at H7 and H9 is asking for nothing but trouble: we should then have the first word in column 7 ending with O and the second beginning with N—neither to be recommended, as we learned in the last chapter; and also the first word in column 9 would end with W and the second begin with L—not much better. Shall we move up one space, or down? Which will be more useful to us: a word beginning with O–N, partnered by one ending with W–L, or one ending with O–N, balanced by a word beginning with W–L? The latter, surely; so we insert the two blocks at J7 and F9. In column 7 we want a nine-letter word or phrase ending with O–N. We may think of one in a flash or get held up for a fair time; or we can look it up in a rhyming dictionary (see Chapter 23), which can be very useful for such occasions. FIRST-BORN will fit, so we put it in hopefully; and to balance it in column 9 we enter WALLOWING. A slight pause again to study the diagram (see opposite page) and to decide which part seems to call for our most urgent attention.

As our eyes roam over the exposed letters now tentatively installed in their places, they observe little to cause alarm or despondency in any of the rows (although the B, F, B in row A may be a little awkward and needs watching later) and see that only columns 5 and 11 await their blocks. At all costs we must avoid ending a word in column 11 with A–I. We can either begin a word with –A–I and put a block at E11 (making the resultant four-letter word at E12 have S as its second letter, which is very restricting) or end a word with A–I– and put a block at K11 (making the four-letter word at K12 have E as its second letter, which is excellent). Let's

	1	2	3	4	5	6	7	8	9	10	11	12	13	14	15
A			B				F						B		
B		■	E	■		■	I	■		■		■	R	■	
C			L				R						E		
D		■	O	■		■	S	■		■		■	A	■	
E			W				T						S		
F		■	T	■		■	B	■	■	■		■	T	■	
G	S	C	H	O	O	L	O	F	W	H	A	L	E	S	■
H		■	E	■		■	R	■	A	■		■	D	■	
I	■	C	A	R	D	I	N	A	L	V	I	R	T	U	E
J		■	V	■		■	■	■	L	■		■	H	■	
K			E						O				E		
L		■	R	■		■		■	W	■		■	T	■	
M			A						I				A		
N		■	G	■		■		■	N	■		■	P	■	
O			E						G				E		

do the latter, put in the block, and pause to think of any well-known ten-letter word ending in –ATIC and starting, let's say, with A. AUTOMATIC? A letter short. AUTOCRATIC? Yes, let's put it in, looking to right and left as we do so to see if we've landed ourselves in the soup anywhere. No; that U is unchecked, and for the moment everything else looks manageable.

Symmetry demands a corresponding block at E5 and a ten-letter word to balance AUTOCRATIC, beginning –O–D. AO–D is no good. BO–D? BONDSWOMAN will fit (007's girl-friend?), so in she goes; but we'll have to keep an eye on the W at K5, and if it proves too difficult we'll throw her overboard. These two new blocks have, incidentally, determined the lengths of the two words in row E as well as those in row K, and the situation at present is shown in the diagram below.

	1	2	3	4	5	6	7	8	9	10	11	12	13	14	15
A			B				F				A		B		
B			E				I				U		R		
C			L				R				T		E		
D			O				S				O		A		
E			W				T				C		S		
F			T		B		B				R		T		
G	S	C	H	O	O	L	O	F	W	H	A	L	E	S	
H			E		N		R		A		T		D		
I		C	A	R	D	I	N	A	L	V	I	R	T	U	E
J			V		S				L		C		H		
K			E		W				O				E		
L			R		O				W				T		
M			A		M				I				A		
N			G		A				N				P		
O			E		N				G				E		

Where next? We have reached the stage at which we can now concentrate on one corner at a time; and as often as not, provided that we see no danger-signals elsewhere, the methodical procedure is to begin at the NW corner, continue through to the NE or the SW as the fancy takes us, move on accordingly to the SW or NE and finish in the SE corner. But it would be a waste of time and effort if we did this for three-quarters of the diagram, only to discover that one corner proved too intractable for us and we had in the end to remove the spanner from the works and begin a whole area of the diagram all over again. Experience therefore teaches us that a slight unorthodoxy in sequence is often justified by results.

Now here, for instance, you're still a little apprehensive about the ten-letter word in row K, aren't you? I don't blame you; it looks very awkward and we may be defeated by it. If so, it will be simple enough to remove BONDSWOMAN and substitute something more co-operative; or delete WALLOWING so as to find a more helpful letter than the O at K9. But we must do it now, before things become more involved, so this time we move to the SW corner first.

Can we think of a word to fit those three fixed letters, E, W and O, in row K? Probably not a word, except possibly one beginning with OVER–, so what about a phrase? We're in luck! The proverbial ONE SWALLOW may fail to make a summer, but it has brought the welcome warmth and sunshine into our lives today. In it goes, and since it brings no further problems with it as far as we can see, we shall transfer our attention to the NW corner, where we must decide upon the location of the remaining blocks.

If we insert a block at A6, we must then find a nine-letter word in that row to fit F–––A–B––. Nothing leaps to mind. A block at A8 means finding something suitable for the first word, of which we have ––B–––F. The phrase IN BRIEF will fit, so let's see where it leads us. We pencil in the block, remembering immediately to insert the corresponding block at O8. Now we have two words going down which begin with I. At A1 we can try IMMUNISE, which will give NEWS or NEWT (whichever one we haven't used recently) at E1. In row C it will be better to have the block further along than immediately below A8, because then the pattern will afford more open access from quarter to quarter. So we put one at C10, which leaves room for MILLIARDS as the first word in row C. Before we forget, we must balance the new block at C10 with another at M6, and our pattern is complete. IRIS (or IBIS) in column 5 concludes the conquest of the NW frontier, and as we prepare for an assault on the NE we study the lie of the land at the top section of the diagram.

	1	2	3	4	5	6	7	8	9	10	11	12	13	14	15
A	I	N	B	R	I	E	F	■			A		B		
B	M	■	E	■	B R	■	I	■		■	U	■	R	■	
C	M	I	L	L	I	A	R	D	S	■	T		E		
D	U	■	O	■	S	■	S	■		■	O	■	A	■	
E	N	E	W	S T	■		T				C		S		
F	I	■	T	■	B	■	B	■	■	■	R	■	T	■	
G	S	C	H	O	O	L	O	F	W	H	A	L	E	S	■
H	E	■	E	■	N	■	R	■	A	■	T	■	D	■	
I	■	C	A	R	D	I	N	A	L	V	I	R	T	U	E
J		■	V	■	S	■	■	■	L	■	C	■	H	■	

Which part of the NE shall we fill in first? That's right: the longest one, in row E, which already contains three letters spaced out at intervals. After some thought, the phrase AT ALL COSTS occurs to us. We must now look simultaneously for two words starting at A9, one going across and consisting of ––A–B––, the other reading downwards as ––S–L. The letter A won't do here as the first letter, but we're all right with B, which will give BRAMBLE across and BASIL down. Now with one eye on row C and the other on column 15, we can have THEIC and ENCASH (but THEIC is a bit hard), or TREAD/TREND and ELDEST—we need look no further. Opposite, at top, is our NE corner (with a couple of spaces at the bottom belonging to the SE).

We left the SW earlier on, once we were satisfied with ONE SWALLOW. Returning there, we find that we need two more words across and two down, with no particular literal obstacles. If we stake our CLAIM in row M, we can use MOB-CAP in column 1. Considering row O and column 7 together in order to ensure a viable final letter where they both meet, we hit upon PREENED and LURED or LURID. We put in both alternatives for the time being, and we shall

	5	6	7	8	9	10	11	12	13	14	15
A	I	E	F	■	B	R	A	M	B	L	E
B	B R	■	I	■	A	■	U	■	R	■	L
C	I	A	R	D	S	■	T	R	E	A N	D
D	S	■	S	■	I	■	O	■	A	■	E
E	■	A	T	A	L	L	C	O	S	T	S
F	B	■	B	■	■	■	R	■	T	■	T
G	O	L	O	F	W	H	A	L	E	S	■
H	N	■	R	■	A	■	T	■	D	■	
I	D	I	N	A	L	V	I	R	T	U	E
J	S	■	■	■	L	■	C	■	H	■	

choose the one that we find inspires the neater clue eventually. The lower part of the diagram lacks only the SE corner, and here it is:

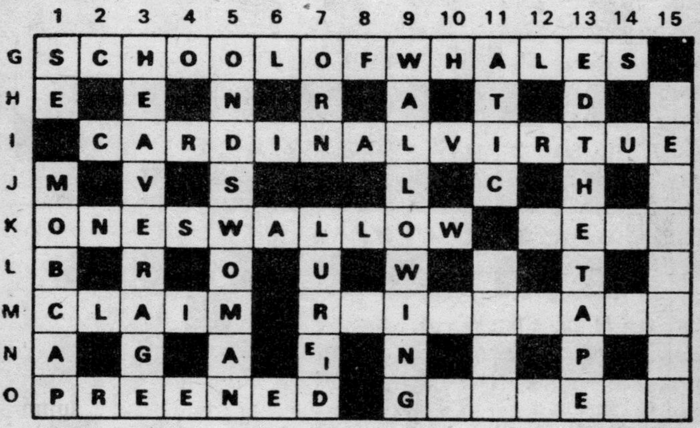

Now it's your turn! And where better to obtain practice than in the SE corner, where both Across and Down words have their final letters at the grid's extreme edges? Try to use only familiar vocabulary, and remember that you may employ single words or phrases. I would suggest that you start on row M, because that is the longest answer, and that you don't let any frustration in this exericse show itself in that four-letter word which goes in column 11! Off you go, and don't read any further until you've finished.

When you have filled in this corner to your satisfaction, perhaps you would like to attempt the final task without which the diagram is not complete: that is, writing in the clue numbers. The method was explained in the previous chapter, so you will probably have no difficulty this time. You will find that, in a diagram of this size and general pattern, the numbers usually go up to 25, 26 or 27. Now have a look at the final version below, and see to what extent your words and mine

1 I	N	2 B	R	3 I	E	4 F		5 B	R	6 A	M	7 B	L	8 E
M		E		B R		I		A		U		R		L
9 M	I	L	L	I	A	R	D	S		10 T	R	E	A N	D
U		O		S		S		I		O		A		E
11 N	E	W	S T		12 A	T	A	L	L	C	O	S	T	S
I		T		13 B		B				R		T		T
14 S	C	H	O	O	L	O	F	15 W	H	A	L	E	S	
E		E		N		R		A		T		D		16 P
	17 C	A	R	D	I	N	A	L	V	I	R	T	U	E
18 M		V		S				L		C		H		N
19 O	N	E	S	W	A	20 L	L	O	W		21 B	E	A	N
B		R		O		U		W		22 S		T		A
23 C	L	A	I	M		24 R	A	I	S	E	C	A	I	N
A		G		A		E I		N		C		P		T
25 P	R	E	E	N	E	D		26 G	A	T	H	E	R	S

coincide. It's my guess that many of you will have arrived at the same answer as mine in row M, if nowhere else.

It remains to be stressed yet again that this, though fairly typical of its kind, has been one diagram only, and that each new composition creates its own little problems from the moment that the first phrase takes its place in the grid. It is hoped, however, that the technique demonstrated here will help new practitioners to avoid situations that lead inevitably to disaster.

Above all, it should be realised that so far we have merely produced a set of answers, which are all words or phrases familiar to most people, within the framework of a symmetrical diagram. It will be impossible, however, to say whether it is a good crossword or not until we have devised the clues; for, granted that the vocabulary and pattern are satisfactory, it is the standard of accuracy and fairness of the clues which will determine whether the puzzle is solvable, and the setter's extra skills which will make it entertaining.

Turning a diagram

Before we leave this chapter, there is a further feature of diagram composition which is worthy of mention: namely, the device whereby we can convert all the Across words to Downs, and *vice versa*. Suppose, for example, that we have completed a diagram and are engaged in concocting the clues, when we suddenly realise that, for technical reasons, an Across word would be neater to clue if it were a Down word instead (because, let us say, the word 'up' makes better sense than 'back' in that particular clue). In that case, we can turn the diagram round; but since the process is not quite as simple as it may sound, it will be best to give here a practical demonstration, using a miniature crossword.

Imagine that you have written the top diagram overleaf on a sheet of transparent material. You notice that the first Across word is DOWN and, to help your clue, you would prefer it to be, literally, a Down word. This is what you must do. Give the diagram a quarter-turn (i.e. 90 degrees) clockwise,

D	O	W	N		P	O	S	H
I		I				I		O
S	T	R	A	N	G	L	E	R
G		E		E				S
U	N	D	E	R	T	A	K	E
S				V		M		M
T	E	M	P	E	R	A	T	E
E		A				Z		A
D	U	P	E		T	E	N	T

then turn over your sheet as you would the page of a book. (Alternatively, if you have written the diagram on thin paper, give the sheet a clockwise turn, turn over the sheet, then hold the paper up to the light). You will be looking at the words in their desired order (with DOWN now the first Down word) but written askew. When you have rewritten the letters normally, your original diagram will have become the following:

D	I	S	G	U	S	T	E	D
O		T		N		E		U
W	I	R	E	D		M	A	P
N		A		E		P		E
		N	E	R	V	E		
P		G		T		R		T
O	I	L		A	M	A	Z	E
S		E		K		T		N
H	O	R	S	E	M	E	A	T

To complete the metamorphosis, you must scrap the old clue numbers and supply new ones. Q.E.D.!

22 A cryptic crossword—the clues

When preparing to devise a set of clues for a crossword, we must have in mind certain standards: those of difficulty, accuracy, fairness and entertainment value. A popular puzzle such as we contemplete here will tend towards the easier standard, while still offering a challenge to the solver's brain cells. Accuracy, and its travelling companion, fairness, ought to be ensured by a consistent adherence to the principles expounded in Part II of this book; and whether our clues are on an easy or a difficult level, according to the readership we envisage, those same principles are totally applicable and need no modification.

Entertainment value is less easily measurable and difficult to guarantee, for what one solver finds dull, despite its accuracy, another may consider the perfect clue; and conversely, some solvers will always prefer a witty idea, for all the clue's defects in the eyes of the purist, to whom it is unacceptable. Ideally, of course, every clue should be both accurate and entertaining and thus satisfy everyone; and so, even though we may fail to reach this desirable goal consistently, we must at the very least aim at it by maintaining our accuracy, grasping every opportunity for humour that we see and trying to infect the solver with our own sense of enjoyment.

Style

No matter how many techniques, or combinations of different techniques, we bring into play during the composition of crossword clues, each of us is apt, subconsciously, to favour certain methods of treatment as a first choice: to tend towards lengthy or succinct wording on the average; to concentrate on some familiar abbreviations in preference to others; to include a high proportion of anagrams; and so on. Discriminating solvers have a habit of noticing such idiosyncrasies on regular acquaintance and so of recognising a setter's 'style', which helps them to get behind his mind, as it were, and to fall progressively less and less for his little tricks. Many a clue-writer, indeed, though he may appear anonymously in print, appends his signature, in a sense, unmistakably by his style in much the same way as do other producers of creative work, such as artists, musicians and novelists.

There is therefore little need to fear that a willingness by clue-writers to abide by the spirit of prescribed rules means condemning themselves to a cheerless uniformity—as would almost certainly be the case if computers took over the job! There is always, as we shall see shortly, ample scope for variety within a framework of orthodoxy, so that several different setters, given the same crossword to clue, would produce puzzles of quite different styles, as well as standards, without necessarily infringing a single rule.

The clues for our puzzle

We naturally can't hope to exploit, in a single crossword of twenty-eight clues, all the techniques that we have learned. We shall, however, endeavour to introduce as much variety of treatment as the words in the diagram which we completed in the last chapter will allow; and as we deal with each clue in turn we shall sometimes examine more than one possibility before deciding on the neatest wording for our final version. Here and there we shall even discuss a clue of a harder standard than the one we are aiming at here, if an interesting idea suggests itself; but for the purposes of this 'average' puzzle we shall always settle in the end for the problem that is least difficult for the solver.

Many setters, no doubt, habitually clue a crossword by working in sequence through the Acrosses and continuing likewise until the last of the Downs: an admirably methodical system. My own practice deviates slightly from this, in that I always prefer, for two reasons which I shall explain, to deal first with the four long phrases around which the diagram has been constructed. Firstly, whereas one is apt to clue single words predominantly on the basis of their literal make-up, a phrase is more likely to suggest a treatment from the mental picture that it evokes rather than from its letters. For example, the word SHAMED quite quickly reveals itself to a clue-writer's eye as AM inside SHED, from which this clue might be devised:

Am kept in hut, disgraced (6)

A solver will soon spot that he has to discover a word meaning disgraced, consisting of AM which is kept inside a word for a hut, which is SHED. But faced with, say, the phrase MONEY FOR OLD ROPE, one begins to wonder what kind of old rope will bring in money, and maybe an antique rope of pearls comes to mind. From that idea a clue then forms itself, such as:

Easy financial gain—from selling antique pearl necklace? (5,3,3,4)

Secondly, if a long phrase does not happen to inspire an amusing idea, we may very well have to employ an anagram to deal with some or all of its letters: and it is always important, if we ration the number of anagrams that we use in each crossword, as I do, to know at the start how many of them the phrases will demand. If we then have very few left, we must clue our shorter words by other means; or if the phrases have not needed any after all, we can spread a few anagrams around the puzzle to give solvers some extra help if they're stuck. Let us therefore write our clue numbers in their correct numerical sequence on our sheet of paper—Across first and then Down—and, to start with, examine our four phrases in turn.

14 Across: SCHOOL OF WHALES. When we were putting this in the diagram we scribbled 'Welsh academy' in the margin to remind us of our original idea. Can we pursue it now? Do most people pronounce 'whales' as 'Wales'? The truth is that some do and others don't, so we mustn't use that pun, which would simply mystify those who don't. Yet it's too tempting to abandon altogether, so let's see. Apart from that H, it really is a Welsh academy, and—here's a thought!—whales are creatures that spout water. What is more appropriate in schools than spouters? If we can think of a word beginning with an H that suggests speaking, we can say that spouters are beginning to h—— in a Welsh academy. What about 'harangue'? So here we are:

Spouters start to harangue in Welsh academy (6,2,6)

Is every word correctly used? 'Spouters' defines the answer. 'Start to harangue' means a start to the word 'harangue', namely the letter H, which is 'in Welsh academy', or inside SCHOOL OF WALES. Thus the definition and the subsidiary indications both lead to the answer and the solver is doubly certain that he is correct.

17 Across: CARDINAL VIRTUE. What can we do with something like justice, fortitude, temperance, etc? Any of these qualities can apply to the Church type of CARDINAL.

Can we make the reverend gentleman appear to fall below such standards, just for fun? VIRTUE consists of VI (Roman numeral for six) and RTUE (a mixture of the letters of TRUE). If we make the Cardinal have half-a-dozen drinks, which is far from true temperance, we've got the basis of a clue, which eventually becomes:

> **Church VIP having half a dozen with questionably true temperance? (8,6)**

An amusingly misleading picture thus emerges of a tipsy ecclesiastic displaying the opposite of a cardinal virtue; but when analysed, the clue really shows CARDINAL (Church VIP) having (next to it) half-a-dozen (VI), (together) with RTUE (questionably, or an anagram of, TRUE), followed by the definition 'temperance?' Note the question mark, which is essential when only one of several possibilities is suggested and is equivalent to saying 'temperance, perhaps', 'temperance, for example' or 'could the answer be temperance?'

2 Down: BELOW THE AVERAGE. Still haunted by the vision of the elbow-bending Cardinal, we notice that this phrase begins with BE and ends with VERAGE, and we wonder how to connect a beverage with the overall meaning. A nice ambiguous word for average is 'mean', because it normally makes one think first of something like miserly. Anything below the average is less than the mean, so we can define it as 'worse than mean'. Now we want to suggest some action connected with drink that is very mean, such as deliberately spilling someone's whisky or surreptitiously putting something unpleasant in it. Examining our phrase again, we find LOW THE A inside BEVERAGE. LOW can mean vulgar, and both THE and A are, grammatically, articles. It's going to work! We're going to drop the word LOW (meaning vulgar) and the two articles into BEVERAGE to make BE-LOW-THE-A-VERAGE, and the clue is going to make good but misleading sense, as follows:

Vulgar couple of articles dropped in the drink—that's worse than mean (5,3,7)

7 Down: BREASTED THE TAPE. This phrase, used of an athlete winning a race, doesn't immediately suggest any unusual mental picture from its sound or meaning, as some phrases are apt to do. Since no obvious pun, nor any fanciful way of visualising this scene comes readily to mind, we must examine the phrase's literal make-up instead. It doesn't conveniently split up into separate words that might be suitable for a charade type of clue, nor does it have some words inside others; so let's see if an anagram can be formed which will fit in with the general sense of finishing first in a race. After some trial and error, we extract the word AHEAD and then BETTER, both of which are apposite, leaving PETS, PEST or STEP. One who finishes first is often at least a step ahead of, and better than everyone else in the race. Well, then, let's try to convey the idea of a well-organised runner by the wording of our clue, thus:

Finished first, step ahead, better adjusted (8,3,4)

The first two words form the definition, and the anagram is indicated by the statement that STEP AHEAD and BETTER have been adjusted, or set in a proper order. Before we move on to the next clue we must recheck each letter of the anagram carefully against the phrase to ensure that we have made no mistakes; and we must also make signs in the margin beside this clue and that of 17 Across (which we shall erase later) to remind us that we have now used one full anagram and one part-anagram. That done, we are ready to work our way systematically through the remaining twenty-four clues.

1 Across: IN BRIEF. The word BRIEF stimulates two immediate reactions: conciseness and barristers. Fortunately, both ideas can be connected, since it is easy enough to imagine a barrister reading information in his brief which has been succinctly presented. If we put the two different meanings side by side, we have:

Where barrister will get facts succinctly (2,5)

Here we have two helpful definitions, with the solver left to supply his own pause before 'succinctly', the second of them. Of course, the clue as you read it is not necessarily true, but each 'half' separately is perfectly correct and the whole makes good sense.

5 Across: BRAMBLE. This prickly shrub consists of B + RAMBLE or BR + AMBLE. Both involve walking, which is most suitable for the idea of coming across shrubs, but of the two the single letter B is more awkward to clue than BR, the abbreviation for British Rail, so the railway is certainly the 'line' that we'll work on. BR AMBLE gives 'railway walk', which isn't very sensible—let's try again. It's an Across word, so we can have 'walk *beside* railway', which is a very natural phrase. (Note that if this were a Down answer, something like 'walk *below* railway' would be required.) All we need now is to put the pieces together neatly and say that we can find our answer, a shrub, in the letters BR plus AMBLE. Here's one way:

Shrub seen in walk beside railway (7)

9 Across: MILLIARDS. We must have very large numbers as our definition here, but what activity are they going to indulge in? We can see IARD (a mixture of the letters of RAID) inside MILLS, so one idea might be on the lines of:

Very large numbers make a wild raid in mills (9)

Not a very convincing picture? I quite agree! For one thing, it really should be '*on* mills' to make good English; for another, we ought not to rush into an anagram, or even a part-anagram, as our first thought in case we exhaust our ration too quickly; but most of all, it's extremely dull and needs livening up. A second look at the letters reveals LIAR in MILDS—and a fibber surrounded by drinks of beer, whether milds or bitters, presents a more interesting scene altogether. Can the definition be further improved? A synonym for a lie is a tale, so a liar is a tale-teller. That leads to a slight change of thought: we'll have a man telling a story, while his fascinated listeners keep plying him with lots of drinks—and that must all be conveyed in a clue of average length, as follows:

Tale-teller surrounded by drinks of beer—lots and lots (9)

Anyone reading this clue will have no difficulty in visualising the story-teller's recital, so that, although we haven't made it noticeably harder than our very first thought, the extra polishing has certainly improved both its appearance and its credibility.

10 Across: TREAD or TREND. Which of them seems the more promising? The sensible thing is to work out a clue for each, and if they are both usable we'll save one of them for a future occasion. TREAD, as a verb, means to set the foot down, to step, to walk, or, as a noun, a track or footprint. Do any of these meanings have a natural association with the word's letters? An anagram of TRADE isn't appropriate, nor, at first sight, is T + READ. If we read it backwards we see DAERT, which is DART (to rush or shoot) around E (East). Here's an idea:

Walk or rush back around the East (5)

This is adequate, without being particularly attractive; but, as we said before, not every clue is going to be a polished gem! Nevertheless, we'll have another go at it before we're satisfied that that's the best we can manage. We haven't used a 'hidden' clue yet, so perhaps this is the right time to give the solver a nice easy one in case he's struggling, such as:

(a) In the centre a distinct footprint (5), or
(b) Walk in Montmartre—adorable (5)

It shouldn't take him long to discover the footprint hidden in 'cenTRE A Distinct', or a word meaning to walk in 'MontmarTRE—ADorable'. And since such clues do tend to be very easy, we pencil 'hidden' in the margin as a warning that we shan't be using any more in a puzzle of this size, unless this is going to be one of the rare occasions when we weaken and admit two.

This word has claimed a fair amount of our time, but we still ought to consider the alternative, TREND, briefly, before we move on. It can mean a tendency, and can be thought of as TO REND minus the letter O, which is commonly clued as 'love'. To rend a garment is to tear it, or to make tears in it, which encourages us to concoct the following very misleading clue:

Tendency to cause tears when love has departed (4)

This should lead the solver to look for a word meaning 'tendency', formed from TO REND (to cause tears or rips) when the O has gone. But in the process he will probably be held up by thinking of 'tears' as weeping—as we have craftily suggested. And since, on reflection, the entire clue is more suitable for a harder standard of puzzle than our present one, we shan't use it here.

11 Across: NEWS or NEWT. Looking at NEWS first, we spot that its four letters are the four quarters of the compass, and at once this short clue occurs to us:

Information coming from all quarters (4)

That didn't take long, so we'll have a quick look at NEWT as well. There isn't much that the letters suggest apart from W in NET, but as it happens they can fit the answer quite nicely, since we can say that we have to net, or catch, around the West, a certain creature, as follows:

Catch, around the West, an amphibian (4)

We have to choose one of these two clues for this puzzle—let's say the one to NEWS—but we shall use the other as soon as NEWT turns up in a future crossword.

12 Across: AT ALL COSTS. This phrase, meaning 'no matter what the cost may be', makes us think, among other things, of inflated food prices, especially since most of its letters spell A TALL COS, or a big lettuce! All that remains is TS, or ST (the abbreviation for Street) backwards. We can therefore provide our solver with a pound note and send him shopping with this instruction:

> **Get a big lettuce near back-street, whatever the price (2,3,5)**

The clue has told him to obtain A TALL COS beside the reverse of ST, and that the answer means 'whatever the price'. It's lucky for us, by the way, that this is an Across clue, because we couldn't correctly say '*back*-street' to indicate ST going *upwards* in the diagram.

19 Across: ONE SWALLOW. Another phrase, which can be interpreted in two ways: firstly as part of the proverb, 'One swallow doesn't make a summer', and secondly as a single little drink. It won't make sense to say that one drink doesn't make a summer, so we must work out a form of words for summer which will make the idea acceptable. Summer is a time for hot weather—what about 'a hot time'? That suggests a really lively party, and the imbibing, no doubt, of more than one little drink. The general idea may be evoked by a clue such as:

> **A single little drink—it hardly guarantees a hot time (3,7)**

This statement, compounded of two different aspects of the same phrase, makes good sense, which is the basic requirement of every clue. It is also mildly amusing, which is always an asset. And finally, when the solver has suddenly recognised the disguised familiar proverb in the second half, he is likely to enjoy the solution all the more.

21 Across: BEAN. Not an inspiring-looking word, this common item of food, but you never really know a word's potentialities until you experiment with it. The definition could be 'pulse', with thoughts of a doctor holding one's wrist, but the word itself doesn't suit that notion. It sounds like BEEN—that's not promising either; besides, many people are apt to pronounce BEEN as BIN. A different approach is needed. What about the expression 'I haven't a bean', meaning 'I'm penniless'? Does the word help us there? A in BEN (one in a Scottish mountain), or BAN around E (embargo about the East)—both hopeless. BE + AN, or to live with one—ah, the germ of an idea at last! Living with a bean is not a recognised phrase, but living without a bean certainly is. Here's a slightly tricky clue, based on this thought:

Live with one—it's hard to live without one! (4)

Tricky it may appear, but in fact the synonyms used in the subsidiary part are easy ones: 'live' equals BE and 'one' is AN. The definition in the second part is a complete sentence, with 'live' intended to be read in the sense of 'to enjoy life' rather than merely 'to exist'. The deception is completed by making the whole clue appear to concern a man and woman inseparably attached to each other. The exclamation mark is optional, depending on how strongly we feel about living without money.

23 Across: CLAIM. There is little scope for maneouvre with these letters, so we must do our best with the only apparent treatment, which is I in CLAM. I can't sensibly be found inside a clam, obviously, but I can, as the slang expression puts it, get stuck into one, or start eating it with gusto—an idea that prompts the following:

Demand shellfish—I'll get stuck into that (5)

The solver must pause after the definition, 'demand'. Then we have CLAM, indicated by 'shellfish', and the statement that I—i.e. the letter I—will be placed, or stuck, inside that. Note that, as was explained in Chapter 5 (p. 77), we must never say anything like 'I *am* getting stuck into shellfish', since what we really mean is '(The letter) I *is* getting . . .', and that the remedy is to say, for instance, '(The letter) I *will* get stuck into shellfish'.

24 Across: RAISE CAIN. Many of you, I fancy, put in this phrase when you filled in your own SE corner in the last chapter. Did you have any immediate thoughts about a suitable clue for it? Some reference to Cain's parents seems inescapable, since presumably they raised him from his infancy, so let's have:

Make a fuss, as Adam and Eve had to? (5,4)

Thus we have two different interpretations of the phrase: to make a fuss, which is the meaning in normal use, and the fanciful one in which we wonder whether Cain was in fact raised by Adam and Eve—hence the question mark.

25 Across: PREENED. One thinks here automatically of peacocks or smaller birds arranging their feathers or pluming themselves. The definition, then, might be 'plumed'. The word itself suggests nothing on these lines—in fact, it hasn't any familiar words in its parts, and it isn't all that easy to treat. Having reached almost the end of the Acrosses with only one part-anagram used in them so far, perhaps we ought to help the solver here by giving him a full anagram for a not too commonly used word. END PEER or PEER NED? That's nonsense. NEED REP? Not much better. DEER PEN, or an enclosure for deer—sensible, but no obvious connection with 'prided' or 'plumed'. REED-PEN? A distinct possibility, this, since the oldest type of pen one thinks of is either the calamus, which was a hollow reed, or the quill, which is a feather; and we realise that the word 'plumed' can also mean 'feathered'. It's true that reed-pens didn't have feathers, but ours will! Here we are, then:

Variety of reed-pen, plumed (7)

On reading the clue, we see at once in our mind's eye a type of hollow pen, rather like a quill, with feathers on it. In other words it is a convincing picture. 'Variety of' clearly indicates that the answer is a different arrangement of the letters of REED-PEN which will produce an answer meaning plumed in some sense.

A marginal note is required before we proceed, to tell us that we have used a full anagram again, and a quick glance over the sheet reveals a total of two so far out of our ration of four, as well as one part-anagram, so we're nicely in hand.

26 Across: GATHERS. There are several interesting possibilities in this word, which not only has a plentiful variety of synonyms for its definition, such as assembles, picks up, collects or infers, but also seems to be capable of being split up in several ways. Without making things too complicated, let's see which treatment of the letters is most practicable. There's (a) GAT (a slang term for a gun) + HERS (the girl's, or belonging to the girl); or from a slightly different angle (b) HER inside, or surrounded by, GATS; (c) THE (an article, grammatically) inside GARS (a mixture of RAGS); or (d) GAS (empty conversation or talk) about THE and R (the abbreviation for a king). What clues do these arrangements inspire?

(a) Picks up the gun belonging to the girl (7)

The definition is 'Picks up', and the answer is GAT + HERS. Alternatively, if we're thinking of a machine-gun which one takes apart for cleaning and then reassembles, we could change the definition to 'assembles', as follows:

(a) Assembles the gun belonging to the girl (7)

Both these clues make good sense and are eminently solvable.

(b) Picks up the girl, surrounded by guns (7)

This time, the definition is followed by HER surrounded by GATS, so that we have employed the same synonyms but a different treatment.

(c) Picks up article wrapped in tattered rags (7)

The definition could be 'Collects' instead, and it would make equally good sense. The article (THE) is wrapped in, or placed inside, an anagram of 'rags', and the adjective 'tattered' suggests that this word has been subjected to rough treatment and is no longer in its original shape.

(d) Picks up empty talk about the king (7)

This shows GAS placed about THE R, with the definition coming first. Our final choice from this batch will depend on how each clue attracts us, whether we would rather not use another part-anagram yet, the number of abbreviations we're likely to need before we've finished and so on. Let us delay our decision, then, until we see what problems await us in the Down clues, which we are now ready to tackle.

1 Down: IMMUNISE. Unlike the previous word, this one doesn't offer a wide choice of definitions, nor does it neatly separate into helpful component parts. I'M + MUSE about the reverse of IN isn't exactly inspiring; what else is there? An anagram seems the best bet here so we begin to experiment: ME, US, MINI? These words aren't even remotely on the same wavelength as to vaccinate, which is what the answer means. ME MINUS I? That's plain nonsense, I'M US, ME IN? No, but if we change the order to ME, I'M IN US, we've made some sense at last, and after some more pondering we can try the following:

Vaccinate me—I'm in US, ill (8)

The clue presents an easily understandable sentence, with 'Vaccinate' as the definition, a pause which the solver supplies, and an anagram of the words ME I'M IN US, which we are told are written 'ill', meaning badly, or not in their normal order. The main deception here is that one naturally reads 'ill' as an adjective meaning unwell, whereas it really has to be taken as an adverb. Another mark in the margin brings our tally of full anagrams to three, so we have only one left, except in an emergency.

3 Down: IBIS or IRIS. The wading bird comprises I + BIS (meaning twice), I + the reverse of SIB (a kinsman or kinswoman) or IB. (abbreviation of *ibidem*, meaning in the same place) + IS. Whatever clue we devise on any of these lines, therefore, it is going to be on the difficult side, since BIS, SIB and IB. can hardly be called well known to our average solver. But while we are considering this word, we can think of a couple of possible clues which we might find useful for a harder puzzle at another time, such as:

(a) The bird's a kinswoman—one that's stuck up (4)

This indicates that the bird (IBIS) is SIB-I when stuck up, or written upwards. Note that if this had been an Across clue we should have had to change 'stuck up' to 'brought back', or something similar.

(b) I twice get the bird (4)

We have said that I + BIS get IBIS, and have incidentally created, in very few words, an amusing picture of a music-hall turn's hostile reception by the audience. We make a note of this for possible future use and move on now to consider IRIS, a girl's name, or a plant which is known also as the flag.

Treatments which suggest themselves on sight are: (a) the reverse of SIR + I; (b) I + the reverse of SIR; (c) IRISH minus the last latter. From these we can devise several clues.

(a) Teacher and I hoisted the flag (4)

SIR (a synonym of teacher) and I hoisted, or lifted, means that the letters are to be written upwards in a Down clue; and the definition is 'the flag'.

(b) I, teacher, raised the flag (4)

A slight variation on (a), this keeps the letter I where it is, after which SIR must be raised, or written upwards, the whole resulting in IRIS, the flag.

(c) This girl's Hibernian, mostly (4)

The clue says that IRIS is the word IRISH, or Hibernian, mostly, or except for its final letter. Which one shall we adopt? My preference is for (a), but you may like one of the others better.

4 Down: FIRST-BORN. What shall we say about the eldest child? Well, he's been to university and got a FIRST. Then he has to ROB upside-down, followed by the letter N, which is the compass-point for North. So to begin with a FIRST, then ROB up, because it's a Down clue, and finally North. Here, then, is the melancholy story of the brilliant student's descent into pretty crime, told in this clue:

Eldest child, with excellent degree, having to steal up North (5-4)

Thus we see the FIRST-BORN, with FIRST having (after it) the reverse of ROB + N.

5 Down: BASIL. A man's name and a herb. Come to think of it, Herb is short for Herbert, which is also a man's name! We mustn't miss this opportunity for a neat clue, like:

Herb is a man's name (5)

The solver, after a short period of bafflement at this statement of the obvious, will soon realise that he has to find a type of herb which is also a man's name. Neither the name nor the herb happens to be among the most common of its kind, but with the assistance of a letter or two from intersecting words the answer should not be long in coming.

6 Down: AUTOCRATIC. We still have one anagram awaiting our call, and experience tells us that a word like this, if we intend to help the solver to find it, will have to be given the anagram treatment; for anything else is certain to involve bits and pieces which will make the whole thing difficult, obscure or forced. So we jumble the letters, looking for something that might merge with the idea of tyrannical or despotic, which the answer means. The word COURT raises thoughts of a Star Chamber, and that leaves AATIC. What about A COURT I ACT? After a couple of false starts, at last we come up with:

Reassembling a court, I act like a despot (10)

We have here reassembling, that is coming together anew or in a new form, the words A COURT I ACT; and the definition is 'like a despot'. A feature of the deception here is that a solver is bound to read 'reassembling' as a transitive verb, whereas we really mean it to be used intransitively.

Having now exhausted our self-imposed ration of four complete anagrams, we must try to clue the remaining words without having recourse to this device again in this puzzle.

8 Down: ELDEST. It means most senior. Its letters seem more suitable for a foreign language than for English, with its EL (the, in Spanish) and DE (of, in French) before we get to ST (the abbreviation for street). 'The Spanish of French Street' would do nicely for the title of a novel, but how do we fit in the definition? Better, perhaps, to have DE inside EL and ST, which will lead to:

Most senior of French seen in the Spanish street (6)

These words clearly indicate that in the answer—meaning most senior—of, French (DE), is seen inside the, Spanish (EL), street (ST). As was stated earlier (p. 135), we do not intend to include any foreign words which are not, in our opinion, widely familiar; but even those of us who have neither learnt Spanish nor spent holidays in Majorca have at least heard of the word EL, and similarly nobody capable of solving a crossword will complain that the French word DE is beyond his linguistic grasp.

13 Down: BONDSWOMAN. We thought at once, as we put this word in the diagram, of 007's girl-friend. Can we incorporate this idea in a neat clue that is consistent with the word's meaning of a slave? We can try:

007's mistress is a slave (10)

James Bond is well known as 'Secret Agent 007'. One of the definitions of WOMAN is 'mistress'. Hence BOND'S WOMAN may be clued as 007's mistress, and the complete answer is defined by the word 'slave'.

(A clue of this kind, featuring as it does a character from popular fiction, raises the interesting question of topicality, which it will be appropriate to consider here while we are in the process of concocting clues. There is often a strong temptation to include an allusion to a person or event in the news at the time, or to eminent people, regardless of topicality, whenever such a treatment is relevant to the answer or the clue's wording. This is an excellent way of making clues lively and up to date, but on the other hand there are some attendant risks which must be carefully weighed.

Firstly, unless you are sure that your crossword will be published almost immediately after its composition, the topicality which you have introduced may prove to have been so short-lived that it makes little sense to the solver who reads the clue some months after the event. Secondly, a famous person, though apparently in excellent health at the time of writing, or installed in an office such as that of Head of State for several years to come, is apt most inconsiderately to die, or to be deposed or replaced, without the elementary courtesy of postponing such extreme action until the crossword in which he appears has been presented to the public. And finally, whenever a living notability is referred to, it is always prudent to examine your clue's wording from every angle so as to ensure that you have not inadvertently, however innocent or flattering your intention may have been, used a form of words which could be construed as libellous by any casual reader, whether he knows anything about crosswords or not.

A further consideration, and one that each setter must decide according to his own judgment, is the extent to which allusions to real or fictional names are fair to the solver. For example, in the clue which we have just completed and which provoked this digression, we have assumed that James Bond and his numerical pseudonym of 007 are both well known to solvers. Are we justified in this assumption? Well, since films on the subject are still doing the cinematic rounds, it is reasonable to believe that we are, although probably with somewhat less confidence than, say, ten years ago when the Bond vogue was at its height. And this is the point: that it is all too easy for a setter who, let us say, has grown up in an era of world-renowned film stars like Gary Cooper and Shirley Temple, or popular literary figures such as Professor Moriarty, the arch-enemy of Sherlock Holmes, or Harry Wharton and Co., the schoolboy friends of Billy Bunter of Greyfriars, to forget that a new generation of solvers has since emerged which has been nurtured on a far different diet and may know very little, if anything, of these names.

In short, a clue-writer needs to remind himself constantly that topicality is ephemeral and that popular favourites in any sphere are apt to become merely a blurred memory.)

15 Down: WALLOWING. Which is more useful for clueing purposes: W + ALLOWING, or ALLOW inside WING? The definition must lead the solver to an answer that means rolling about in mud, and we are going to suggest in some way that this activity is permitted. Since the odd letter W does not readily contribute to this idea, as far as we can see, let us use the two complete words instead and see what picture they produce:

Permit, in part of the building, rolling about in mud (9)

We have given the solver the information that a word meaning permit (ALLOW), written inside a word for part of the building (WING), will result in the answer WALLOWING, defined as 'rolling about in mud'. What scene of decadence or debauchery we have invited his imaginative brain to contemplate we cannot say, but the mind boggles!

16 Down: PENNANTS. We had one kind of flag in 3 Down when we clued IRIS, and now we have different ones, but flags nonetheless. They can be seen as consisting of PENN. (the abbreviation for Pennsylvania) and ANTS (the clue-writer's favourite workers). A sensible-sounding clue, which treats the words in this way, is:

Flags made by American State workers (8)

The word PENNANTS, we have said, is made, or produced, by combining PENN., an American State, with ANTS, which are workers. Observe once again the misleading nature of the clue's wording, which suggests that pennants are made by State employees in America. We don't mean what we appear to say, of course, but we have correctly said what we mean about the make-up of the answer.

18 Down: MOB-CAP. This article of feminine head-gear, though now out of date, should be familiar enough not to cause real difficulty. However, it is always a good principle, whenever we have a word that is just a little harder than the average for the particular puzzle it is in, or a place-name capable of more than one acceptable spelling, to make its clue rather easier than average by way of compensation or in order to ensure that the spelling required in the diagram in question is unmistakably indicated. In the present case, we shall call the MOB the rabble, which is its most obvious meaning, and treat CAP as the reverse of PAC, which is the word PACK without its final letter, or 'almost PACK'. The following clue, then, should not pose any serious problem:

Feminine head-gear makes the rabble almost pack up (3-3)

The general picture is one of a mob exasperated by the current fashion in women's hats.

20 Down: LURED or LURID. In the former word, which means enticed or decoyed, we have LED around UR (the famous old city of the Chaldees which clue-writers find so convenient to call at) or LUD (the form of the word Lord by which a judge is addressed in court) around RE. Both will make quite neat clues.

(a) Decoyed, and escorted, around ancient city (5)

That is to say, we have a word meaning decoyed (LURED), and we also have another way of arriving at it, by using a word for escorted (LED) around an ancient city (UR).

(b) Law-Lord shuts up about being enticed (5)

This is a shade harder to solve, although the amusing mental picture of the embarrassed judge has its attractions. The clue says that a legal type of Lord (i.e. LUD) shuts up (i.e. encloses) 'about' (RE, as in the commercial expression 'Re your letter . . .', meaning 'concerning' or 'about'); the whole answer being a word for enticed, which is LURED. The fact that the solver must read 'shuts up' as if it meant 'keeps silent', whereas it really means 'encloses', is what helps to make this a more difficult clue than (a). So unless we find something better with LURID, which we shall now consider, we shall adopt (a) for this puzzle.

It looks as if the ancient city will have to be used for LURID too, this time with LID around it, leading to:

Ghastly hat seen around ancient city (5)

LURID means ghastly, and it consists of LID (hat) seen around UR (ancient city). It is a perfectly satisfactory clue, but since we've just been talking about feminine head-gear in the clue to MOB-CAP, let's stick to clue (a) after all and put LURID aside for another time.

22 Down: SECT. A school of opinion or a body of followers will be our definition here, and this may neatly fit in with the fact that the word consists of SET, meaning a clique or group of persons, about C, the Roman numeral for a hundred. We can select one of these two:

(a) A hundred in clique, forming a body of followers (4)
(b) School group, about a hundred (4)

Clue (a) shows C in SET, forming SECT. In (b) the definition comes first with the word 'School', and then after a pause which the solver supplies, as he has learned to do by now, there is SET (group) about C (a hundred). There's almost nothing to choose between the two clues, but since choose we must, let's have (b), shall we?

We realised, when we began to clue this crossword, that we couldn't hope to include in one puzzle every technique available to us. Nevertheless, we have been able to produce a very typical set with a reasonable variety of treatments, including four complete anagrams and one part-anagram, which should be nice and helpful without becoming tedious from excessive use. We have also limited the 'hidden-clue' device to a single appearance only, and this too we regard as our norm. At times we were well content to be able to concoct one sensible-sounding clue to a not very tractable word; at others we had more versions than we needed and so had to discard some nice clues. In the process, however, I hope that this exercise has enabled you to catch a glimpse of some of the artifices that may underlie the wording of clues and to gain an insight into the workings, however contorted, of one clue-writer's mind.

Now that we have finished it, have we composed an easy or a difficult puzzle? It is not so easy to judge as we go along, clue by clue, so let us now remind ourselves which clues we have chosen and present the crossword as a complete entity, exactly as it will appear in print (see pp. 246 and 247). In this way, and by checking the clues individually against their solutions, we shall be able to form a clearer impression of its standard of difficulty, and also of its fairness and, incidentally, its entertainment value.

Let us also be sure, when we have written it all out in sequence, that we check both the clue numbers and the figures in brackets for accuracy, since mistakes can occur here, as elsewhere, through undue haste or simple human fallibility.

It is possible that some of my readers, inspired by reading these chapters on diagram composition and clueing to devise puzzles of their own, may become so impressed by the artistry of their efforts that they will be anxious to have them published so as to allow others to share their enjoyment. It might first be preferable, however, to try out the crosswords privately among friends in order to discover whether they really are solvable, as well as fair and accurate in all respects, or whether perhaps some revisions and amendments might improve them.

Those who are members of organisations large enough to have their own periodical 'house magazines', whether in printed or cyclostyled form, might then try to have their puzzles included in some issues; or, if no crossword has hitherto been featured, they might urge their editors to consider starting one, at least for a trial period. If their puzzles prove to be popular among a limited readership, they might be encouraged to submit further compositions to other editors.

Opportunities for publication, it must be made clear, are far from numerous, for the bulk of the British press, certainly as far as crosswords are concerned, is outside the sphere of amateur freelance contributions. Most of the national dailies and weeklies have their own regular contributors, while magazines and other periodicals, as well as local evening papers, are either similarly placed or are contracted to receive their puzzles from one agency or another. It would therefore be a waste of time and postage for setters to offer casual crosswords to these publications.

Notable exceptions are the *Birmingham Post* and the *Birmingham Evening Mail*, which do print such freelance crosswords as they consider to be of a satisfactory standard. Aspiring contributors would be well advised to study over a period the general character and degree of difficulty of these papers' puzzles, and also to observe whether the same grid designs regularly recur, before attempting to compose their own on similar lines. Occasionally other papers too invite readers to submit a crossword, with the chance of publication offered for the best one. In addition, it should be realised that even setters on a regular contract are mortal, so that one may sometimes see an advert in a Personal Column inviting applications for a post which has become vacant.

The *Listener*, the BBC's weekly publication, prints crosswords composed by freelance contributors only. As was mentioned in Chapter 1, the *Listener*'s puzzles are almost invariably thematic and of a much harder standard than the average. However, anyone with a novel or ingenious idea, who also has the skill to translate it into a puzzle incorporating accurate standards, is at liberty to offer it for consideration to the paper's Crossword Editor, by whom it will be accepted or rejected entirely on its merits.

Freelance puzzles of *Listener* standard appear in *Crossword*, the monthly magazine of the Crossword Club, which

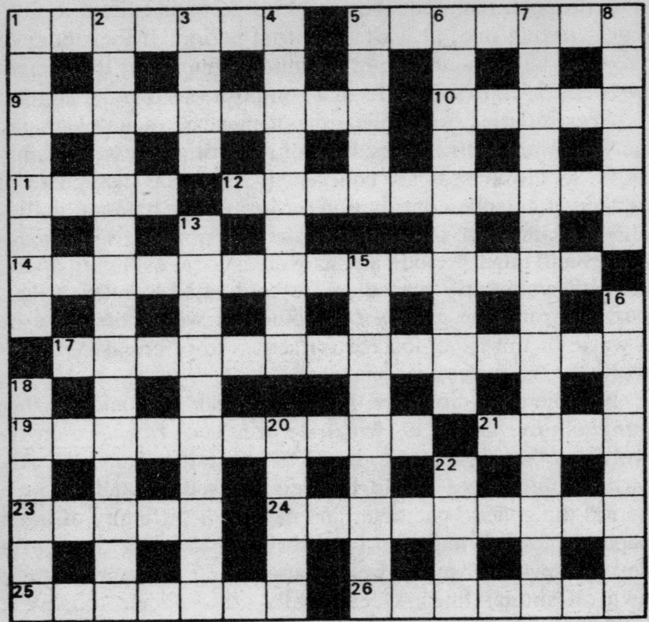

ACROSS

1 Where barrister will get facts succinctly (2,5)
5 Shrub seen in walk beside railway (7)
9 Tale-teller surrounded by drinks of beer—lots and lots (9)
10 In the centre a distinct footprint (5)
11 Information coming from all quarters (4)
12 Get a big lettuce near back-street, whatever the price (2,3,5)
14 Spouters start to harangue in Welsh academy (6,2,6)
17 Church VIP having half-a-dozen with questionably true temperance? (8,6)
19 A single little drink—it hardly guarantees a hot time (3,7)
21 Live with one—it's hard to live without one! (4)
23 Demand shellfish—I'll get stuck into that (5)
24 Make a fuss, as Adam and Eve had to? (5,4)
25 Variety of reed-pen, plumed (7)
26 Picks up the gun belonging to the girl (7)

DOWN

1 Vaccinate me—I'm in US, ill (8)
2 Vulgar couple of articles dropped in the drink—that's worse than mean (5,3,7)
3 Teacher and I hoisted the flag (4)
4 Eldest child, with excellent degree, having to steal up North (5-4)
5 Herb is a man's name (5)
6 Reassembling a court, I act like a despot (10)
7 Finished first, step ahead, better adjusted (8,3,4)
8 Most senior of French seen in the Spanish street (6)
13 007's mistress is a slave (10)
15 Permit, in part of the building, rolling about in mud (9)
16 Flags made by American State workers (8)
18 Feminine head-gear makes the rabble almost pack up (3-3)
20 Decoyed, and escorted, around ancient city (5)
22 School group, about a hundred (4)

Solution

also contains articles and correspondence devoted to this subject. For details of membership, etc., write to The Editor, *Crossword*, The Crossword Club, Hilberry Farm, Awbridge Hill, Romsey, Hants SO5 OHE.

As for the crosswords that are supplied to daily and weekly newspapers and to magazines from outside their own organisations, many of these are produced by an agency in Fleet Street called Morley Adams Ltd. In their office in Hulton House they have a regular staff turning out crosswords during office hours every day, and they also employ half-a-dozen others who work at home. It must always be assumed, however, that they have all the staff that they need unless they advertise for replacements in such papers as *The Times*, the *Guardian* and the *Daily Telegraph*.

Finally, there are currently several monthly magazines which cater exclusively for that large section of the public which is interested in puzzles of all kinds. Most of them have a variety of crosswords, mainly depending on definition-type clues, but also include a modicum of cryptics. Those whose editors have informed me that they are prepared to consider freelance contributions, with a view to possible publication, are the following, complete with their editorial addresses:

New Crossways, 54 Gurney Drive, London N2 ODE.

Puzzle Corner, same address as *New Crossways* above. There are additional bumper issues quarterly.

Puzzled, Aidfairs Ltd., Causton Hall, Cross Rd., Croydon, Surrey.

(*The*) *Puzzler*, 320 Regent Street, London W1R 5AH.

Puzzlers World, Model & Allied Publications Ltd., PO Box 135, Bridge Street, Hemel Hempstead, Herts HP1 1EE.

Puzzles Digest, Model & Allied Publications Ltd., same address as *Puzzlers World* above.

With each of these entertaining magazines, it is most important to adapt your own compositions to the appropriate standard and style, and to submit neat and legible puzzles, preferably typed.

23 Useful books of reference

It is sometimes assumed that composers of crosswords must be surrounded by shelves crammed with books of reference from floor to ceiling. If this happens to be true in some cases, it is probably incidental to their composition of crosswords and not essential to it. Indeed, for the majority of those who produce the daily or weekly puzzles, whether of the plain-definition or the cryptic type, a reasonable dictionary and a school atlas are, more often than not, entirely adequate; and the same applies to the solvers of such crosswords too.

For the setters and solvers of crosswords of a more difficult standard, however, such as those based on a particular literary theme, or a general knowledge type, or one containing many classical allusions, a more extensive personal library will naturally be required. To compile a fully comprehensive list of such books is impracticable here: hundreds of titles could justifiably demand mention as being potentially useful in some degree for some puzzles at some time. What will be practicable and, I believe, helpful at this point is a much smaller catalogue of books written and compiled specifically as works of reference, each of which in its own way has something to offer to both composer and solver. And even if some of them may not need to be consulted by either from one year to the next, there may well be other times when they prove to be just what is required for completing an awkward corner or solving a particularly intractable clue.

Some of the books listed below may be out of print, but possibly still obtainable from second-hand bookshops. Most are dictionaries of one kind or another, sometimes covering more or less the same ground as each other. In each case the name of the publisher is given, but not the purchase price, since the latter is unlikely to remain constant. Here, then, with a brief description of their contents and functions, is a collection of books which I hope readers will be pleased to know about and to possess.

Brewers's Dictionary of Phrase and Fable (Cassell). A revised and enlarged version of *Brewer's Reader's Handbook* (*q.v.*). Many old references have been replaced by more modern expressions. A fascinating book for dipping into, it contains the main figures of the world's mythologies, customs ancient and modern, explanations of the origins of common phrases, stories of characters from legend and folklore, etc.

Brewer's Reader's Handbook (Chatto & Windus). A dictionary of famous names in fiction, with many references and allusions to historical, mythological and proverbial characters. Includes many references that do not appear in the more modern *Dictionary of Phrase and Fable* mentioned above. Now out of print.

Chambers Biographical Dictionary (W. & R. Chambers). Over 15 000 biographies of the famous and infamous of all nations, past and present. A fascinating book to glance through at leisure.

Chambers Words (W. & R. Chambers). A list of about

115 000 entries from *Chambers Dictionary* (see next item), not including the 1977 Supplement. Arranged by computer alphabetically from two-letter words upwards. A good short-cut and time-saver for busy crossworders and sceptical Scrabblers.

Chambers Twentieth Century Dictionary, 1977 Revised Edition (W. & R. Chambers). The most versatile dictionary of its size and strongly recommended for crossword addicts, especially those who prefer tough puzzles. Contains a wealth of obsolete and Scottish vocabulary in addition to the latest technical and scientific terms, with Americanisms, colloquialisms and slang well represented.

(The) Concise Oxford Dictionary, New Edition (1976) (Oxford University Press). This Sixth Edition, thoroughly revised and edited by Dr. J. B. Sykes (himself a brilliant crossword solver), incorporates many new words and phrases unknown to the compilers of earlier editions.

(The) Concise Oxford Dictionary of English Literature (Oxford University Press). Based on the larger *Oxford Companion to English Literature*, this abridged version is less bulky and less expensive. Authors, works and characters of importance, as well as historical and mythological information relevant to English literature, have all been retained.

(The) Crossword Anagram Dictionary (Barrie & Jenkins). With words grouped according to length (but with allowance having to be made for plurals, tenses of verbs, and so on), this book enables one to solve any anagram of a normal word very quickly. A boon if you are occasionally stumped and driven to distraction, but a wicked temptation to lazy solvers!

(The) Crossword Companion (Stanley Paul). Contains over 45 000 items, ranging systematically from two-letter to twenty-letter words, with separate additional lists including UK Counties, States of the USA, birds, plants, etc. Very useful for setters and solvers alike.

(A) Dictionary of English Synonyms (Warne). This book offers a large selection of words bearing exactly equal meanings. For any clue-writer held up by being unable to think

of a neat definition, and for struggling solvers also, there is a plentiful variety of vocabulary here. Beware, however, of American spellings.

Everyman's Classical Dictionary (Dent). Covers the bulk of historical and geographical references from 800 BC to AD 337 as well as Roman and Greek mythological places and characters.

Everyman's Dictionary of Fictional Characters (Dent). The revised edition (1973) contains over 20 000 entries. Names appearing in all well-known works of British and American writers are to be found here, as well as two handy indexes of authors and titles. Each entry tells you who the character is, the title of the work and, where appropriate, the other members of the character's family.

Everyman's Thesaurus of English Words and Phrases (Dent). Based on Roget's original classification and categories, this book contains long lists of words and phrases with their synonyms and antonyms. It includes a great many of today's technical terms, slang, Americanisms, etc. It also has a vast and revised index.

Everyman's other reference books include a *Dictionary of Literary Biography*, *Quotations and Proverbs*, *Non-Classical Mythology* and *Shakespeare Quotations*.

(The) Modern Crossword Dictionary (Pan Books). Particularly helpful for phrases in common use, this dictionary is arranged alphabetically according to the number of letters in a phrase. Ranges from eight to fifteen-letter phrases. Also has a section with three to nine-letter words, grouped alphabetically.

(The) Nuttall Dictionary of English Synonyms and Antonyms (Warne). Similar in function to the *Dictionary of English Synonyms* (*q.v.*) by the same publisher, this book has the added attraction of providing antonyms, where they exist, as well as plentiful lists of single-word synonyms.

(The) Oxford Companion to Classical Literature (Oxford University Press). An authoritative book, covering not only the literature of Greece and Rome but also classical allusions

in modern European literature. Most useful for ensuring the correct spellings of awkward and unfamiliar names, and for helping composers of difficult crosswords out of tight corners when no word in the English dictionary will fit.

(The) Oxford Dictionary of Quotations (Oxford University Press). For those setters who insist on including quotations in their puzzles, and for their solvers and others who need to check literary references in Shakespeare, the Bible and nursery rhymes, for example, this is the standard work.

Oxford dictionaries and companions (some also available as paperbacks) are many and various. The famous *Oxford English Dictionary* with its thirteen volumes, now modernised by extra supplements, is too expensive for most crossworders to own. But many libraries have it on their shelves; and as the ultimate authority on the meaning and history of English words it is unrivalled.

For those with special interests, the following are worthy of mention: *Oxford Companion to Art; Oxford Companion to Music; Concise Oxford Dictionary of Opera;* and *Oxford Companion to the Theatre*.

Pears Cyclopaedia (Pelham Books Ltd). This book is revised annually and therefore is more up to date in some respects than many weightier and more pretentious tomes. Useful for quick reference to such items as medical terms, a world gazetteer and atlas, famous people, historical events, and many more.

Smaller Slang Dictionary (Routledge & Kegan Paul). Compiled by the celebrated Eric Partridge, this is a handy book for clue-writers and solvers alike. It concentrates on the slang of the twentieth century, unlike its more ambitious big brother, *A Dictionary of Slang and Unconventional English*. Naturalised Americanisms, service expressions and a certain amount of rhyming slang are all included.

Excellent sources also for useful phrases (quite apart from the incidental pleasure inherent in the late Eric Partridge's work) are his *Dictionary of Catch Phrases* and *Dictionary of Clichés*, both published by Routledge & Kegan Paul.

Addicts of definition-type crosswords, especially the bumper American ones, will be greatly helped by the same publishers' *Bernstein's Reverse Dictionary* which, instead of conventionally giving words alphabetically, followed by their meanings, gives meanings (i.e. the definition clues) alphabetically, followed by their 'answers'. Two successive entries taken at random should make this clear: stormy, severe: INCLEMENT; stormy, violent: TEMPESTUOUS.

(*The*) *Synonym Finder* (Rodale Press). This revised and updated edition, containing over a million synonyms, is the largest and most comprehensive dictionary of synonyms available. Each entry is accompanied by numerous synonyms, often arranged in several related groups. Particularly helpful is the indication of which synonyms are British or US slang, and which are idiomatic, informal, rare or obsolete.

Walker's Rhyming Dictionary (Routledge & Kegan Paul). Intended originally as a help to budding poets, this book has become a most useful aid to crossworders who know the end of a word but can't work out its beginning. The words are arranged alphabetically in reverse order, the entries progressing from those ending in -aa to -ba, -ca, -da and so on. If you are composing or solving a puzzle and have got stuck at, say, a seven-letter word which must end in -OP, a glance at this dictionary will show you more than a page of words ending with these two letters, among them several of seven letters, from DEVELOP to OVERTOP, which may be what you need.

Part IV

Illustrative Crosswords

24 Hints for solvers

The reader has by now, it is hoped, been presented with so detailed an explanation of all aspects of cluemanship that he ought to have more than a shrewd idea of what store of tricks a setter is liable to draw from in order to divert his public, in both senses of the verb. Before turning their attention to the various types and standards of the crosswords that follow, however, some solvers may be grateful for a reminder of some of the main features of cryptic clues—as well as for a few further hints of a practical nature, even if, on reflection, they prove to be fairly obvious.

For a start, it is only common sense to use a pencil rather than ink while solving a crossword, especially one that you intend to send in because a prize is offered for a certain number of correct solutions, or when some kind of competition is involved. For one thing, you may put in a wrong answer through haste or through some misunderstanding of a clue. For another, even if you are confident that your answer fully satisfies the wording of its clue, it may turn out to be a 'red herring', unsuspected by the clue-writer himself, which will have to be erased later when intersecting letters from other words force you to replace it with the answer really intended. (Incidentally, since red herrings, strictly speaking, are deliberately laid across the trail in order to confuse, it might be advisable to allude to a purely accidental alternative solution as a 'cook'—a term used in exactly similar circumstances in chess problems.)

Next, let us assume that you have picked up an unfamiliar crossword and, having read through all the clues once, have so far failed to solve a single one on sight. If the general tenor of the clueing leads you to suspect that a degree of literary or specialist knowledge not to your taste is called for, abandon it forthwith and forget it. But if it appears to be a normal daily cryptic which merely calls for a little patience until you can get behind the setter's mind and style, there are some things that you can do at once.

The most promising procedure, initially, is to look through the clues again until you find an anagram or two—most cryptic crosswords will have a few—bearing in mind that any clue-writer who aims to be fair will have employed some significant word or phrase to indicate them, like 'twisted', 'horrible', 'in a way', 'somehow' and others on the lines of those included in the examples in Chapter 12. Once you have identified the anagram part of the clue by counting the number of letters required in the answer, you will then be left with the definition part and will know what kind of answer, and what part of speech, you are looking for. Some solvers find it useful, when working out an anagram, to write its letters on a sheet of paper in haphazard order. The new pattern thus formed sometimes suggests the answer's make-up. If you can solve only a couple of clues in this way, you will have at least one letter as a starting point to several other intersecting words. Study the clues to each of these words in turn, and perhaps the single letter now established in each case will prove to be helpful and will lead to an avenue of thought that is worth exploring.

Temporarily stumped once more, look for signs of a 'hidden' answer: that is, the actual letters of the answer concealed within the words of the clue, following some such indication as 'among', 'in', 'contributing to' and so on, a variety of which can be seen in Chapter 10. Some setters use this device regularly, even if not more than once or twice in any one puzzle, while others do so rarely; but it is always a possibility worth investigating.

Even after making progress in one quarter of the diagram, you may have another quarter still completely blank and begin to despair anew. Don't give up yet! Concentrate on each clue for that quarter in turn, and you should find something, however small, to get you restarted. For example, if you are pretty certain that the required answer is a plural word, put the final letter S in its correct place in the diagram; and the same applies to an answer in the third person singular of the present tense. Each of these letters, unless it is enclosed between blocks or bars, will contribute, perhaps significantly, to another word that crosses it. Similarly, if a clue's definition points to a past tense, try writing ED at the end of the answer; or if a present participle is indicated, enter the letters ING in the answer's last three spaces. Or again, where a phrase is being clued, the figures in brackets may be revealing. For instance, with something like (4,1,4) you can bet that middle word is A, or with (6,3,6) there is a fair chance that the three-letter word is AND or THE—try them out in turn, and see if their exposed letters give you new thoughts about other uncompleted answers in that vicinity.

Some of these suppositions, of course, may turn out to be wrong—if the plural, for instance, is a word like WORKMEN, the past tense something like BECAME, or the three-letter word ITS, FOR, HIS, etc.—but they won't all be wrong every time; and those that do prove helpful may provide just the breakthrough for which you have been praying. Many a solver has reached a dead end in a corner of the diagram, and almost resigned himself to defeat after a long and noble struggle, when suddenly daylight has dawned in one clue, after which the rest, with the extra help provided by a new letter, have very quickly yielded up their secrets too.

Parts of answers, if not the complete words, can also be firmly established by the recognition of familiar abbreviations wherever they appear in clues. See a clue beginning with such favourites as 'holy man' or 'good fellow', or perhaps 'thoroughfare', 'highway' or 'street', and you can enter ST as the answer's first two letters with confidence. Similarly, an 'artist' or 'the artillery' will give you RA somewhere in the answer, just as 'sappers' or 'engineers' will make you a gift of RE. Sometimes you have to get to know your setter before being so sure, for where one may say 'quarter' when he means North, South, East or West, another prefers 'point', yet another regularly sticks to 'direction' and one who is more generous still may give the actual compass-point by name. Ever-increasing familiarity with those abbreviations which frequently recur in your favourite crossword, and about which much was said in Chapter 16, will fill in at least a letter or two of the answer towards which you are striving.

Chapters 14 and 15 contain numerous illustrative clues in which surgical treatment of various kinds has been applied to whole words or to parts of them. With these operations in mind, far from being mystified upon seeing such indications as 'headless', 'losing heart', 'cut short', 'capital of', 'last of', etc., you will automatically translate such words and phrases as, respectively, 'without its first letter', 'minus its middle letter or section', 'with the final letter missing', 'the initial letter of', 'the concluding letter of', etc. Some of these will give you a letter which you can immediately enter in the square, and the rest will serve as a useful corroboration when the answer is eventually discovered.

Apart from the undoubted helpfulness of odd letters, however, there are other points in the structure of clues to look for which, without necessarily leading at once to the correct answers, will make you fairly certain that you know what type of clue, or what combination of types, is confronting you. For instance, if a clue in a puzzle that you can trust consists of two words only—e.g. 'Game jumper (7)'—that means that there is only one word beside the essential definition, and one word cannot do anything more than give a second definition. You know, therefore, that you are looking for a word of seven letters which in one sense means game and in another a jumper. You may not think of the answer there and then but as soon as the letters, say, C–––K–– have appeared in the diagram from intersecting answers it should not be long before you identify both the game and the jumper as CRICKET.

The mere sight in a clue of words like 'backward', 'up', 'returning' and the like should be enough to warn you at once that part or all of the answer can be read as another word in reverse. Examples of this technique are to be seen in Chapter 9.

Other revealing phrases are 'by the sound of it', 'we hear' and similar indications of puns, as described in Chapter 11. Here again, even if the correct answer does not immediately suggest itself, at least you will have understood what the clue is telling you and how you are expected to proceed in working out its solution.

It follows from all this that none of us should be too ready to give up a crossword in disgust simply because it is not to a large extent solvable fairly soon after the clues have been scanned. Most addicts will not need this advice, for they feel that with each new puzzle they are accepting a challenge and, having once begun, will be reluctant to withdraw from the contest without first making every possible effort to succeed; and this applies to solvers of comparatively easy puzzles no less than to those who like them to be as tough as possible. No matter what standard of difficulty is involved, though, the most successful results are likely to be achieved by a careful and methodical approach, based on the suggestions offered in this chapter, and summarised as follows in what we might call 'A Solver's Ten Commandments':

1 Read each clue carefully and see if you can isolate the part of it which forms the definition—it must be there, or you are beginning an unfair puzzle and are asking for nothing but grief!
2 Try to identify the type of clue—e.g. anagram, hidden, charade, etc.—and then see if the answer strikes you within a minute or two.
3 If not, move on to the next clue, and the next, until you meet one that you can solve. But on the way, don't forget to write in the diagram any odd letter, group of letters or part of a phrase that you can at the beginning, middle or end of a word, even though you don't yet know the complete answer. These may be suggested by plurals, past tenses, participles, abbreviations and so on.
4 As soon as you have an answer confidently fixed in its place, go in turn to each of the clues of its intersecting words, for which you now have at least one letter of their respective answers.
5 Continue this process of building on firm foundations, and don't attempt any clue for which you have no letters in the diagram until you can make no further progress with the letters that you already have. Taking advantage of the help that one answer provides towards the solution of others is, after all, the basis of crosswords, presenting a system of cumulative rewards, as it were, which distinguishes them so fascinatingly from all other forms of puzzle.
6 Whenever you are forced to a temporary halt, examine the part-answers of words that you have scattered over the grid *en route*. It is by no means rare to find among them a pattern of alternate letters—though often enough with some omissions here and there—which may suggest the 'shape' of the answer, such as an ending in –ATION, –ALLY or –ENCE, or, if it is a long word, its likely

rhythm of syllables—in a phrase, its 'English word-probability'. With the answer's rough pattern in mind, study the appropriate clue once more and see if further inspiration is now forthcoming.

7 If nothing seems to work and you are well and truly stuck, put the puzzle aside for a while, do something completely different, and forget about the unsolved clues. When you return to the task later with a fresh outlook, certain ideas with which you were unprofitably obsessed earlier will give way to new ones, and the chances are that at least one stubborn clue will be fathomed and so contribute further welcome assistance to the remainder. Every experienced solver knows that in any normal crossword, even one of a difficult standard, a cryptic clue can be solved eventually, though it may take several attempts, each after a longish interval.

8 If a clue doesn't seem to make sense, don't rush to the conclusion that the setter has made a mistake, but look again, harder. He may indeed, being human, have erred or been the victim of a misprint, as sometimes happens, unfortunately. Reserve your judgment, however, and give him the benefit of any doubt until you have tried all angles. You may be rewarded by something particularly pleasing when the penny drops, which you would have missed by an over-hasty assumption. If he has really blundered, then exercise your divinity by forgiveness—unless he makes a regular habit of it!

9 When the diagram is complete, if you intend to post it to the paper in quest of a book token or other prize, rewrite everything in ink, and most carefully revise the final version in case you have made a slip or omitted a letter—a human failing of solvers which is sufficiently common to be worthy of mention here.

10 If, however, in spite of all your efforts, there are still too many clues which baffle you, so that you begin to despair of ever completing a solution on your own, there remains one more practical way of helping yourself. Stick

to the puzzle of your choice, solve what you can each time and then study the answers of the rest on the following day, or week, when the solution appears, and try to see how each answer satisfies the wording of its clue. Some paperback collections of crosswords have annotated solutions, which would be even more helpful in this respect.

Not until you have given a crossword a fair chance will you be able to judge whether it measures up to the standards of ease or difficulty, of fairness, accuracy, wit and ingenuity that happen to suit your own predilections. On the basis of such considerations you will accept or reject puzzles of that general standard for the future.

The crosswords that follow are intended to illustrate the wide range of styles, types and standards of puzzle to be found in newspapers and periodicals at the present time, as well as to revive several examples from the past. Nos. 1 and 2 are old-fashioned puzzles of different kinds: the first crossword published in the *Manchester Guardian* in 1929, and the alternative-type crossword for which large cash prizes used to be offered, especially in the 1930s (see Chapter 1). No. 3 is a definition-type puzzle, sometimes referred to as the 'quickie', for which the diagram from Chapter 20 has been used. Those of you who had a shot at filling in this same diagram will now be able to see whether any of your answers are the same as mine: probably very few. Puzzles 4 to 9 are cryptic crosswords, easyish at first, but of gradually increasing difficulty; and Nos. 10 and 11 are novelties, for the benefit of solvers who like an occasional change from the normal kind of cryptic puzzle.

Nos. 12 to 17, all previously published in the *Listener*, are designed chiefly for the more advanced solver, combining the element of novelty with a more difficult level of clues and vocabulary, while at the same time aiming to offer some light-hearted entertainment. Finally, Nos. 18, 19 and 20 are a sample each of the work of the three famous practitioners referred to in Chapter 1: Torquemada, Afrit and Ximenes.

The solutions are fully annotated, the object being to enable beginners in particular, but older hands too, to understand exactly how every answer is arrived at from the wording of its clue. In the harder puzzles also, explanations are given for all the clues, but they are sometimes spelled out in slightly less detail than in the earlier ones.

It is hoped that you will have a good look at all the crosswords in this section, that you will attempt those which you think you can solve and that you will study all the solutions, even of those puzzles that seem at present too difficult to tackle. You may be surprised to discover that, once you have analysed the answers, many of the clues were not so impossible after all. Furthermore, only by examining a reasonable number of examples in detail will it be possible to appreciate to the full the great scope, variety, ingenuity and potential of the crossword puzzle.

The Puzzles

First *Manchester Guardian* Crossword, 5 January 1929

(Contains the names of several well-known politicians.)

ACROSS

1 One of our Elder Statesmen.
6 Investigation.
10 A highly taxed commodity.
11 Whatever is fast is this.
12 Glaring, but, says the dictionary, is also scandalous.
15 Those who remember the Boer War will remember this statesman.
17 Wet clothes are no use until they are this.
18 Describes poetry concerned with love.
20 Some fellows call themselves this.
21 A river in Russia and a gentleman in Spain.
22 When staff is added this fish is very plain.
24 Well known in the cotton mill.
26 An important pronoun.
27 A fairly common prefix and suffix.
28 A Locarno statesman.
32 An American author.
33 Where Cain went to.
34 The Tiger.
38 A bill sometimes becomes this.
39 Instrument favoured by Orpheus.
41 Men have sought its relics in Armenia.
43 To uplift.
45 Means the same.
47 Gets tidings of.
49 Insurrection.
50 Begins a famous Miltonic sonnet.
51 A 't'-less blow.
53 Abbreviation for Canadian province.
54 Compass point.
55 An orthodox Chancellor of the Exchequer.
56 A negative in more than one Latin language.
57 A French novelist or a London editor.
58 A Labour MP who became a Minister and left his party.

DOWN

1 The head of the Government.
2 Wing-shaped.
3 Military formations of the past revived in the Great War.
4 The vessel which the poet Gray called 'storied'.
5 Assigned fixed value to.
6 A politician as prominent in India as here.
7 Prepare a book for the press.
8 A Liberal leader.
9 A Tory ex-Chancellor.
13 Labour dislikes being called this.
14 Christopher not Joseph.
16 Part of the face.
19 One of Scott's heroines.
23 What new planets swim into.
24 Minister with historic feudal name.
25 To make one.
29 A once-familiar royal name.

1

30 A popular novelist.
31 The reverse of timid.
32 Less than anger.
35 A politician now in the City.
36 A member of the Labour Government.
37 A financier whose name has become proverbial on the Continent.
40 Won a notable by-election for Liberalism.
42 A Liberal politician prominent before and during the war who became an ambassador.
43 Peer who gave his name to a famous committee and edited a queen's letters.
44 One of Liverpool's MPs.
46 One of Manchester's MPs.
48 Very eager.
52 Heroine of a Greek legend.

Alternative-type crossword

2

■	1	■	■	2	3 H	I	4 P
5	E	A	6 L	■	O	■	A
■	F	■		■		■	
7	E	A	R	L	E	S	S
■	R	■	K	■	D	■	E
8	E	N	■	9	■	■	D
■	N	■	10	O	A	11 D	■
■	C	■	■	R	■	A	■
12	E	A	S	T	■		■
■	■	■	■	13 H		K	E

ACROSS

2 Handling a —— without proper control sometimes causes much damage.

5 There's usually a recognised way to —— something.

7 It's often hard to remain —— when surrounded by disaster.

8 Special skill is frequently needed to make best use of ——.

10 Some animals soon become familiar with a ——.

12 One type of person has much experience with ——.

13 There are many who enjoy —— regularly.

DOWN

1 Job-seeker is often prepared to show —— at interview.

3 Things are generally improved by being well ——.

4 In some schools certain things must be —— from time to time.

6 Men who —— about are apt to make some people nervous.

9 It's always best to be warmly clothed when going —— in winter.

11 Many greatly dislike being in a —— place.

Definition-type crossword: the 'Quickie'

3

ACROSS

1 Impede (8)
9 Danger (5)
10 Error (7)
11 Non-attendance (7)
12 Flavour (5)
13 Craving for food (6)
14 Respect (6)
18 Ascend (5)
20 Taken for granted (7)
21 Emotion (7)
22 Wash (5)
23 Simultaneously (8)

DOWN

2 Equilibrium (7)
3 Meddle (6)
4 Overturn (5)
5 Changing (12)
6 Spatter (6)
7 Foreboding (12)
8 Lake (4)
15 Notice (7)
16 Steering device (6)
17 Object aimed at (6)
18 End of sleeve (4)
19 Fetch (5)

Cryptic crossword

ACROSS

1 Feminine car? That's a very pleasing touch (6)
4 Go on, go right back, surrounded by the press (8)
10 This fan has a plastic rim, dear (7)
11 Liberal artist gets bit of clay in face (7)
12 Decline a student's allowance, about to die (8)
13 One of the watery features of Norfolk, but not in this country (6)
15 Negatives one's badly developed (4)
16 Apt to take on various duties, showing natural abilities (9)
19 One who finishes in test is most gentle (9)
21 Monster who spills gore (4)
25 A king, sullen, showing warmth of passion (6)
26 One in rage after short March wedding (8)
28 She serves drinks, making froth help out (7)
29 The recluse is 'ere with the little child (7)
30 Agreements, we hear, to produce a written composition (8)
31 Alert about start of business chain (6)

DOWN

1 A hundred being suspended? Times *must* be! (8)
2 Search has Mum jumping about in rage (7)
3 Kind of jacket suitable for mad artist! (6)
5 Unusual combination of artillery and engineers (4)
6 An expert in gout, he rushes from place to place (8)
7 Fence without limits, lose, and shut up (7)
8 South African young men are apt to be green (6)
9 Buses, trains, etc. bring ecstasy (9)
14 Girl had shortened pen, all twisted (9)
17 Officer having wild jaunt at about first of December (8)
18 Eastern people stay in tent for dwelling-place (8)
20 Back the gee-gee that's last 'ome? (7)
22 Get weaving, embracing Rani — it's very hard (7)
23 Poor player upset bar a little (6)
24 Hard trial, or bargain (6)
27 Poems included in good essays (4)

4

Cryptic crossword

ACROSS

1 Eccentric stranger gets ship to go off course (10)
6 Refuse to add up without computer, initially (4)
9 More mature reprobate attracts 'er (5)
10 Leader that is getting feet caught in fetter (9)
12 Stupid act, Ivan ruling—he's quite mad (6,7)
14 He entertains a thousand in the street, getting about a pound (8)
15 Groom, RE Lieutenant, so taken aback (6)
17 It wipes out a complete series of games (6)
19 Badly out in sum, becoming insubordinate (8)
21 Wide old coppers, yes—not heavy, it's very clear (5,8)
24 Tinned meat gives browbeater muscle (5-4)
25 Make a speech, having nothing to chide (5)
26 Hindu ascetic can make you almost a soldier (4)
27 They're seen in Canada, providing Peter, oddly, with meals (5-5)

DOWN

1 Sailor on northern lake (4)
2 Havin' ambitions, you need a sedative (7)
3 Quiet stroll with rambling duet, say, when you have pancakes (6,7)
4 Stormed around Fleet St area, and revoked former statement (8)
5 Even so, it's calm (5)
7 Old property allowed to be put up after chat (7)
8 One skilled with hands in art, music, dancing (10)
11 Perfecting the job is a runner's goal (9,4)
13 Young scamp, to rob efficiently, in an unlikely way (10)
16 I lug fuel all over the place—it's tricky (8)
18 Smuggle liquor, and kick a member (7)
20 Atrocious act abroad, followed by great anger (7)
22 Where gladiators fought, coming in bare, naturally (5)
23 Catches the gun that's tossed up (4)

5

Cryptic crossword

ACROSS

1 Strolling minstrel going round posh street gets the bird (7)
5 Move slowly in the main channel (4)
9 Scented fish (5)
10 Associate has a horse—eight, we hear (9)
11 After studies, I, Old Bob and Eddie were composed (9)
12 Receiving payment, have a meal (4)
14 He likes picking up bits of sticky paper (5-9)
15 His crazy notion, that keeps his car buzzing along? (3,2,3,6)
19 This feature, if repeated, will bring cheers! (4)
20 Upset by squeeze, the cause of useless tears? (5,4)
22 Found her a rattle—that's never been known before (7-2)
23 A blemish—it isn't vulgar (5)
24 The front part inclines downwards (4)
25 Compensate, as nudes must do eventually (7)

DOWN

1 Cut the early part of the Bible class (6)
2 Looking at an article, unimportant, and becoming converted (6,3,5)
3 The process of getting a crumpled mat in a tent (10)
4 The doctor 'as the twitch, and is violent (7)
5 Heathen that Castro's supporters believe (7)
6 Frozen fish, about a pound (4)
7 I can mend it, Pete, if it's broken—it may heal (6,8)
8 The low-down on the German's sexy affair (6)
13 Control said to be re-established (10)
15 Reverse support (4,2)
16 Guts needed in teams (7)
17 He gives instructions, comparatively concise (7)
18 Catherine hides in the ship—there may be rollers below (6)
21 Henry, love, let's have a luminous ring (4)

6

Cryptic crossword

ACROSS

1 Bags, sort that gets returned when employer's in (8)
5 What detectives' chief did is bad (6)
10 Pocket fortune that's taken by surprise guests (3-4)
11 Novice whose wage is a pound (7)
12 In which astronauts may be televised, or snapped (5)
13 Being alone, I ain't solo, oddly enough (9)
14 Warder's act in prison concert? It adds to the torture! (4,2,3,5)
16 Broke a rule at soccer, as dance manager did? (7,3,4)
21 When a lobe is damaged, a stiffener is needed (9)
22 See me yearn endlessly for fruit (5)
23 Give way to in'abitant of India with broken leg (7)
24 He takes in Nellie, a Greek (7)
25 Tough is returning to New York's leader (6)
26 Animated, as mediums are? (8)

DOWN

1 Ulster, perhaps, to Irishman, imprisoning CO (7)
2 A month to live—Dr, losing head, comes round (7)
3 Vessel parked in street—part of students' rag? (5)
4 Affluent roué to act as croupier (4,2,3,5)
6 Lots of falling snow have mingled with canal (9)
7 Study the penalty—it's the limit (7)
8 Fearless old copper receives a phone-call (6)
9 China's position when beefy visitor's left? (3,4,3,4)
15 Member of secret organisation takes rum to cove (9)
17 Leave an orchestra performing (7)
18 Disorder in jail—men tortured (7)
19 Source of oil? Nothing's come up, children (7)
20 I'll be embraced by birds—won't we all? (6)
22 Runner, one with happy face, losing the lead (5)

7

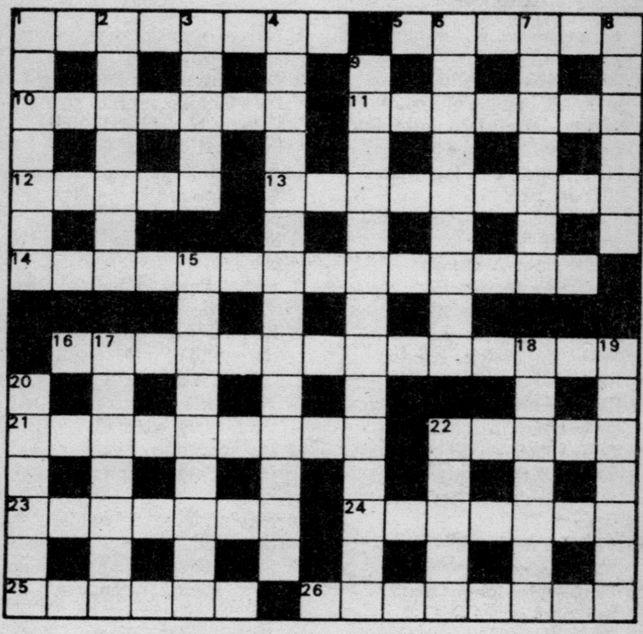

Cryptic crossword

ACROSS

1 About the actors—mould some more (6)
4 What treasure-hunters hope to do? It's on the nail (4,4)
9 Lapse—lapse often noticeable with male language (4,2,3,6)
11 He's absorbed in Japanese copper lustre (5)
12 Some must have a range that's shared (8)
13 French money in a S. American country (9)
15 Partnership not easily disturbed (4)
18 When this crawler is battered, he's in a hole (4)
19 Stop me dithering about one set of compositions (4-5)
21 Italian lines keeping one in (8)
22 The leaderless home circle that space-travellers leave behind (5)
25 Possible fate of big fish or big hit? (6,2,3,4)
26 Here's a poisonous plant, husband—duck (8)
27 Turn over, making anxiety almost stop (6)

DOWN

1 He's in opposition, is Brown, among others (9)
2 Does this region sound right for a Chinese murder? (5)
3 P. loves N.—sing about it, making a scoop (8)
5 Arranging things in advance is ruinous for the modern painter (13)
6 Storm-raiser chopping tool chest (6)
7 Fish with the knowledgeable, to find how lines converge (9)
8 Rushed to get out of sight, by the souhd of it (4)
10 Give him a gratuity, the Western writer's friend, and tell him the secret (3,3,3,4)
14 Put accent on change—patient's condition can take it (5,4)
16 Having spine and hams distorted? (9)
17 Short letter at the border takes an age—and they haven't long to live (8)
20 Rage quietly over the girl's squirrel (6)
23 Magistrate helps to make the score even (5)
24 The rabble total about a hundred (4)

8

Cryptic crossword

ACROSS

1 The beetle is dead, squashed by the Queen (6)
5 Furnish in a flexible way (6)
9 Lay around to study brief (7)
10 Tout's dog (6)
12 Is severely dealt with, like a victim of the guillotine? (4,2,2,3,4)
13 At the end of the night the staff danced (4)
14 He's a ranting preacher, but is taken aback by a big fib (3-7)
18 Try one, duck, getting American red as a brick (10)
19 Part of the tariff is collected for the public revenue (4)
21 Intent on pleasure—that's what the KO'd boxer may be (3,3,1,4,4)
24 Contended about arrival being changed (6)
25 Want a mineral? Ring the bus-company around four (7)
26 Henry's in the front of the picture displaying the medicine (6)
27 Keep on jabbering—that will torpedo the treaty (6)

DOWN

2 Places where you may find a lost coin going mouldy (9)
3 Catch up and slip up—it's all in the game (6)
4 It's rough going around a London district with a bird—you need integrity (9)
5 What's afoot? It's upsetting to bachelors (5)
6 The newly-rich snatch up a beautiful piece of sculpture (8)
7 Subject has to remain on the outskirts of Greece (5)
8 The first signs of fluster, followed by excitement—that's entreaty (11)
11 Docker's tyke, going mad, shot up in the air (3-8)
15 Needless repetition got lay-out quite muddled (9)
16 Antiquated mine I have around the Border (9)
17 They give food some value, and look into tooth-decay (8)
20 The notice gets split and cut loose (6)
22 Tories' leader, lacking caution, scraps (5)
23 When Scotland Yard raised a detective agency (5)

9

Novelty crossword

Each clue is an anagram leading to one word. In the case of the Across clues, a synonym of each word should be entered in the diagram; in the Down clues an antonym is required.

ACROSS

1 Ten-ply (9)
10 Gal has inn (7)
11 Sue GI, Sid (7)
12 I quell boy (9)
13 Ushers (5)
14 To be us (4)
15 Sugar and I (10)
17 Sire in belt (10)
20 Dies (4)
22 Abet (5)
23 Purler's end (9)
25 Trot, mouse (7)
26 Ecarté (7)
27 Gate adit (9)

DOWN

2 Models hide (5)
3 Can reel (7)
4 Rod-men (7)
5 Pax, Ned (8)
6 We're old (6)
7 I? I'll fly a bit (13)
8 No use—go home (13)
9 Peons (6)
16 The ray (8)
17 In duty (6)
18 Often at Ur (7)
19 No curve (7)
21 Valse (6)
24 Me, I can do a PC (5)

10

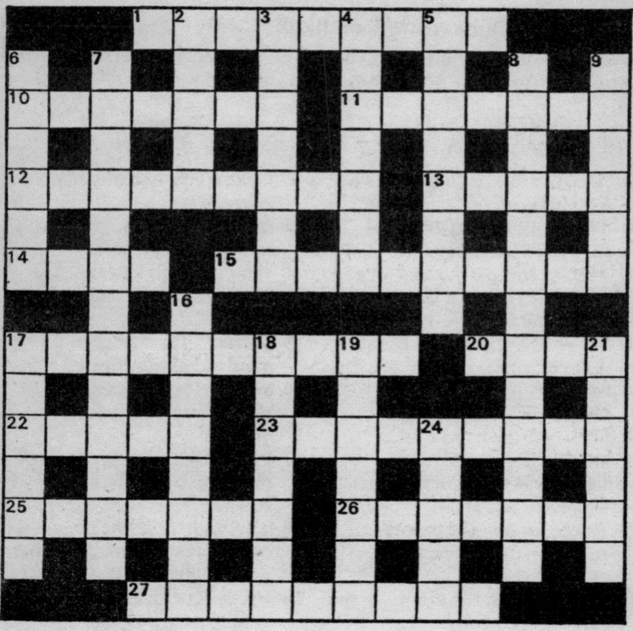

Novelty crossword

The Across clues are given haphazardly. The location of their answers in the diagram will be helped by a correct solution of the Down clues, which are normal.

ACROSS

(a) A bit of stuffing in straw hats for big heads!
(b) Trees split by half-branch—they have to be dug out.
(c) Marine company, stuck in a rock, may have to be hoisted.
(d) What a pencil-shield should do in a certain position.
(e) Specially made core for centre—it's very hard.
(f) Shave off the front of the shelf's rim.
(g) Love record is held by apes: expresses regret.
(h) Raced among the moors in reverse—that's where the stock is.
(i) Archbishops, the pi lot—some rant disgracefully.
(j) Sign of hesitancy in tot may prove a life-saver.
(k) It's useful for one who fiddles and is about to go wrong.
(l) Short line at end of letter fires reactionary.
(m) Spirit's arriving shortly? A rotten lie.
(n) It isn't good to live as a backslider.

DOWN

2 It can make one bite black rubber (7)
3 A pogrom policy, yet there's room for frolic in it (4)
4 Who gets fights to take place? The Head at the end of the year? (8)
5 Subjects, for example, involved in fibs (6)
6 Silent people, they give odd tips when surrounded by gins (9)
7 I must hide among the more inquisitive and the more rowdy (7)
8 There's little in the street—an old copper and lots of paper—good night! (5,6)
10 Escapes before eleven, to give vent to anger (3,3,5)
14 Confer about form losing its leader—one who keeps the rules (9)
16 See the Navy, after getting nothing, pining (8)
18 Southern commanding officer with a yen for the whip (7)
20 MOs tend, somehow, to be extremely remote (7)
21 Songs given by Bill, a wind-bag (3-3)
24 Get the dress—we're not quite finished (4)

11

Listener-type

Cook's Tour

The sixteen items of food or drink are clued (in italics) simply by the name of the regions in which they are normally found. Their unchecked letters may be arranged as: SEE OUR EGG COMING, CILLA? Every word in the diagram is in *Chambers Twentieth Century Dictionary,* 1972 edition.

ACROSS

1 Half the manuscript's undecipherable, being scratched (8)
9 Crown and a cloak worn by a don (4)
12 *Scotland* (11)
13 A crude sort of violin that makes one shudder (4)
14 Jock's aim—to take up permanent abode, abandoning Scotland's capital (5)
15 The girl with a small masculine bust (4)
16 A sleeping-tablet is so clean, somehow (7)
18 *Spain* (4)
20 *Brazil* (7)
24 *Malaysia* (6)
27 Allowance rarely seen—there's a preposterous row about it (5)
28 Dilapidated old car causes accident rounding end of avenue (4)
29 Open place where nations' spokesmen have a drink together? (5)
30 Railways carrying gold—that should amuse Scotsmen (4)
31 A female nude's first appearance, white-faced and wooden (5)
32 *USA* (6)
33 Fringed sash made from waste raw silk, with a splash of colour added (7)
35 Looks likely to succeed in audition (4)
38 *Turkey* (7)
41 Ostrich grass can provide good camouflage for the hare (4)
43 Ancient lighthouse seen in a lake after a little sail (5)
45 Yarn that's been spun by a bishop (4)
46 *Germany* (11)
47 Left before the lesson, in the old days (4)
48 *Scotland* (8)

DOWN

1 Short, sudden shower around the North (5)
2 Wooden bowl supplied together with present in Aberdeen (5)
3 *W. Indies* (4)
4 *Australia* (10)
5 *E. Indies* (8)
6 *England* (5)
7 Star dead—prayer offered up (5)
8 Turkey's weight is satisfactory—it's a mirth-provoker without its head (3)
9 No gentleman wants love quickly (4)
10 *Persia* (5)
11 *Germany* (8)
17 *Ireland* (10)

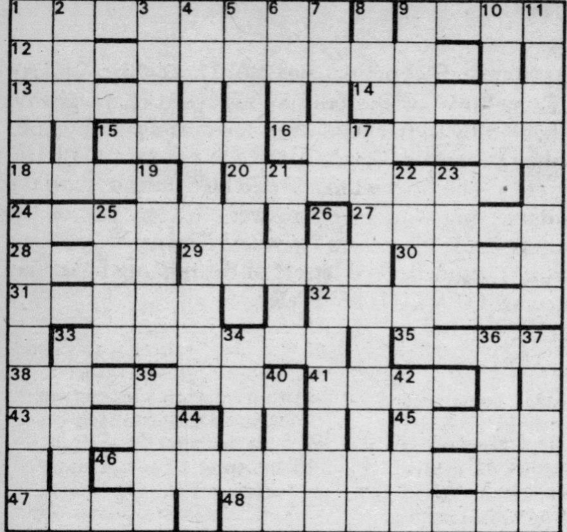

12

19 Translator holds copy in feeble light (5)
21 Prophet doing the rounds of British pulpits (5)
22 Israeli making trouble for Arabs (5)
23 Scottish stuff that upsets Irishmen (4)
24 Dismal hut with flags fluttering (8)
25 In Kashmir a huzoor is regarded as a demon by Hindus (4)
26 To live without a palpitation, you need a dressing-gown in New York (8)
33 The old longing makes me go after a feminine supporter (5)
34 *Britain* (5)
36 Note base of bronze in BC type of viol (5)
37 Beau displaying poise in tartan shirt? (5)
39 Animosity is evident, just a wee bit (4)
40 I'm an old woman, past it, and am not standing around for all to see (4)
42 The nobleman will require attention before long (4)
44 Law made by the sovereign, formerly (3)

Listener-type

Missing links

The chain: 26–5–9–16–32–19–36–41–40–37–42–20A–14–1A–33A–26. Each 'link' of the continuous word-chain above, from the beginning to the beginning again, is a synonymous clue to its successor (e.g. LID-COVER-HIDE-PELT-STRIKE, etc.). The fifteen links are to be deduced, with the help of intersecting words. All answers, except one of the proper names, are in *Chamber's Twentieth Century Dictionary*, 1972 edition. The unchecked letters of the missing links may be arranged as: O! A LOUTS' BAR.

ACROSS

6 Sponge cake I once needed after spirit (7)
11 The Frogs? There's a type of drama with a distinctive character about it (6)
12 Translation of German can make a permanent impression (6)
15 Peak pulled back reveals the nose (3)
18 Adventurous girl, one having to swallow lies—not half! (5)
21 Degenerate, having abandoned Scripture for a number of years (6)
23 River in the South of France, running westward (5)
28 Scheme will require a couple of months (6)
30 Generous Scottish lightweight admits former reputation (7)
35 Specially designed boats that will guide things through the bore (5)
38 Riverside bird having to migrate around the start of Easter (5)
39 Look warm and dry in Nairobi (3)
43 Still comes in after the proper time—it's an extremely childish habit (7)
44 Indisposed, perhaps, as the result of a plot (4)

DOWN

1 Begins showing knife to incite rising (5)
2 Auntie's reforming Oriental Christians (7)
3 The writer without work becomes a listless person (4)
4 Deceitful one, offering Oriental fruit full of seeds (6)
6 Rum-soaked cake upsets a sailor repeatedly (4)
7 Right storm coming up will make soil fit for cotton-growing (5)
8 Turn in, beginning to cross the equator (7)
10 Bully using birch endlessly (4)
13 Timid female, grabbed by the doctor, cried like an animal (5)
17 Jar with no lid is outside (4)
20 Weak and, according to Caesar, ineffectual (3)

13

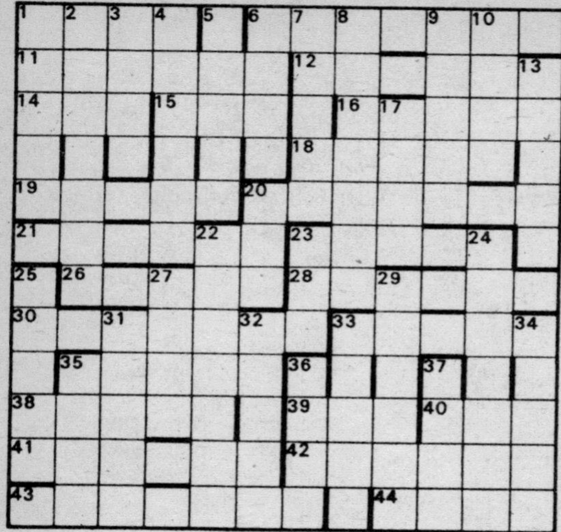

22 Mac's drenched, all right—you've a legal claim about that (7)
23 Fish that's lying around dead (3)
24 One who barters as of old, supplied from various sources (7)
25 No longer experiences violent bursts of passion (5)
27 Though able, in need of correction (4)
29 An unenjoyable task leads to a nervous disease (6)
31 Boggy ground sticks to bottom of grizzly bear (5)
33 A fine jet, taken up for single journeys (5)
34 Sly fellow, embracing you, dallied amorously (5)
35 Rigid one that makes you bristle (4)

Listener-type

Justyn Print

Each clue in italics is the imaginary title of a new book by an unknown author. Solvers are asked to deduce the authors' names from the broad hints given by their titles: for example, if the clue to 51,35 were *The Broken Window* (3,5), the author's name might be EVA BRICK. The unchecked letters of the authors are: A. C. D. E. G. G. G. G. L. L. L. M. M. M. M. N. O. O. P. R. T. T. T. Y. Answers to normal clues are all in *Chambers Dictionary*. Ignore an accent in one word.

ACROSS

1 You can see the Indian ox, cruelly laden, sag (8)
7 The chrysanthemum, though old-fashioned, is pleasing around the lake (5)
10 See 18
12 Lay back, embracing love beside the road, being affectionate (7)
13,34 Ac. *The Excursion* (5,5)
14 Good old Bess is in a low haunt, scoffing (8)
16 See 37
17,56 *Over The Stile* (3,7)
18,10 *Sick In Transit* (6,5)
19 Chinese official bringing back the old head-master (5)
21 Froth on beer that's become stale when standing in still (5)
22 I'm extremely busy, and am not wanting to miss the plane (3)
23 Terns become mad, we hear, after start of swoop (6)
25 Discarded letter one found stuffed in tin (3)
27 Panegyric that brings a certain amount of wet stuff into Jock's eye (5)
30 Opportune time to tie up and finally settle (4)
32 See 6
33,42 Ac. *Upon My Word!* (5,6)
34 See 13
35 See 51
36 Remained soft, wrapped in Scotch matted wool (4)
38 Short sword presented in the forces to commanders (5)
41,47 *Under The Birch* (3,5)
42 See 33 Ac.
43,42 Dn. *Lucky Dip* (3,6)
44 See 52
46 Strangely divine in 'allowed setting (5)
49 Neat US dodge to get rid of an elected member (6)
51,35 *The Compulsive Voyeur* (3,5)
52,44 *The Language Mistress* (5,5)
54 Laws do, in the circumstances (8)
55 This crossing may make you pause, even if you look both ways (5)
56 See 17
57 Pamper the infant—it's only little (5)
58 There's no going back into time that's past (5)
59 Guard's khaki uniform? (8)

DOWN

1 Bad money brings ruin, and society muddle (5)
2,9 *The Habitual Drudge* (7,6)

14

3 Commercial book (abridged version) will get you to speak extempore (2-3)

4 Indo-Europeans vote against being brought up in Classical art (6)

5 An old game like cribbage will do for simpleton or knave (5)

6,32 *The Marriage Beneath* (6,5)

7 Young salmon, back from the sea, left in alarm (6)

8 Magnetic force gets sailor upset—what a surprise! (4)

9 See 2.

11 No Scots nor old English should hold one (3)

15 This diner is more elegant, being topless (5)

20 Indian waiting-maid ducks away from a boorish lout (4)

24 The viola vibrates a lot (4)

25 Ancient mount, where gross debauchery once took place(4)

26 The right iron to use at St Andrew's? Sandy's own is about right (4)

28 I was an evil god all right, in life only half-visible (4)

29 First single—leg-side, first of extras—anybody can get that (3)

31 Address the leaders of all railway trades-unions—it calls for cunning (3)

33 Man the highway—the rabble tend to drive together (4)

34 To strike once over you and me—that youngster's yet to be born (5)

37,16 *Farewell, Culture!* (7,5)

39 Knitted cape that women can't get into on being confined (6)

40, 41 Dn. *Tiger On My Tail* (6,6)
42 See 43
45 A hard shell that's in a crumbling state (5)
47 See 41 Ac.
48 Peasants who cause disturbances of the peace, from what we hear (5)
50 He was a big man, Oriental, having difficulty getting up (4)
53 It's deadly with Henry missing—one has to suffer delay (3)

***Listener*-type**

Snakes and Ladders

The answer to each Across clue appears in the diagram in two parts: it runs first from the clue number as far as a bar; then, after descending a snake or climbing a ladder to another numbered square (not clued), continues as far as the next bar. The snakes and ladders, which the solver must imagine, may travel either obliquely or vertically. Down clues are normal. All words, except for one name, are in *Chambers Dictionary*.

ACROSS

1 Here's a little monkey, Mum, with broken toes.
6 Hell, a student can't expect good tuition from this!
11 Expert's deliberate falsification—a heavy blow.
12 Cheeky one gets a disease.
16 Having a couple of gills etc. in bar, I had become tipsy.
19 Is tucking into a lot of herrings—discomfort's sure to result.
23 It's a strain, having a painter about one.
24 You have to restrict students' freedom to go out wearing a gown.
25 Cure is far too costly—what you need is smack.
30 High water, caused by tide's first arrival North.
31 Unusually tasty gourd found about the East—tasty indeed.
42 Boisterous wind has lost worker a franc.
43 Idlers are not kept in responsibility endlessly.
44 Former operation to treat rust.
46 Sovereign in the grip of magnetic force is abandoned.
47 Language one mouths in Scotland after a reverse.
48 A set of bells for the band.
51 They're washed up on beaches, wrecked in a gale.
52 One gets it in rope that's tightening.
55 Everything I get right I call almost symbolic.
58 Ring given product of nitre shows purity of lustre.

15

DOWN

1 Hartnell, for example, evokes the lyricist in me (7)

2 I'm appearing in one commercial with the Queen—he disapproves (12)

3 Song that's crazy, getting a girl crazy (8)

4 A duck—a sign for a type of margarine (4)

5 Religious one, about to corrupt other, very low forms of animal life (11)

7 King gets stuck into a morsel—a sprat (4)

8 Console one having received a knock (5)

9 Aldgate girls looking dishevelled—they're sluts (7-5)

10 Thomas, enthralled by bawdy language (5)

13 A large antelope's pitched us in a tree (5,6)

14 A pun on one in charge of an eastern language (7)

17 Once a very hard worker had a spot of vermouth in a drink (5)

26 You can use it for varnishing a defective gun, protected by a net (4-3)

28 Old Greek living abroad, wanting to lie sprawled under a palm (8)

32 Row about the race—this oil's unsuitable for engines (5)

34 Ornament of twisted shape, depicting grave within large moulding (7)

38 Violent burst of passion over love shows zest (5)

40 I award turned-up, wide-brimmed hat (5)

45 Depression—what's needed is a new deal (4)

49 Lodges within the borders of the Netherlands (4)

Listener-type

Head-hunting

The first letter of every answer is out of place. Thus, if the answer to a clue were SLEEP, it would be entered as LSEEP, LESEP, LEESP or LEEPS. The diagonals 5–30, 1–41, 19–40 form an appropriate excerpt from an old music-hall song (included in the *Oxford Dictionary of Quotations*). *Chambers Dictionary* is recommended, but it does not give the one place-name, nor the phrase at 8.

ACROSS

1 A stimulant will get you free from stress (6)
7 There's vehemence about the Queen because of this (6)
12 Public-school pupil comprehends Southern Baltic language (8)
14 Scottish seer about to cut and run (5)
15 Is brought in to repair slightly defective piece of electrical apparatus (8)
16 I leg it, a vulgar vagabond, in a holiday in the country (13)
18 I'm on the fiddle, where only one brand of beer is served? (4-3)
19 Eat away in a back-street chop-house (4)
20 Race, by the sound of it, with one swimmer (3-4)
21 One dips into a crib—it's a habit (4)
22 Extremely closed circle (3)
24 Stir love in a young maiden (4)
25 Old salts, by sprinkling, can make a remarkable red soup (7)
28 See a wreath, and there'll be something like depression (4)
32 A judge that's beginning to speak dries up (7)
35 Window-screens, curiously soft ones, absorbing dazzle (7-6)
36 One sees the langur of Ceylon prowl round and round (8)
37 Walk back with an escort, being glanced at amorously (5)
38 My Pa's embarrassed by your pity (8)
39 Rushes around the East, unfolding ancient tales (6)
40 The girl is stuck in a sandy tract (6)

DOWN

1 Mac's directions needed for turning over a furrow (5)
2 Abstainer forced into opening a magnum? (6)
3 A Scot's keen to make sales around the North (5)
4 Part of the bridle has to tinkle a little (7)
6 Aged gentleman invokes Norse gods (5)
7 No longer denies fantastic yarns about the East (6)
8 Flogs dress at jumble—it's hardly see-through material (7,5)

16

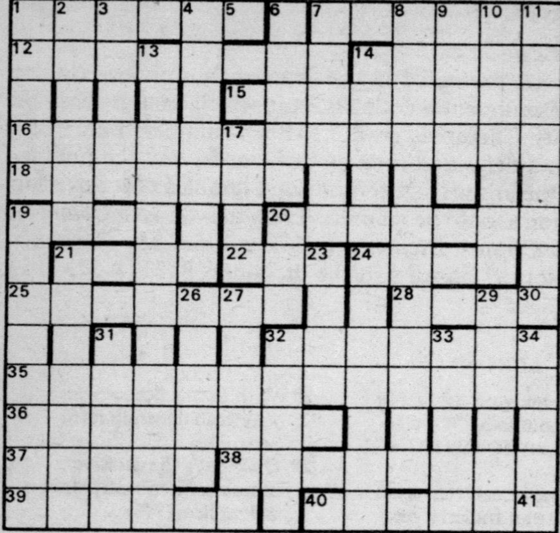

9 Get ready to drive and drink, by the sound of it, all the way (3,2)
10 To excel when taking an exam, try this tobacco (7)
11 The thing, 'e reckoned, will be done again (8)
13 Oh, ref's in trouble, trouble we had presaged (12)
14 Quick one before mischievous rising (5)
17 Discount on foreign bill I obtained in past (4)
19 Period of culture that finds vocal expression in the philosopher (5,3)
20 Group determined to decline local lease (3)
21 Former foster son irritated with rule (7)
23 Scots love East Cornish town (4)
24 Brightly-dyed leather—natural and almost fade-resistant when stuck up (7)
26 Circular yellow plant (5)
27 English king's units showing the effects of current changes (6)
29 Marked man had got round the surging river (6)
31 Died in disorderly flight northwards of a Welsh family (5)
32 Type of grass found in British capital (5)
33 Stops, losing head, and colours slightly (5)
34 A double-bend always is a trial (5)

Listener-type

Christmas crackery

The clues are presented in the form of those jokes, riddles, limericks, sentimental couplets, etc., which emerge from the best-quality Christmas crackers. Each numbered clue contains both a definition (one or two words) and the jumbled letters of the answer. Definitions and jumbles never overlap. Punctuation should be ignored. Every answer is in *Chambers Twentieth Century Dictionary*, 1972 edition. My Christmas wish for solvers appears in the diagonals 8–20, 5–32, 1–52, 24–51, 41–50.

ACROSS

1 When's an igloo-dweller like some mountain? When he's snowed on (SNOWDON)! (6)

6 A: Name insects that seem most like an Indian river plant (6)

11 B: Garden ants—they're about the best examples of INDUS TREE (5)

13 Q: Why's the captain of a side starting extra time like a good conductor? (5)

16 A: Each of his players tries to add something to the score (3)

17 To his rose-tree the same crack each day (4)

18 Made the Dean (seeking praise)—'Let us spray!' (7)

19 'I'll cap that', his tree vowed (5)

21 'Don't delay—watch me, boughed' (bowed)—(4)

22 'Twas a gentle quip, neat in its way (7)

24 These rude words, pointed at your charms resplendent, (5)

27 With bardic licence warm your cold dependant (6)

29 Q: What's the decisive moment when a carpenter is sick at heart? (6)

30 A: When he stakes his AWL on the slowest nag in the race! (5)

33 A: Why's a cactus-lover like the fan of a dagger or a lance expert? (7)

39 B: I can tell you without hesitation—I don't know (4)

41 A: Because 'e'll stop a long time watching 'is xerophyte ('is 'ero fight)! (5)

43 S: A dance band organist, Ah s'pose, entirely differs from a factory strike (7)

45 R: Dat's true, Sambo. But does yo' really know why? (4)

46 S: Yes, Rastus. De first will plant de feet, de second defeat de plant (3)

47 R: No, Sambo. A person at de organ works de stops: a strike stops de works! (5)

17

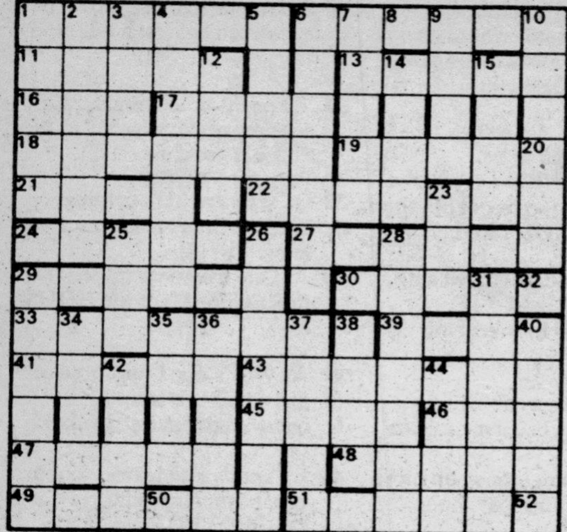

48 What Royal person is often seen making a loud lament? The Prince of WAILS! (5)

49 A: Can you tell (or reveal) the difference between a canary and a monarch's wise captives? (6)

51 B: Yes, old man: one sings, held by a cage—the others are sages, held by a king (6)

DOWN

1 A: Why does the star fiend-killer suggest at first a good penalty-taker? (5)

2 B: Because he shoots, and then, I presume, gets a GHOUL (goal)! (6)

3 A: Plucky salmon take longer to disembowel than little fish —why? (4)

4 B: They've got more guts than sardines, silly! (7)

5 Q: I stun weasels. How does a gross Indian peasant resemble me? (5)

6 A: In either case you see a STOAT FELLER in me! (stout fellah) (7)

7 'Idle men interfere with scab at factory.' Won't it get worse if you PICKET? (5)

9 What noble estates are like deserts? BARON lands (4)

10 The Mormon sect, at least, believes the plural of spouse is SPICE! (6)

12 'That's the limit!' once cried (with some truth) (4)

14 A shop-girl, quite a prude, name of Ruth; (4)

15 'Any colour but blue (4)
23 For that costume would do, (3)
25 When the bride is so long in the tooth!' (3)

26 Q: Why's a solar eclipse like a fish that's glad to be decapitated? (7)
28 A: When its face is cut off, the sun is DE-LIGHTED! (7)

29 With ardent carol may I sing to thee (6)
31 My ceaseless love beneath thy linden tree? (6)

34 Q: How does a cabbie's tip differ from a beehive on open mud? (4)
35 A: One makes money on hire; the other, contrarily, honey on mire (4)

36 Set tangle against pip? That's a seaweed against a wee seed (5)

37 'Opposition to hanging will save my neck', says killer. No noose is good news! (5)

38 Q: Why are MPs coming home at breaks like vases set in niches? (4)
40 A: One may perhaps see them in RECESSES of the HOUSE (5)

42 A: Why's one London street girl equal to a couple entertaining in a strip club? (4)
44 B: That's a stale one: 'cos a bird in the STRAND is worth two in the BUFF! (4)

Torquemada

By the Waters of Shannon

Note: Clues consist of one word or consecutive words in each line.

ACROSS

1 I issue this warning to them
10 Who praise the uproarious Brem:
13 Ere you visit the lair
14 Of a newly wed pair
16 Have notches cut out of your hem.

18 Should it ever befall that the Grung
19 Simply must disinherit its young,
21&24 It will first climb a tree
22 And glean sprats for their tea
23 By a weird rise and fall of its tongue.

26 If a Michaelmas daisy should please
28 The green-crested Pot-stick or Kreze,
32 'Tis a custom of old
33 That the bird should be told
34 rev. That the thing is a deadly disease.

35 Little Edward once pelted a Plo
36 With fragments of glacial snow

18

DOWN

1 Till it fell from the swing:
2 I regret that its wing
3 Now extends nearly down to its toe.

4 When the Snats move away in the Spring
5 They're remarkably swift on the wing,
6 And I think that they coin
8 (As they tear to the Boyne)
9 **rev.** That they coin little lyrics to sing.

11&7 A Snail is a fool to a Woft;
12 I have seen a Woft seat itself oft
15 At my aunt's little Zoo
17 **rev.** On a slip of bamboo
20 Since a slip of bamboo is so soft.

24 With enough beer and bromide and borax
25&30 To fill a crustacean's thorax
27 Any may sheep can be
28&31 In a threefold degree
29 Concealed from the fangs of the Lorax.

Afrit

From *Armchair Crosswords* (Warne, 1949).

ACROSS

1 He may be a'richt in the heid, but he's aye wandering (5)

4 Curious fellow: he usually has to pay sixpence (6)

8 The fragrance of an old *amour*. It seems to have gone off a bit! (8)

9 Pat says he made all the running, and of course things have to be to run smoothly (5)

11 The sum I do here has chemical results (6)

12 They have ends, but they're really beginnings—twelve a year (7)

13 Summary way of making a cab start (8)

14 Stop!—or proceed slowly if the road is (5)

15 To make these you begin with leaves, and end with roots—even if they end in smoke (8)

19 Is it his unnatural need and baffled rage which makes him so false, the rat? (8)

22 Men go like this, little man (5)

24 Truly rural, he is, though not till he's had his beer! (8)

27 It takes two on 'em to do it properly (7)

28 Not experienced, so if you haven't got the right 'un try the left 'un (6)

29 It's dear and old when you sing about it, but it sings for the camper when it's new and cheap (5)

30 Hides away, but shows that the island lies between the South and South-east (8)

31 You may safely do so to the baby; otherwise you might get landed! (6)

32 Lots and lots, though they may be reduced to a shred (5)

DOWN

1 You can't say *he* hasn't got a shilling to his name (5)

2 He'll keep you in order, and the motor, too. There's something in that (7)

3 A laying down of the law. Still, it doesn't tell you to follow Father (5)

4 Do as the doctor does, and the praise will be equally divided (8)

5 There's a hindrance *en route*, and that makes the game merely one of chance (8)

6 It really is a moving spectacle to see Mother after the cows! (6)

7 'Tear asunder a broken reed' is one account of it, but it's another kind of account which usually is (8)

8 A design which is revealed in the name of the Law (6)

10 An untidy study is naturally bound to be (5)

16 She doesn't sound as if she were mass-produced, so she should render good service (8)

17 Considerably abashed, as Vera would be by a proposal like this! (8)

18 To get across, let art go one way and poetry the other (8)

19

20 You can't approve his way of getting money, especially as he's got enough under his head to keep a roof over his head (7)
21 Foxes had them long before the wireless was thought of (6)
22 This is desire in an immoderate degree, so the degree should be modified and diminished (5)
23 Spoil a good drink? Why, it's the outside edge! (6)
25 Pitch and toss. If you're right in this you won't be left in this (5)
26 They make an end of themselves, being mere creatures of fancy (5)

Ximenes

Misprints

Half the Across and half the Down clues contain a misprint of one letter only in each, occurring always in the definition part of the clue: their answers are to appear in the diagram correctly spelt. The other eighteen clues are correctly printed: their answers are to appear in the diagram with a misprint of one letter only in each. No unchecked letter in the diagram is to be misprinted: each twice used letter is to appear as required by the correct form of at least one of the words to which it belongs. All indications such as anagrams etc. in clues lead to correct forms of words required, not to misprinted forms. Every word is in *Chambers Dictionary.*

ACROSS

1 Essentially Latin school—dark blue (5)
5 Windmill pieces, with it—the admiral's type (7)
10 Crash of gate stops you with a colossal jump (12)
11 Get farmer to show what's wrong (4)
12 Vulgarian boldly interrupts girl without respect (7)
13 Deliberate collision in London street—I'm fired (6)
15 He would evade work but proverbially never lies (5)
17 Nasty hook—reverse of what a fisherman uses (4)
18 I may be called lather-proof, therefore most fit (8)
21 Sheep in having got lost calls for finesse (8)
22 To steal the dog's dinner is very hard (4)
24 Pocket picker to be seen in funds (5)
26 Soft clots: get the doctor—a very short distance (6)
28 Fish like carp among catch in rough water (7)
29 Very nifty round hat (4)
30 Trying to cure Ma, hugging her, deary? No! (12)
31 Is this slayer more infernal? (7)
32 Marriage no longer violated by Sepoy (5)

DOWN

1 This is old hat, darling, like you and me (7)
2 Once simple mixed emotions, typical of a wish (12)
3 This old royal fish is always fed (7)
4 The Painted Perch can be upset by oats (4)
5 Arch-binder will give you an evening in Paris (8)
6 The sea's sounding very rough, my boy (5)
7 I used to be sweet: now I'm a slut (4)
8 Jobs for operators become suddenly slack afloat (12)
9 I'm moping in a place of confinement (5)

20

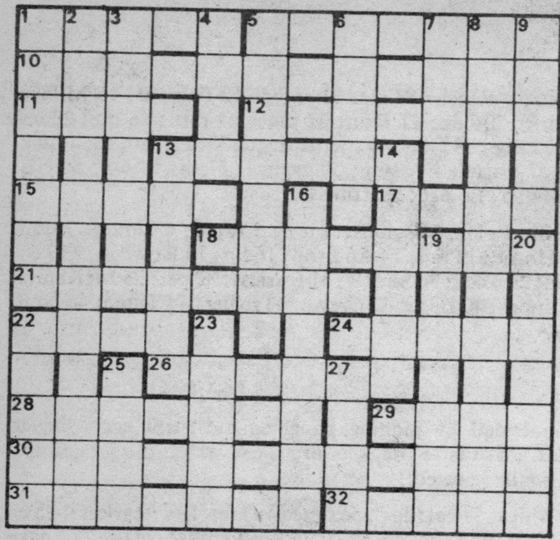

13 A household makes husbands get senile (6)

14 Trip off? That was well known in Scotland (6)

16 Formerly peaty ground, light, for tall plant (8)

19 A livery upset? Try old-fashioned French thyme (7)

20 Stuff the French play casually (7)

22 Female don, by no means a lovable woman (5)

23 Lesson's no use to me: I sound opposed to it! (5)

25 Turn upside down a brat with a flat bottom (4)

27 A notion that is somewhat less than perfect (4)

The solutions

No. 1

Across: 1 Balfour; 6 search; 10 ale; 11 rapid; 12 flagrant; 15 Milner; 17 dried; 18 erotic; 20 odd; 21 Don; 22 pike; 24 pirn; 26 me; 27 en; 28 Stresemann; 32 Poe; 33 Nod; 34 Clemenceau; 38 act; 39 lute; 41 ark; 43 elate; 45 id; 47 learns; 49 rising; 50 avenge; 51 hi; 53 NS; 54 NE; 55 Snowden; 56 ne; 57 Lesage; 58 Roberts.

Down: 1 Baldwin; 2 alar; 3 legions; 4 urn; 5 rated; 6 Simon; 7 edit; 8 Runciman; 9 Horne; 13 red; 14 Addison; 16 lip; 19 Rowena; 23 ken; 24 Percy; 25 wed; 29 Teck; 30 Soutar; 31 fearless; 32 pet; 35 McKenna; 36 Slesser; 37 Stinnes; 40 Edge; 42 Crewe; 43 Esher; 44 Tinne; 46 Nall; 48 agog; 52 Ino.

No. 2

Solution recommended by judging panel as most apt according to wording of clues. (Words in brackets are those which the judges also considered but finally rejected.)

Across: 2 ship (whip); 5 heal (deal, peal, seal); 7 fearless (tearless); 8 pen (gen, hen, men); 10 road (goad, load); 12 feast (beast, yeast); 13 hake (hike).

Down: 1 reference (deference); 3 honed (hosed); 4 passed (parsed); 6 lark (lurk); 9 forth (North); 11 dark (dank).

No. 3

Across: 1 obstruct; 9 peril; 10 mistake; 11 absence; 12 taste; 13 hunger; 14 honour; 18 climb; 20 assumed; 21 feeling; 22 rinse; 23 together.

Down: 2 balance; 3 tamper; 4 upset; 5 transforming; 6 splash; 7 presentiment; 8 mere; 15 observe; 16 rudder; 17 target; 18 cuff; 19 bring.

No. 4

Across: 1 caress: car-ess, feminine of car?; 4 progress: go-R (right), backwards, in press; 10 admirer: anagram of rim, dear; 11 radical: RA (artist) + c(lay) in dial (face); 12 gradient (a decline): grant (student's allowance) about die; 13 abroad: a (Norfolk) Broad; 15 noes: anag. of one's; 16 aptitudes: apt + anag. of duties; 19 tenderest: ender (one who finishes) in test; 21 ogre: anag. of gore; 25 ardour: a R. (king) + dour (sullen); 26 marriage: I (Roman one) in rage after Mar. (short for March); 28 barmaid: barm (froth) – aid (to help out); 29 eremite: 'ere –

mite (little child); 30 treatise: sounds like treaties (agreements); 31 albert (watch-chain): alert about b(usiness).

Down: 1 changing: C (Roman 100) – hanging (being suspended); 2 rummage: anag. of Mum, in rage; 3 strait: anag. of artist; 5 rare: RA + RE; 6 gadabout: a dab (an expert) in gout; 7 enclose: (f)enc(e) – lose; 8 salads: SA (South African) – lads (young men); 9 transport: two meanings; 14 misshapen: miss (girl) – ha(d) – pen; 17 adjutant: anag. of jaunt at, about D(ecember); 18 tenement: E – men (Eastern people) in tent; 20 endorse: the end 'orse; 22 granite: anag. of get, round Rani; 23 rabbit (a poor games player): reverse of bar + bit (a little); 24 ordeal: or – deal (bargain); 27 odes: hidden in goOD ESsays.

No. 5

Across: 1 transgress: anag. of stranger + SS (ship); 6 scum: sum without (= outside) c(omputer); 9 riper: rip – 'er; 10 chieftain: i.e. (that is)+ft (feet) in chain; 12 raving lunatic: anag. of act, Ivan ruling; 14 minstrel: M (thousand) – in – St (street) – re (about) – 1. (pound); 15 ostler: RE – Lt. (Lieutenant) – so, all reversed; 17 rubber: two mngs.; 19 mutinous: anag. of out in sum; 21 broad daylight: broad – d. (old pence, coppers) – ay – light; 24 bully (browbeater) – beef (muscle); 25 orate: O (nothing) – rate (to chide); 26 yogi: yo(u) – GI; 27 maple-trees: anag. of Peter, meals.

Down: 1 tarn: tar – N; 2 aspirin: aspirin(g); 3 Shrove Tuesday: sh! – rove + anag. of duet, say; 4 recanted: ranted around EC (London postal district); 5 still: two mngs.; 7 chattel: chat + rev. of let; 8 manicurist: anag. (indicated by 'dancing') of in art, music; 11 finishing (perfecting) post (job); 13 improbably: imp – rob – ably; 16 guileful: anag. of I lug fuel; 18 bootleg: boot (kick) – leg (member of the body); 20 outrage: out (abroad) – rage (great anger); 22 arena: hidden in bARE NAturally; 23 nets: rev. of sten (gun).

No. 6

Across: 1 bustard: bard round U – St (posh street); 5 inch: hidden in maIN CHannel; 9 smelt: two mngs.; 10 affiliate: sounds like a filly – eight; 11 consisted (were composed): I – s. (old shilling or bob) – Ted (Eddie) after cons (studies); 12 feed: two mngs. (receiving a fee, and have a meal); 14 stamp-collector (cryptic definition only); 15 bee in his bonnet; 19 chin (feature of the face): 'chin-chin!' = 'cheers!'; 20 spilt (upset) milk (to squeeze): 'no use crying . . .'; 22 unheard-of: anag. of found her a; 23 taint: 'taint = it isn't; 24 bows: two mngs.; 25 redress: re-dress.

Down: 1 bisect: Bi (early part of Bible) – sect (class); 2 seeing (looking at) the (an article) light (unimportant); 3 attainment (the process of getting): anag. of mat in a tent; 4 drastic: Dr – 'as – tic (the twitch); 5 infidel: in Fidel (Castro); 6 cold: cod about 1£ (a pound); 7 patent medicine: anag. of I can mend it, Pete; 8 gender (an affair of sex): gen (low-down) – der (the, German); 13 reinstated: rein (control) – stated (said); 15 back up: two mngs.; 16 insides (guts): in – sides (teams); 17 briefer: two mngs.; 18 skates: Kate in SS (ship); 21 halo: Hal (Henry) – O (nothing, or love).

No. 7

Across: 1 trousers (bags): rev. of sort round user (employer); 5 rancid: ran CID; 10 pot (to pocket, billiards) - luck (fortune; 11 learner: £ (pound) – earner; 12 orbit: or – bit (snapped); 13 isolation (being alone): anag. of I ain't solo; 14 turn of the screw (warder); 16 handled the ball; 21 whalebone: anag. of when a lobe; 22 melon: me – lon(g); 23 indulge (give way to): 'Indu (Hindu) + anag. of leg; 24 Hellene: he round Ellen (Nellie); 25 sinewy: rev. of is + New + Y (York's leading letter); 26 spirited: influenced by spirits.

Down: 1 topcoat (e.g. an Ulster): to Pat, round CO; 2 October: be (to live) in (d)octor; 3 stunt: tun (vessel) in St (street); 4 rake (roué) in the money (affluent); 6 avalanche: anag. of have, canal; 7 confine: con (study) – fine (penalty); 8 daring: d. (old penny or copper) – a ring (phone-call); 9 all over the shop (bull in a china-shop); 15 oddfellow: odd (rum) – fellow (cove); 17 abandon: a band (an orchestra) – on (performing); 18 ailment (disorder): hidden in jAIL MEN Tortured; 19 linseed: rev. of nil (nothing) + seed (children); 20 swains (lovers): I inside swans; 22 miler: (s)miler.

No. 8

Across: 1 recast: re (about) – cast (the actors); 4 spot cash: two mngs.; 9 slip of the tongue: slip (lapse) – oft (often) – he (male) – tongue (language); 11 sheen: he in sen (Japanese copper coin); 12 partaken: part (some) – a ken (range); 13 Argentina: argent (money, French) – in a; 15 firm: two mngs.; 18 toad: toad-in-the-hole, dish cooked in batter; 19 tone-poems: anag. of stop me, about one; 21 Veronese (Italian): verse (lines) around one; 22 earth: (h)earth (home circle); 25 caught in the deep: cricket; 26 mandrake: man (husband) – drake (duck); 27 careen: care (anxiety)-en(d).

Down: 1 resistant: is tan (brown) amongst rest (others); 2 clime: Chinese pronunciation of crime?; 3 spooning (making a scoop): P – OO (nothings, or loves) – N, in sing; 5 preordainment: anag. of modern painter; 6 thorax: Thor (storm-raiser) – ax (chopping tool); 7 anglewise: angle (fish) – wise (knowledgeable); 8 hied: sounds like hide (get out of sight); 10 tip him the wink: tip him + the W (Western) – ink (writer's friend); 14 grave (accent) turn (change); 16 misshapen: anag. of spine, hams: a 'read it again' clue (see No. 4, 14 Down, for easier clue to same word); 17 ephemera (short-lived insects): Ep. (Epistle, letter) – hem (border) – era (an age); 20 gopher: go (the rage) – p (piano, quietly) – her (the girl's); 23 reeve: hidden in scoRE EVEn; 24 scum: sum (total) about C (Roman 100).

No. 9

Across: 1 elater: late (dead) in ER (the Queen); 5 supply: in a supple way; 9 laconic: laic (lay) around con (to study); 10 barker: two mngs.; 12 gets it in the neck; 13 trod: t (end of night) – rod (staff); 14 tub-thumper: tub (rev. of but) – thumper (a big fib); 18 testaceous (brick-red): test (try) – ace (one) – O (nothing, or a duck) – US (American); 19 fisc: hidden in tarifF IS Collected; 21 out for a good time: two mngs; 24 varied: vied (contended) about ar. (arrival); 25 olivine: O (a ring) – line (bus-company) about IV (Roman 4); 26 physic: Hy's (Henry's) in pic (front part of picture); 27 yatter: anag. of treaty.

Down: 2 locations: anag. of a lost coin; 3 tennis: rev. of net (catch) + rev. of sin (slip); 4 rectitude: rude (rough) round EC (London district) – tit (bird); 5 sabot: rev. of to-BAs (bachelors); 6 parvenus: rev. of rap (snatch) + Venus (de Milo); 7 liege: lie (remain) – ge (outside letters of Greece); 8 flagitation: fl (first letters of fluster) – agitation (excitement); 11 sky-rocketed: anag. of docker's tyke; 15 tautology: anag. of got lay-out; 16 primitive: pit (mine) – I've (I have) around rim (border); 17 calories: lo (look) in caries (tooth-decay); 20 adrift: ad. (notice) – rift (split); 22 trash: t (leading letter of Tories) – rash (lacking caution); 23 Asdic (detecting apparatus): as (when) + rev. of CID (Scotland Yard).

No. 10

Words in brackets are the synonyms (Across) and the antonyms (Down) which were clued as anagrams.

Across: 1 abundance (plenty); 10 agnails (hangnails); 11 conceal (disguise); 12 slantwise (obliquely); 13 reeds (rushes); 14 dull (obtuse); 15 protectors (guardians); 17 debauchees (libertines); 20 team (side); 22 pulse (beat); 23 pillagers (plunderers); 25 extreme (outermost); 26 produce (create); 27 flustered (agitated).

Down: 2 built (demolished); 3 nastier (cleaner); 4 ancient (modern); 5 contract (expand); 6 raised (lowered); 7 infallibility (fallibility); 8

heterogeneous (homogeneous); 9 closes (opens); 16 funereal (hearty); 17 dapper (untidy); 18 hapless (fortunate); 19 eclipse (uncover); 21 master (slave); 24 alone (accompanied).

No. 11

Letter in brackets indicates where each clue originally appeared.

Across: 1 metropolitans (i): anag. of pi lot, some rant; 8 storm-cone (c): RM – co. (Marine company) in stone (rock); 9 Ariel (m): ar. (arriving) + anag. of lie; 11 evil (n): rev. of live; 12 cover-point (d): position on cricket field; 13 trenches (b): trees, interrupted by (bra)nch; 15 serif (l): rev. of fires; 17 resin (k): re (about) – sin (to go wrong); 19 boasters (a): s(tuffing) in boaters (straw hats); 22 apologises (g): O (love) – log (record) – is, in apes; 23 edge (f): (l)edge; 25 serum (j): er (sign of hesitancy) in sum (to tot); 26 storeroom (h): tore (raced) in rev. of moors; 27 ferro-concrete (e): anag. of core for centre.

Down: 2 ebonite: anag. of one bite; 3 romp: hidden in pogROM Policy; 4 promoter: two mngs.; 5 lieges: e.g. (for example) in lies (fibs); 6 Trappists: anag. of tips, in traps (gins); 7 noisier: I in nosier (more inquisitive); 8 sweet dreams: wee (little) in St (street) + d. (old copper) – reams (lots of paper); 10 let off steam: let-offs (escapes) – team (eleven); 14 conformer: confer about (f)orm; 16 lovelorn: lo (see) – RN (the Navy) after love (nothing); 18 scourge: S (Southern) – CO (commanding officer) – urge (a yen); 20 endmost: anag. of MOs tend; 21 air-sac: airs (songs) – a/c (account, or bill); 24 wear: we ar(e).

1 S	2 C	R	3 A	4 B	5 B	6 E	7 D	8 O	9 C	A	10 P	11 A
12 C	O	C	K	A	L	E	E	K	I	E	I	M
13 A	G	U	E	R	I	L	N	14 E	T	T	L	E
N	I	15 H	E	R	M	16 S	E	17 C	O	N	A	L
18 T	E	N	19 T	A	20 B	21 A	B	A	22 S	23 S	U	C
24 G	U	25 R	A	M	I	M	26 B	27 R	A	T	I	O
28 H	E	A	P	29 U	N	B	A	R	30 B	A	U	R
31 A	S	H	E	N	G	O	32 T	A	R	P	O	N
S	33 B	U	R	D	34 A	S	H	G	35 A	I	36 R	37 S
38 T	R	E	39 H	A	L	40 A	41 R	H	42 E	A	E	P
43 F	A	N	A	44 L	L	U	O	E	45 A	B	B	A
U	M	46 S	T	E	I	N	B	E	R	G	E	R
47 L	E	R	E	X	48 S	T	E	N	L	O	C	K

No. 12

Across: 1 (M)S-crabbed; 9 cap-a; 13 a-gue; 14 settle minus S(cotland); 15 her-m.; 16 anag.; 27 rev. of oar (to row) about it: preposterous = backwards; 28 hap round (avenu)e; 29 UN-bar; 30 Au in BR: see bar (2) in Chambers; 31 a-she-n(ude), and two mngs.; 33 bur-dash; 35 sounds like heirs; 41 anag. and two mngs.; 43 a L after fan; 45 abb-a; 47 L-ere.

Down: 1 scat round N; 2 co-gie: see coggie in Chambers; 7 d. + rev. of bene; 8 (j)oke, and two mngs.; 9 cit-O; 19 ape in tr.; 21 Amos round B.; 22 anag.; 23 rev. of Pats; 24 anag.; 25 hidden; 26 be without (= outside) a throb; 33 me after bra; 36 re + (bronz)e in BC; 37 p (= poise) in sar.; 39 two mngs.; 40 an't (= am not) round U (type of film that all may see); 42 ear-l.; 44 L-ex.

1 D	2 U	3 M	4 P	5 B	6 B	7 R	8 I	O	9 C	10 H	E
11 A	N	O	U	R	A	12 E	N	G	R	A	13 M
14 T	I	P	15 N	E	B	G	16 C	17 R	A	Z	E
E	A	E	I	A	A	18 A	L	I	C	E	W
19 S	T	O	C	K	20 W	R	I	N	K	L	E
21 D	E	C	A	22 D	E	23 I	N	D	U	24 S	D
25 G	26 S	T	27 A	R	T	28 D	E	29 C	O	C	T
30 U	N	31 C	L	O	32 S	E	33 S	H	O	O	34 T
S	35 S	A	B	O	T	36 R	P	O	37 S	U	O
38 T	E	R	E	K	U	39 A	I	R	40 T	R	Y
41 S	T	R	A	I	N	42 C	R	E	A	S	E
43 L	A	Y	E	T	T	E	T	44 A	B	E	D

No. 13

The chain: start – break – crack – craze – stunt – stock – race – strain – try – stab – crease – wrinkle – tip – dump – shoot – start.

Across: 6 che (obsolete word for I) after brio; 11 no in aura: see anurous in Chambers: play by Aristophanes; 12 anag.; 15 rev. of ben; 18 ace, including li(es): a 'read it again' clue; 21 decadent minus NT; 23 in + rev. of Sud; 28 Dec.–Oct.; 30 unce, with los in it: unclose = not stingy; 35 anag.; 38 trek around E(aster); 39 two mngs. and hidden; 43 yet in late; 44 a-bed.

Down: 1 da + rev. of set; 2 anag.; 3 me outside op.; 4 Punic-a; 6 rev. of AB–AB; 7 R + rev. of rage; 8 in – c(ross) – line; 10 haze(l); 13 ewe in MD; 17 (g)rind; 20 w. – et; 22 OK in droit: see drouk in Chambers; 23 i.e. around d.; 24 anag.; 25 two mngs.; 27 anag.; 29 chore-a; 31 carr-(grizzl)y; 33 rev. of trips; 34 tod round ye; 35 set-a.

S	E	L	A	D	A	N	G	M	G	O	O	L	D
M	U	N	D	Y	R	O	C	O	R	D	I	A	L
A	S	A	L	L	Y	D	E	R	I	S	I	V	E
S	T	E	I	N	A	D	A	G	L	O	R	I	A
H	A	M	B	A	N	Y	E	A	S	T	A	N	T
S	C	R	A	Y	S	S	A	N	E	L	O	G	E
S	E	A	L	A	T	T	I	C	H	O	N	O	R
F	O	R	T	H	D	I	R	G	E	K	E	P	T
E	S	T	O	C	B	E	N	B	R	I	G	H	T
T	O	M	G	L	O	T	T	O	D	D	L	Y	R
U	N	S	E	A	T	L	E	W	P	O	L	L	Y
S	T	A	T	U	T	E	S	L	E	V	E	L	O
L	A	M	E	D	O	G	T	E	P	E	T	I	T
A	G	O	N	E	M	W	A	R	D	R	E	S	S

No. 14

Across: 1 anag.; 7 good round L; 12 rev. of laic (lay) round O + Rd; 14 ER (Good Queen Bess) + is, in dive; 19 rev. of nab-MA; 21 as in yet; 22 ant, an't (= am not), and wanting minus wing; 23 sound of craze after s(woop); 25 a in Sn (tin); 27 log (Hebrew liquid measure) in ee; 30 three mngs.; 36 p (soft) in ket; 38 hidden; 46 DD (a divine) in 'oly (holy, hallowed); 49 anag.; 54 ut (= do, the note) in states; 55 two mngs., palindrome, and 'read it again' clue; 57 pet-it; 58 rev. of no in age; 59 war-dress.

Down: 1 two mngs. and S-mash; 3 ad. – lib.; 4 rev. of nay in ars (Latin); 5 three mngs.; 7 L in grise; 8 od + rev. of OS; 11 ne around a; 15 (n)eater; 20 a-Yah(OO); 24 anag.; 25 two mngs.; 26 ain about R; 28 OK in li(fe); 29 three mngs., and on + e(xtras); 31 initial letters, and two mngs.; 33 he-Rd, and three mngs.; 34 fet-us; 39 stag round on; 45 anag.; 48 sounds like riots; 50 E + rev. of net; 53 let(Hal), and two mngs.

1 M	2 A	R	3 M	4 O	S	5 P	6 A	7 B	8 A	9 D	10 D
11 O	N	12 M	A	L	13 A	R	14 A	R	N	15 R	Y
16 D	I	17 B	D	18 E	G	O	R	I	C	A	L
I	19 M	20 E	R	21 O	N	22 T	23 A	24 T	O	G	A
25 S	A	V	I	26 T	27 U	O	M	28 I	29 N	G	N
30 T	31 D	E	G	U	S	T	A	T	32 O	33 L	34 T
35 E	V	36 R	A	N	C	H	I	A	T	E	37 O
38 G	39 E	40 T	41 L	G	A	E	C	42 L	T	43 T	R
44 U	R	E	45 D	46 O	47 S	48 R	49 I	50 I	A	51 A	S
52 S	T	R	A	I	T	I	N	O	53 R	I	A
54 T	E	55 A	L	L	56 U	A	N	T	S	57 L	D
58 O	R	I	E	N	S	59 I	S	E	A	S	E

No. 15

Across: Pairings were as follows: 1–39 marm + anag. of toes; 6–21 a bad don; 11–20 three mngs.; 12–50 malar-I-a; 16–36 anag.; 19–59 is in mease; 23–53 a RA about I; 24–54 to-gate, two mngs., and togate; 25–33 three mngs.; 30–14 t(ide)-ar.-N; 31–15 anag. about E; 42–35 lev(ant); 43–56 an't (= are not) in trus(t); 44–37 ure-do; 46–57 L in od; 47–27 rev. of I-mous; 48–29 two mngs.; 51–41 anag.; 52–38 a + it in string; 55–18 all-ego-R-I-cal(l); 58–22 O + anag. of nitre

Down: 1 odist in me; 2 I'm in an advert + ER; 3 mad + anag. of a girl; 4 O (a duck, cricket)-Leo (sign of the zodiac); 5 pi-a about rot-other; 7 R in bit; 8 an-con; 9 anag.; 10 Dylan Thomas, poet: hidden; 13 a-gnu's-cast-us; 14 a-ram-a-i/c; 17 v(ermouth) in beer; 26 anag. of gun in toil; 28 anag. of to lie under ita; 32 oar (to row) about TT (race); 34 sad in tore; 38 gust-O; 40 rev. of I-aret; 45 anag.; 49 in-N(etherland)s.

1 T	2 O	3 N	A	4 I	5 C	6 E	7 E	H	8 R	9 E	10 A	11 T
12 S	T	E	13 O	N	I	A	N	14 L	O	E	P	E
R	T	L	R	R	15 E	S	R	I	S	T	O	R
16 I	L	L	E	G	17 G	I	A	V	T	U	R	A
18 A	B	S	S	B	A	R	Y	E	E	P	A	T
19 T	E	C	H	I	I	20 E	S	A	D	A	C	E
S	21 O	C	A	T	22 O	T	23 O	24 A	G	O	L	D
25 O	U	P	D	26 R	27 E	S	O	F	28 L	V	29 E	30 I
N	R	31 U	F	B	H	32 R	E	F	A	33 I	E	34 S
35 E	S	T	O	O	N	B	L	I	F	N	D	S
36 A	N	D	W	E	R	O	O	S	S	T	E	A
37 G	L	O	E	D	38 Y	M	P	A	S	T	H	Y
39 E	E	R	D	E	S	E	40 E	N	I	S	D	41 E

No. 16

Quotation in diagonals: 'Carve a little bit off the top for me' (Fred Murray).

Across: 1 a-tonic; 7 heat about ER; 12 Etonian takes in S; 14 ee about lop; 15 is in restor(e); 16 villeggiatura: anag.; 18 Bass-bar; 19 etch: hidden; 20 sea-dace: sounds like seed (race) + ace (one); 21 a in cot; 22 to-O; 24 O in gal; 25 poudres: anag.; 28 v-lei; 32 a-ref. – i.e. – s(peak); 33 festoon-blinds: anag. of soft ones, round blind (to dazzle); 36 wander-O-O; 37 rev. of go + led; 38 sympathy: anag. of my Pa's + thy; 39 reeds round E; 40 is in dene.

Down: 1 rev. of airts; 2 TT (teetotaller) in bole; 3 sell round N; 4 ring-bit; 6 ae.-Sir; 7 renays: anag. of yarns about E; 8 frosted glass: anag.; 9 tee up: sound of tea + up; 10 cap-oral; 11 it-'e-rated; 13 foreshadowed: anag. of oh ref's + ado-we'd; 14 a + rev. of evil; 17 agio: I in ago; 19 Stone Age: tone in sage; 20 four mngs.; 21 noursle: anag.; 23 loo-E; 24 rev. of naif-fas(t); 26 or-bed (to plant); 27 Henry's, henrys; 29 heeded: he'd (= man had) round rev. of Dee; 31 Tudor: d. in rev. of rout; 32 B-Rome; 33 (s)tints; 34 ess-ay.

E	S	K	I	M	O	E	M	M	E	T	S
A	N	E	N	T	S	R	E	P	A	C	T
R	I	T	S	E	A	M	D	R	R	Y	A
S	P	A	I	R	G	E	L	I	L	A	C
T	E	N	D	M	E	L	E	G	A	N	T
U	R	D	E	E	E	I	C	I	C	L	E
C	R	I	S	I	S	N	A	N	T	E	S
A	N	E	L	A	C	E	T	I	O	T	A
N	O	P	A	L	O	N	E	S	T	E	P
T	O	E	I	G	L	E	A	L	E	R	S
O	P	E	R	A	A	M	M	E	A	N	E
R	O	L	L	E	R	Y	O	D	L	E	S

No. 17

Definitions were as follows:

Across: 1 igloo-dweller; 6 insects; 11 about; 13 extra time; 16 score; 17 crack; 18 spray; 19 tree; 21 watch; 22 neat; 24 pointed; 27 cold dependant; 29 decisive moment; 30 stakes; 33 dagger; 39 I; 41 xerophyte; 43 dance; 45 true; 46 plant; 47 works; 48 lament; 49 canary; 51 sings.

Down: 1 at first; 2 he shoots; 3 salmon; 4 guts; 5 Indian; 6 stoat; 7 interfere; 9 noble; 10 spice; 12 limit; 14 prude; 15 blue; 23 do; 25 long; 26 fish; 28 cut off; 29 I sing; 31 ceaseless; 34 tip; 35 mire; 36 seaweed; 37 opposition; 38 set; 40 recesses; 42 strip; 44 bird.

1 P	2 R	3 E	4 M	O	5 N	I	6 T	7 O	8 R	9 Y
10 E	U	L	O	11 G	I	12 S	E	13 D	E	N
14 N	E	O	G	A	M	I	S	15 T	N	N
16 D	E	N	17 T	S	18 B	E	T	I	D	E
19 U	20 N	G	E	T	L	21 G	E	N	I	P
22 L	E	A	S	E	23 E	E	R	Y	24 A	25 P
26 A	S	T	27 E	R	28 T	29 H	30 I	31 B	L	E
32 T	H	E	W	33 O	R	I	O	L	E	R
E	34 T	S	E	P	35 E	D	36 N	E	V	E

No. 18

Definitions concealed in the verse were as follows:

Across: 1 warning; 10 praise; 13 lair; 14 newly wed; 16 notches; 18 befall; 19 disinherit; 21 & 24 tree; 22 glean; 23 weird; 26 Michaelmas daisy; 28 pot-stick; 32 custom; 33 bird; 34 rev. deadly disease; 35 little Edward; 36 glacial snow.

Down: 1 swing; 2 regret; 3 extends; 4 move away; 5 swift; 6 coin; 8 tear; 9 rev. coin; 11 & 7 a snail is; 12 seat; 15 little; 17 rev. slip; 20 soft; 24 beer; 25 & 30 crustacean's thorax; 27 may (maid) sheep; 28 & 31 threefold; 29 concealed.

No. 19

Across: 1 nomad: no, Scots for not; 4 parker (Nosey P.); 8 malodour: anag.; 9 oiled: Oi, Irish for I; 11 sodium: anag.; 12 calends: contains ends; 13 abstract: anag.; 14 tarry: two mngs.; 15 cheroots: ends with roots; 19 renegade: anag.; 22 gnome: anag.; 24 villager: contains lager; 27 embrace: 'em-brace; 28 unfelt: anag.; 29 dixie: 'dear old Dixie', and camper's can; 30 secretes: SE-Crete-S; 31 dandle: anag.; 32 herds: anag.

Down: 1 nabob: n. (name) – a bob (shilling); 2 monitor: mo-ni-tor; 3 dogma: dog (follow) – ma (mother); 4 practise: pra-ct-ise; 5 roulette: let (hindrance) in route; 6 kinema: ma after kine (cows); 7 rendered: rend (tear asunder) + anag. of reed; 8 mosaic: two mngs.; 10 dusty: anag.; 16 handmaid: sounds like hand-made; 17 overawed: O Vera, wed!; 18 traverse: rev. of art + verse; 20 grafter: g-rafter; 21 earths: foxes' lairs; 22 greed: anag. of degre(e); 23 margin: mar-gin; 25 lurch: 'left in the lurch'; 26 elves: end of themselves.

1 P	2 E	3 R	S	4 S	5 V	A	6 H	E	7 S	8 S	9 A
10 S	T	E	A	T	O	P	Y	G	O	U	S
11 T	H	A	W	O	12 U	P	S	T	O	R	T
A	E	L	13 M	A	N	N	O	14 N	T	G	I
15 S	O	G	E	R	S	16 H	N	17 L	E	E	R
U	S	A	N	18 S	O	A	P	T	19 V	S	20 T
21 S	T	R	A	T	I	G	Y	O	I	N	W
22 B	O	N	G	23 M	R	T	24 P	U	R	S	E
I	M	25 K	26 M	O	H	A	27 I	R	E	H	E
28 T	I	E	E	R	I	P	D	29 O	L	I	D
30 C	N	E	M	O	T	H	E	R	A	P	Y
31 H	E	L	L	I	E	R	32 P	O	Y	S	E

No. 20

Definitions misprinted in the clues are given in italics.

Across: 1 Perse, per-se; 5 vanes-s.a.; 10 anag.: *rump*; 11 anag.: *warmer*; 12 ups-tart; 13 cannon: three mngs.; 15 = shirker: *dies*; 17 rev. of reel: *look*; 18 soap-test: so-aptest; 21 stra-teg-y; 22 bone: three mngs.; 24 three mngs.: *pucker*; 26 MO-hair: *cloth*; 28 t-ide-rip; 29 O-lid: *niffy*; 30 che-mother-apy: cheapy = not deary!; 31 i.e. more Helly: *slater*; 32 anag.: *carriage.*

Down: 1 pet-as-us; 2 ethe + anag. of emotions: *fish*; 3 real-gar: *red*; 4 anag.: *Porch*; 5 vous-soir; 6 sound of high+son: *tea*; 7 *smut*; 8 surge-on-ships; 9 a-stir: *moving*; 13 men-age; 14 no-tour; 16 hag-taper; 19 anag.: *rhyme*; 20 tweed-le; 22 *dog*; 23 moron: sounds opposite of less on; 25 *boat*; 27 idea(l).

Index